Mediation and Law in China I

As the first volume of a two-volume set on mediation in China, this book examines the legal foundations of Chinese mediation and proposes feasible paths to the institutionalization and professionalization of mediation.

Grounded in traditional dispute resolution practices throughout Chinese history, mediation is born out of the Chinese legal tradition and considered to be "Eastern" in nature. Volume I discusses the legal principles that underpin mediation in China, rooted in a legal tradition that pursues the rule of law and morality as well as the concept of harmony in Chinese society. It first revisits traditional notions and models of Chinese mediation and then puts forward approaches to innovating the concept, its institutionalization, and mechanism of mediation. The book also discusses how to promote professionalization and special legislation dedicated to mediation in China, thus establishing a mediation system that fits into and is properly tailored to Chinese society. It introduces diverse styles of mediation and social governance in different cultural contexts and demonstrates the effectiveness of China's experience in dealing with a litigious society.

This book will serve as a crucial reference for scholars, students, and related professionals interested in alternative dispute resolution, civil litigation, and especially China's dispute resolution policy, law, and practice.

Liao Yong'an is Professor in the Law School at Xiangtan University, China, and Vice-President of the China Civil Procedure Law Research Association. His main research interests are dispute resolution and civil litigation.

Wang Cong is Assistant Professor in the Law School at Hunan University, China. His main research interests are dispute resolution and civil litigation.

Mediation and Law in China I

The Past, Present, and Future

Liao Yong'an and Wang Cong

Routledge
Taylor & Francis Group
LONDON AND NEW YORK

First published in English 2023
by Routledge
4 Park Square, Milton Park, Abingdon, Oxon OX14 4RN

and by Routledge
605 Third Avenue, New York, NY 10158

Routledge is an imprint of the Taylor & Francis Group, an informa business

British Library Cataloguing-in-Publication Data
A catalogue record for this book is available from the British Library

Library of Congress Cataloging-in-Publication Data
Names: Liao, Yongan, author. | Wang, Cong (Legal researcher), author.
Title: Mediation and law in China / Liao Yong'an, Wang Cong.
Description: Abingdon, Oxon [UK] ; New York, NY : Routledge, 2023. |
Includes bibliographical references and index. | Contents: v. 1. The past, present, and future: Re-discovering of legal principles of mediation in China – Transformation and remolding of China's traditional mediation idea – New ideas and new thinking of China's modern mediation – Transformation and changes of mediation model in China – Road for professionalization of mediation in China – Practical exploration of mediation procedural prerequisite in China – Basic conception for formulation of mediation law in China – Structuring of mediation discourse system with Chinese characteristic |
Identifiers: LCCN 2022053948 (print) | LCCN 2022053949 (ebook) |
ISBN 9781032473499 (v. 1 ; hardback) | ISBN 9781032478319 (v. 1 ; paperback) |
ISBN 9781032473529 (v. 2 ; hardback) | ISBN 9781032478302 (v. 2 ; paperback) |
ISBN 9781032472713 (hardback) | ISBN 9781032478326 (paperback) |
ISBN 9781003385882 (v. 1 ; ebook) | ISBN 9781003385776 (v. 2 ; ebook)
Subjects: LCSH: Mediation–China. | Dispute resolution (Law)–China. |
Conciliation (Civil procedure)–China.
Classification: LCC KNQ1758.S47 L54 2023 (print) |
LCC KNQ1758.S47 (ebook) | DDC 347.51/09–dc23/eng/20230403
LC record available at https://lccn.loc.gov/2022053948
LC ebook record available at https://lccn.loc.gov/2022053949

ISBN: 978-1-032-47349-9 (hbk)
ISBN: 978-1-032-47831-9 (pbk)
ISBN: 978-1-003-38588-2 (ebk)

DOI: 10.4324/9781003385882

Typeset in Times New Roman
by Newgen Publishing UK

Contents

Preface vii
Acknowledgments xi

1 Rediscovering the Legal Principles of Mediation in China 1

2 Transformation and Reshaping of China's Traditional Mediation Idea 37

3 New Ideas and New Thinking about China's Modern Mediation 70

4 Transformation and Changes in the Mediation Model in China 90

5 The Road to Professionalization of Mediation in China 104

6 Practical Exploration of the Mediation Procedural Prerequisite in China 125

7 Basic Conception for the Formulation of the "Mediation Law" in China 164

8 The Structure of the Mediation Discourse System with Chinese Characteristics 202

Index 237

Preface

Roscoe Pound held that justice, as the purpose of law, is the idealized concession between an individual's activities and the activities of all people in the crowded world. Mediation provides diverse opportunities for such an "idealized concession" in realizing justice.

To understand the institution of mediation in China, it is necessary to go deep into Chinese politics, economy, society, and grass-roots governance to "understand China." As is well known, mediation has a profound historical and cultural tradition in China and the local authorities and the people both followed the social customs of preferring mediation. However, in China's legal governance construction, mediation discourse has not always had an "orthodox" status. In the late Qing Dynasty and the early period of the Republic of China, China started to modernize its legal governance and especially since the reform and opening-up period, China has transplanted a huge number of Western legal institutions. Thus, mediation was perceived as a heavy historical burden and was criticized and excluded from legal circles. Mediation was marginalized. However, since the social transformation resulted in a huge number of prominent contradictions, the litigation-centered institutions could not deal with them all and was overwhelmed. In the new era, according to the changes in social contradictions and based on the modern strategy of national governance capacity and the governance system, the Communist Party of China regarded the perfection and improvement of diverse dispute resolution mechanisms as an important part of comprehensive governance according to the law and （并提出）"pushed forward the alternative dispute resolution." In this context, mediation has eventually returned to its true features of alternative dispute resolution.

From the fate of moving by fits and starts and the rise and fall encountered by mediation in China since the 1980s, we have obtained two main kinds of enlightenment: (1) in practical terms, in the unscientific sense of social stability, mediation was once simply taken as the peacemaking tool to patch up quarrels and reconcile the parties concerned and was excessively emphasized by official policy, resulting in institutional distortion and impacting on the judicial final resolution principle, even encroaching on judicial authority to some extent; and (2) in theoretical terms, due to the fundamental difference between China's idea of mediation and the Western concept of legal governance of formal rationality, mediation was deemed to be the opposite of modern legal governance, so many researchers of law fretted and fumed about the mediation practice, and the more importance that the official authority attached to mediation, the more the academic circles criticized it.

The main reason for this paradox is that, for a long time, under the domination of Western centralism and the traditional influence of Max Weber, the discourse of China's law theory understood mediation as a substantive irrational institution and disdained mediation. Because of law theory's contempt for mediation and the pragmatism of official practice, the mediation institution did not enter the field of legal governance and thus mediation was stigmatized as a way to "blur the line between right and wrong by compromise (trying to mediate a dispute by sacrificing principles)." Therefore, it is one of the theoretical aims of this book to correct the subjective discourse prejudice attached to mediation, underline its practical value, reshape the new idea and new thinking about mediation, bring mediation into the field of legal governance, and return mediation to its origins as a dispute resolution mode.

Law is not the art of dragon slaying and should respond to practical demands. This is the inherent reason why this author changed his focus, in recent years, from research on civil procedure institutions to research on civil dispute resolution institutions. During the process of research on dispute resolution, the author increasingly felt that the world is always thinking in binary oppositions, one or the other, and this has caused us to fail to understand the operational logic of real-life society. The Western social science theory placed mediation and litigation, state and society, and rationality and emotion as opposing positions in binary logic, one or the other, black or white, pursuing the seamless, abstract, and generally applicable legal institution of formal rationality. Yet, when dealing with particular cases, the Chinese dispute solvers are not subject to the formalism of law, but, according to the actual circumstances of cases, flexibly apply mediation modes and means for mediation where possible, judgment where possible, mediation first and then a combination of mediation and judgment. This is a way of thinking to overcome the binary opposition as well as the basic logic of Chinese-style dispute resolution. Therefore, it is another objective of this book to rediscover the "Chinese legal principle" of mediation, tell a proper "Chinese story" of mediation, and structure a "Chinese discourse system" of mediation in contrast to Western culture and show the poly-logic of virtue and law combination, Confucianism and law in parallel, harmony, and an easy-going attitude, both this and that, weighing up the matter and deliberating on the reasons, and the golden mean pursued by Chinese society and culture.

In 1991, American scholar Olson published a book entitled, *The Litigation Explosion*, pointing out sharply:

> American society has many successful aspects, but our civil procedure institution is a ridiculous failure, ridiculed by the world for being expensive, vicious and unreasonable. The American litigation explosion has greatly wasted properties, bringing shame to manyo ccupations respected by people. It has destroyed valuable enterprises and brought pain to broken families.

Currently, Chinese society is also experiencing the transformation pain of a "litigation explosion." We should not take the same disastrous road as the Western litigation-centralized doctrine but should take as our foundation our own institutional advantages to facilitate the simultaneous resonance of mediation and litigation, rather than favoring one over the other, and encourage the mutual cooperation of the state and society rather than their binary opposition.

Differences and misunderstandings between cultures will often affect individuals' behavior. Due to the wide differences between the formal judicial institutions of different countries, demands for mutual benefit dispute resolution are rarely met in the international sphere and cooperation is found only by relying on litigation. As a local dispute resolution mode with a higher neutrality of law culture, mediation provides a diversified interface for dispute resolution in the age of globalization. Therefore, as a kind of judicial system in which the public participates and has "access to justice," mediation is no longer the unique "Oriental experience" but is spreading as a dispute resolution mode across nations and cultures and is becoming active all over the world. While completing this book, COVID-19 was indulging in wanton massacre worldwide, and humanity has never been as it is today, becoming the closely related "community of a shared future," but some Western politicians still persist in Cold War thinking, contrarianism, unilateralism to spread the theory of "China as a threat," leading to tension in international relationships. China has always pursued the path of peaceful exchange, cooperation, and a win-win situation with all the countries in the world and has constantly strived to create a harmonious international environment to avoid contradictions and conflicts. We hope that mediation will be a dispute resolution mode not only between individuals but also should become a dispute resolution mechanism for countries facing conflicts of interest. Mediation will strive to build a community of shared interests by seeking common ground, while reserving difference, keeping harmony in diversity and incorporating things of a diverse nature. Therefore, when the editor of Renmin University of China told the author that a British publishing house was interested in this book and intended to translate the book, the author agreed with pleasure. He sincerely hopes to present, through this book, China's national image of "harmony is most precious" and the global outlook of "all within the four seas are brothers," to Western readers, and contribute as much as possible to the inclusive and mutual benefit of cultural exchange and cooperation between countries. A Chinese poet in the Tang Dynasty, Wang Bo, wrote a verse that has circulated for thousands of years: "A bosom friend afar brings a distant land near." Western readers are thousands of miles away, but the author believes that the interchange of ideas on mediation discourse can narrow the cultural gap to some extent.

Acknowledgments

Finally, special thanks should be extended to my research team. Faced with the prospect of mediation in China with so long a history and such rich contents, any scholar would feel that task was far exceeding his ability. Therefore, research on the mediation in China requires an academic community to undertake this task. In recent years, during my teaching and research on mediation, I have attracted a number of excellent students who cherish the same ideals and follow the same path to join in research in the field. Like me, they are full of enthusiasm for mediation research. Without their assistance and participation, it would have been impossible for me to complete this basic work of law theory. Therefore, this book is a product of the cooperation between my students and me in the interaction of teaching. They are: Dr. Wang Cong, Dr. Duan Ming, Dr. Zhao Yiyu, Dr. Hou Yuanzhen, Dr. Chen Haitao, Dr. Lv Zongcheng, Dr. Zhang Qinglin, and Dr. Xiao Wen.

Liao Yongan
Hometown of Mao Zedong, Xiangtan, Hunan
8 November 2020

1 Rediscovering the Legal Principles of Mediation in China

1.1 Introduction: Starting with *The Story of Qiu Ju*

In 1992, Chinese film director Zhang Yimou shot a movie called *The Story of Qiu Ju*, the plot is as follows. In a small mountain village in Northwest China, Qiu Ju's husband and the village head quarreled over a trifling matter and Qiu Ju's husband accused the village head, who had no sons, of "dying without descendants." The village head became very angry and kicked Qiu Ju's husband in his "fatal place" (crotch). Pregnant Qiu Ju went to the village head to reason things out as she was of the opinion that the village head could kick her husband, but should not have kicked his penis. The village head refused to admit the wrong. Qiu Ju appealed to the township government. The village head was forced to promise compensation, but he threw the money on the ground. Qiu Ju felt disgraced and went on claiming to "ask for an explanation," and appealed successively to the county bureau of public security and the city government. On New Year's Eve, Qiu Ju went into labor and was having a difficult labor, so the village head and the rest of the villagers sent Qiu Ju overnight in the snow and cold to the hospital where Qiu Ju had a successful delivery. Qiu Ju and her family were very grateful and set aside her resentment of the village head. On the occasion of the banquet to celebrate her son's first month, when Qiu Ju was everlastingly grateful, she was waiting for the village head to come to the banquet, but the superior saw, upon investigation, that Qiu Ju's husband was slightly injured and the village head was detained according to the law. Seeing the smoke and dust arising from the police car's arrival, Qiu Ju felt very ignorant and lost: "Why is he being arrested? I just want to ask for an explanation."

This movie is continually ruminated over and discussed by Chinese law practitioners. Dr. Su Li, returning after studying in the USA, was the first person to observe the "puzzles of Qiu Ju": why cannot the judicial institution established, according to the Western universal entitlement theory, give the "explanation" asked for by Qiu Ju? In this regard, Dr. Su Li criticized the idea of Western universal legal governance, pointing out that this formal justice system, established on the basis of objective and universal entitlement, is not the "capitalized truth" and it is surely not better than the informal justice

DOI: 10.4324/9781003385882-1

system, so other contextual "local knowledge" should not be "brutally" made subject to it. Modern legal governance theory forces every citizen to "struggle for their rights" like Qiu Ju, but ignores the social relation network on which the communities depend for their existence.[1] The article by Dr. Su Li challenged the mainstream legal governance theory of China in those days and became a lasting topic in Chinese law research.[2]

In the view of the author, Qiu Ju did not succeed when "asking for an explanation" because this "explanation" was not tolerated by the modern legal governance system, which preset the seamless, universal, and objective entitlement system and is a product of the formalist tradition of Western law. Such formal justice is not consistent with the justice desired by Qiu Ju and her fellow countrymen, thus leading to such a situation. From the puzzled perspective of Qiu Ju, we can see: the "explanation" or justice pursued by the parties is not merely one universal entitlement paradigm, which may include other various contextual factors, such as human environment, morality, and emotion. Only in the limitations of the formal justice system did mediation as the informal justice system find a possible space for its existence in encountering "discourse oppression."

From *The Story of Qiu Ju*, we can see Qiu Ju's dispute was actually a product resulting from the impact of two factors: on the one hand, Qiu Ju was angry and went everywhere appealing, requiring the village head to explain and apologize. Qiu Ju asked for an explanation for vindication, rather than as a "struggle for rights"; on the other hand, the village head would rather pay money as a settlement than apologize, this means that the village head was willing to admit the fact of having done a wrong thing, but was unwilling to apologize due to loss of "face," because apologizing means "being in the wrong" and losing face. Qiu Ju's anger and the village head's "face" resulted in the dispute,[3] as this was not tolerated by the right discourse on which the formal judicial system depends for its operation. Actually, the "right" discourse is a foreign concept transplanted from the West, breaking the native historical tradition,[4] and the migration of the "right" concept has no corresponding and adequately profound foundation in the traditional culture in China.[5] As Professor Ying Xing said:

> In traditional Chinese society, peasants entered into the battle of litigation not necessarily for the monetary interests and the subject matter itself, but they did not struggle for the universal rights under the order of legal governance, but fought for a different position under the order of rite-governance and moral governance and fought for a face and a breath.[6]

It is worth mentioning that they tried initially to resolve the dispute between Qiu Ju and the village head through mediation. According to traditional mediation, in the police station, the policeman criticized both the village head and Qiu Ju's husband for their mistakes and asked the village head to pay Qiu Ju's husband RMB 200 as compensation for medical expenses and loss of working time. The village head was willing to pay the compensation, but refused to admit his mistake and threw the money onto the ground. Obviously, he was not "sincerely convinced" and the act of throwing the money did more damage to Qiu Ju's dignity and further intensified the situation. Without doubt, the mediation failed. The roots of the failure were found in the fact that the mediator was still constrained in handling the dispute under the framework of legal justice. He only paid attention to the economic compensation, but ignored the appeal for an apology, or the repair of moral emotion was concealed.

The Story of Qiu Ju is only a movie, but it was the real epitome of dispute resolution in China's rural society in the early period of reform and opening up and dramatically reflected the impact of modern legal governance on traditional society. Over the last two decades or so, Chinese society has experienced severe social changes, villagers have gradually got rid of their native constraints, the "society of acquaintance" has been gradually replaced by the society of "ripping-off acquaintance" and strangers, interpersonal relationships have been rationalized and "all of the rural society are being remolded, and it moves by force or spontaneously towards the modern society."[7] This greatly improved the gap between the modern legal governance and traditional China, but the sensibilities and ethics of the society of acquaintance are still rooted in Chinese society, so the attitude of dealing with affairs as "harmony is most precious" and the principle of dealing with affairs as being reasonable and fair have been extended until now as a vital part of culture. In the present society, there will still be new "Qiu Jus," the "explanations" they ask for include the right claims based on economic rationality and also the desire and acceptance based on such non-material interests as morality and emotion. Facing these diverse interest appeals, provision of only such formal relief institution as litigation not only may result in the failure of the parties to really access justice, but also may bring about the "puzzles of Qiu Ju."

Therefore, in the new era of structuring the socialist legal governance with Chinese characteristics, it is necessary for us to structure the diversified dispute resolution institution, regard mediation as a dispute resolution mechanism as important as litigation, rediscover the Chinese value of mediation, extract the Chinese legal principle of mediation and tell the Chinese story of mediation properly. Legal principle is a comprehensive and universal concept, condensing the value of law, the virtue of law, the tradition of law, and the axiom of law and exploring the basic principle of a thing.[8] This chapter will discuss the basic legal principles of mediation in China and place its unique connotation and value in the Chinese context and the future development direction of regularization.

1.2 The Concept of Mediation in China

The word "mediation" itself indicates its flexible, easy-to-change and hard-to-understand characteristics. Before understanding Chinese mediation, it is necessary to first define the concept of mediation. Mediation is a dispute resolution mechanism through the intervention of a third party. Article 3 of *Directive 2008/52/EC of the European Parliament and of the Council on Certain Aspects of Mediation in Civil and Commercial Matters* defined mediation as:

> a structured process, however named or referred to, whereby two or more parties to a dispute attempt by themselves, on a voluntary basis, to reach an agreement on the settlement of their dispute with the assistance of a mediator.

Para. 1, Article 1 of the *German Mediation Law* defined mediation as: "a confidential framework-based process, whereby the parties can strive for settlement of disputes upon reaching the consensus on the voluntary basis with the assistance of one or more than one mediator to settle disputes." From the foregoing definitions, it can be seen that in the context of Western legal governance, the connotation of mediation lays stress on the consensus of the parties and the assistance of the mediator. The core characteristics of mediation in the Western context are: neutrality, voluntary consultation, and assistance. Mediators are in a structured neutral position to help the parties in reaching consensus; voluntary formation of "consensus" by the parties is the most essential factor of mediation and the mediation process must be undertaken through completely voluntary consultation. Western scholars are extremely careful about potential coercion in the mediation process, and except where the parties request it, the mediator is not entitled to provide any particular solution for the substantial issues of dispute settlement.

Yet, the general definition of mediation by Chinese scholars is:

> a legal institution and dispute resolution mode of facilitating the parties to a dispute to conclude, on the basis of independent will, an agreement for eliminating the dispute by means of convincing, persuading and educating under the moderation of a third party.[9]

Article 2 of t*he People's Mediation Law of China* provided:

> people's mediation referred to herein deals with the activities of the people's mediation committee to facilitate, in the mode of convincing and persuading, the parties to reach voluntarily a mediation agreement and settle the folk dispute on the basis of equal consultation.

Compared with the definitions in the aforementioned Western law documents, China's mediation institution also emphasized the voluntary will of the parties, but such mediation methods of "convincing," "educating," and "persuading" expressed the active part of the mediator role. It is especially worth mentioning that China had a long history of mediation practice, but in the whole of ancient society, as a discourse, "mediation" had no uniform title. It was not until the Qing Dynasty that in the litigation archives of the prefectures and counties, a dozen names were used to refer to "Tiaojie (mediation)," such as "paijie," "lipo," "lichu," "lilun," "jili," "liquan," "pochu," "tiaochu," "tiaohe," "tiaoting," "lijiang," "lijie," "yaoli," "quanpo," and "lishuo," "chuming."[10] "Mediation" was established as a uniform formal name as early as in *the Civil Mediation Law* formulated in 1930. during the period of the Nanjing National Government.[11] Compared with "tiaojie," the word "tiaochu" reflected the mandatory feature of the Chinese ancient bureaucrats for civil dispute treatment, i.e. to seek the formation of consensus with the substantial ruling of the mediator as the core. Actually, during the time of Mao Zedong, "tiaochu" was extremely popular either as a discourse or as a practice. It was also an important legal heritage left by "Ma Xiwu Trial Mode" in the revolutionary period. The important characteristic of "Ma Xiwu Trial Mode" was to convince and educate the parties in the process of trial and help the parties to promote ideological consciousness and perform by themselves the necessary obligations, so that the dispute was thoroughly settled.[12] Due to such ideological understanding that the formal judicial procedure of judgment and enforcement was observed but with relatively many difficulties,[13] and people's internal contradictions were prevented from intensifying in the social conditions in those days, the mediation of that time presented a strong instructive feature of "convincing – genuinely convinced." As the Japanese scholar Takamieawa Osamu summarized, Chinese dispute resolution is a social drama performed jointly by the third party (the reasoner), who settles disputes by convincing, and the convinced and heart-felt convinced parties (the genuinely convinced persons).[14] In the process of dispute resolution, the mediator tried his best to "convince" the parties to reach a compromise, indicating that the mediation in the Chinese context is directed and it an intervention of a different kind. The mediator is not only in an assisting role of facilitating the two parties in consultation, but also can provide particular solutions and proposals for dispute resolution and even overcome the "pauperization of consensus" by putting pressure to a certain extent on the two parties to agree.

"Mediation" in the English world comes from the Latin word "mediare." and the latter means "intermediary." Yet, in the cultural context of China, the role of the mediator obviously is not only an "intermediary" function and his role and function are often much more active than that of the Western mediator, as it is difficult for the word "mediation" to completely describe it. In a certain sense, mediation in China covers the continuum from the minimum intervention to maximum intervention of the mediator. On one hand, is the complete consensus of the parties, similar to the conciliation of the parties by themselves, and at the other extreme is the complete decision of the mediator, similar to the arbitration award. The real mediation practice is between the consensus and coercion. What most commonly happens is that the conflict between the parties due to conflicting interests leads to the "pauperization of consensus." Complete voluntary will is only an illusion of scholars. To facilitate the conclusion of consensus, it is absolutely necessary for the mediator to introduce properly the mandatory opportunity, as this is just the difference between the mediation and the self-consultation of the parties. Such dispute resolution mode as mediation itself implies the tension between consensus and coercion.

> Voluntary and mandatory are, in the process of dispute resolution by consensus, a pair of objective contradictions, which exclude each other as well as depend on each other. Without voluntary, consensus will lose the soul and reliance. Without coercion, it will reduce the possibility for the formation of consensus.[15]

According to the extent of the mediator's intervention, some Western scholars classified mediation into two modes of "facilitatory" and "evaluative." The role of "facilitatory mediation" is mainly to promote the parties to communicate and understand and encourage them to design their own solution, for they consider it is not appropriate for them to set forth their own evaluation, forecast, and proposal as it will damage external justice. "Evaluative mediation" will provide its own forecast, evaluation, and advice for handling the case.[16] Western scholars often take note of "evaluative mediation," while, in China, "facilitatory mediation" and "evaluative mediation" co-exist and the "evaluative mediation" often operates more effectively. Especially, under the institutional design of the "unification of mediation and trial," when intervening with mediation, Chinese judges obviously have more power than Western judges, in the category of highly evaluative mediation.[17] Chinese judges can hardly avoid, in mediation, disclosing their judgment of cases based on the available facts and law, but they will also carefully avoid making the parties form the implication of "it is just the judgment result," The Chinese judges hold that it is the fact of the "necessary coercion" in mediation that prompts and interprets the litigation risk to the parties, even if mediation fails, it will also make the judgment result be more predictable as well as easier for the two parties to accept. At this level, it is not hard for us to discover that it is a rational and necessary "latent coercion." Just as Professor Fan Yu said:

> In the process of mediation, the neutral mediators actually all have a certain mandatory function, but it is generally indirect, functioning through the parties' right of disposing. But, it cannot be regarded as coercion for the judges to bring forward, at a proper time, the mediation proposal on the basis of consultation of the parties, and even it can be regarded as the natural state of court mediation, because many people participate in mediation based on the trust and reliance on the judges. As long as it does not violate law, procedural justice or principle of honesty and credit, it will be proper to base on the voluntary of the parties.[18]

Therefore, some scholars are worried that the unification of mediation and trial will cause the Chinese judges to undertake mandatory mediation under cover of the modes of "pressing mediation by persuading," "pressing mediation by delaying," "pressing mediation with judgment," "promoting mediation with temptation," which actually ignores the mandatory factor originally in mediation and also exaggerates the conduct of the Chinese judges in court mediation in "bypassing the law."[19]

In short, when discussing the mediation institution in China, in order to avoid the omission of some key characteristics thereof, we cannot completely ignore the cultural context and deem it to be the same as Western "mediation." If it is really necessary to find a word in English corresponding to Chinese mediation, then "reconciliation" may be more appropriate.

1.3 The Cultural Theory of Mediation in China

Law is not at all an isolated social phenomenon and it is always the product of specific social politics, economy, and culture. Mr. Qu Tongzu points out that law is a social product and it has a close relationship to customs and habits. It maintains the existing institution and the moral, ethical, and other value outlooks and reflects the social structure of one particular period and society. As a dispute resolution institution with Chinese characteristics, mediation is also naturally affected by traditional Chinese culture. When talking about the origin of Western legal governance, scholars will definitely mention Ancient Greece and Ancient Rome, when discussing Chinese mediation, we cannot naturally avoid the Confucian cultural tradition in China. Since the "Grand Unification" of the Qin and Han Dynasties, the traditional Chinese society, Confucianism with the emphasis on rite-governance, and legalism with the emphasis on a legal system were integrated, combining rite and law and introducing rite into law. Law was continually made to follow Confucianism, and the concept of class with the emphasis on clans and cardinal guides and constant virtues became the basic spirit of Chinese ancient law, without any fundamental change in the feudal society of more than two thousand years.[20] The influence of such Confucian ideology on dispute resolution modes in China's traditional society was extremely profound.

First of all, it was the final destination of traditional Chinese dispute resolution to pursue "harmony." In the whole traditional Chinese culture, the pursuit of harmony has always been the mainstream value orientation. The traditional Chinese culture claimed the world outlook of the "unification of nature and man" and started with the belief of natural law-nature-harmony to pursue the harmony of the whole natural order. When reflected in handling the social relation between people, such comprehension is just "non-litigation" and harmony-focused. "The function of law is not to provide a legal channel for people to satisfy with selfish desire," but is to "try its best to constrain the selfish desire of people to reach finally the purpose of making people have no disputes."[21] Therefore, in the Confucian classical doctrine, *The Analects*,

Confucius said: "When hearing a lawsuit case, I am like others (without any brilliance). It is important to prevent any lawsuit case from happening." In the view of Confucianism, being "fond of filing a lawsuit" is always the conduct of pursuing selfish desire, which without doubt runs in the opposite direction from moral and rite customs, denying self and returning to propriety, so the state with Confucianism as its ideology dismissed litigation, emphasizing that people should control themselves, exercise forbearance and modesty, compromise out of consideration for the general interest, and even in case of any disputes such as "folk trifles" should also eliminate them through self-mediation of clans and neighbors. In such a society, it was impossible either to produce the lawyer class as in Western society, specialized in advocating a "struggle for rights." In the traditional Chinese culture, lawyers were called "pettifoggers" for disturbing the moral order. All in all, the main tone of the traditional Chinese law culture was to "persuade litigation" and "stop litigation" through mediation, and make, through convincing, educating, and persuading, the parties to compromise with each other and realize the harmony of individuals and even the whole society.[22]

Second, an ethical standard was the social environment for dispute resolution in traditional Chinese society. Confucianism emphasizes the co-construction of family and state, interpersonal relationships are like family relations and traditional judges were also called "parental official (magistrate)." Such family relations obviously did not take litigation confrontation as the normal mode of dispute resolution. Mr. Fei Xiaotong described such a social structure as a kind of "pattern of difference sequence," i.e., self-centered, forming the extendable social relation circle, like ripples when stones are thrown into water.[23] Such a society especially attached importance to sensibility and ethics. Mr. Liang Shuming pointed out: "what the Chinese ethic society takes as precious is in a word: respect for the opposite party,"[24] i.e., the interpersonal contact attaches importance to the opposite party mutually. According to the social mentality of such an ethical stand, traditional Chinese laws were all established on the basis of an obligatory concept, rather than the concept of rights. In such a society, dispute resolution had a moralized feature, while legal governance was only one of the basic modes for maintaining and propagating the social basic morality and "guiding morality and supplementing the law" became the basic choice for social governance. In the meanwhile, an ethical standard also indicates that the social public treasured more the cultural value of family, community, the collective, public order, and social group. Such collectivist or community-based culture formed a significant contrast to the individualist culture of Western society. According to the model of individualist culture, individuals lay more stress on the competitive doctrine of struggling for rights, while under the model of a collectivist culture, individuals prefer to avoid conflicts and take active measures to resolve conflicts, thus providing favorable conditions for mediation culture to come into being.[25]

Finally, the unification of sense, reason, and law became the basic criterion of Chinese social dispute resolution. Under the Confucian ideology, heavenly principles, state law, and human common sense should be united. Dispute resolution should take into consideration sense, principle, and law and especially should understand and sympathize with the normal human sense and normal principles. It indicates that when conducting themselves, being active and handling interpersonal relationships, the Chinese would not like to start with the rational and logic rules like the formalist tradition of Western law, but when applying the rules, traditional Chinese law must refer to the particular and special circumstances for consideration and try as much as possible to make sure to be "logical and reasonable," "fair and reasonable," and "sensible and reasonable." Therefore, some sociologists pointed out: in Chinese society, the principle that most of the people followed when doing things and conducting themselves in society will neither deviate to rationality, nor deviate to irrationality, but hope to balance and mediate between the two.[26] An important feature of Chinese dispute resolution is the emphasis on the balance between law and sensibility and between rationality and irrationality, rather than insisting on the formalized thinking of either this or that in handling disputes. In the view of Max Weber, such a treatment mode is the type of "substantially irrational" law, but it actually corresponds to the practical rationality of the Chinese people.

In the view of some Western scholars, the morality and customs and legal institution of the traditional Chinese society were old and outdated and no relevant contents can be found to match them in Western comparative law, but we cannot exclude them because of these. Law is always the product of national life. Just as Roscoe Pound pointed out:

> The connotation of the traditional Chinese moral philosophy, evaluated from the ethical customs, is widely accepted as the ideological system of legal governance adjusting the social relation and regulating the conduct and manners. As for China, we have adequate reasons to believe this is a kind of advantage.[27]

Since the late Qing Dynasty, Chinese society has been fundamentally transformed, and with the disintegration of traditional society and the acceleration of modernization, the society of acquaintance was transformed into the society of strangers and the society of ethics was transformed to the society of law principle, but up to now, China's state governance still placed the tradition of moral governance in an important position. On December 9, 2016, the Political Bureau of the Communist Party of China (CPC) Central Committee held the thirty-seventh collective study on legal governance and moral governance in the history of China, at which General Secretary Xi Jinping pointed out one significant feature for the socialist governance with Chinese characteristics

> is to insist on the combination of governing the state according to law and governing the state with morality, and emphasize the legal governance and moral governance at the same time and attach importance to both. It is the summary of historical experiences as well as the profound understanding of governance.

The Fourth Plenary Session of the 18th CPC Central Committee proposed explicitly that it was an important principle that must be insisted on when realizing the comprehensive promotion of governing the state according to law to "insist on the combination of governing the state according to law and governing the state with morality." In the meantime, the Communist Party of China also proposed explicitly to integrate the core socialist values into the construction of legal governance, and the social standard or collective feature with the core socialist values is also favorable for the formation of a mediation culture.

Due to the influence of modernization by Western legal governance and the tradition of the socialist law culture, the contemporary mediation institution in Chin is observed to be different from the traditional mediation in terms of ideology as well as regularization, and, therefore, it is somewhat simple and rough to attribute the developed mediation institution and system of contemporary China completely to the traditional culture, but we still can discover, in the present practice of mediation, the influence of traditional culture. In order to display more clearly such an influence, we have selected, as an example, the event propagated and reported by the official journal sponsored by the Supreme People's Court:[28]

JUDGE: You realized last year you agreed to compromise, but up to now, Xiao Chu, you have not paid the amount of RMB 20,000 and you really have not kept your word.

DEFENDANT: I am really short of money, because no money was earned from the investment in excavators and the house loan has to be paid back monthly.

PLAINTIFF: The house and son are both given to you, and you must give me the amount of twenty thousand Yuan.

JUDGE: You are both from Tongcheng, and know the story of "Six Feet Lane."[29] Now I'll let you watch and listen to it, and hope you can compromise with each other."

...

The above is the process of mediating in a case of post-divorce property dispute by the judge of Tongcheng People's Court, Tongcheng Municipal People's Court Anhui Province. The couple divorced through agreement at the bureau of civil affairs and the man had not paid RMB 20,000 as promised. The trial judge organized the mediation before and during the court hearing, but the mediation failed because the woman was angry. After the court hearing, the judge again led the two to the cultural wall of "Six Feet Lane" constructed by the court for mediation. Finally, the woman agreed to extend the time of payment and thus the case was closed through mediation on the spot.

Tongcheng Municipal People's Court Anhui Province followed the wisdom of the traditional culture and made use of the well-known story of "Six Feet Lane" to guide and enlighten the parties to "exercise forbearance and modesty and live in harmony," carrying out the "Six Feet Lane Mediation Work Method" with significant local characteristics through the mediation process of contradictions and disputes, promoting the harmony after case was closed and settlement, and spreading social positive energy.

In June 2015, Tongcheng People's Court summarized the "Six Feet Lane Mediation Work Method" thus:

- start by narrating the anecdotes of the past in alluding to the present and enlighten with the classics of Six Feet Lane;
- focus on observation and analysis and guide using sense, principle and law;
- take the resolution of contradiction as the key point and move people with the idea of harmony being precious;
- take fairness and justice as the fundamental points and make it clear to people in a state of knowing what to expect and then retreat.

In 2016, Tongcheng People's Court published the study, "Suggestions for Promoting the Implementation of Six Feet Lane Mediation Work Method," stating that everyone can tell the story of Six Feet Lane, everyone can use the "Six Feet Lane Mediation Work Method." People must make sure the three segments—pre-litigation, mid-litigation, and post-litigation—and three processes—case filing, trial, and execution—are completely covered to establish the litigation service station and Six Feet Lane Mediation Work Office at Tongcheng Court. People must make use of the fence of the court to set up the "Six Feet Lane" cultural wall, integrating outstanding traditional culture into the court work and making a litigation and mediation brand with unique characteristics.

In the meantime, Tongcheng People's Court also formulated the Operating Norms for Six Feet Lane Mediation Work, requiring everyone to be flexible in handling the "six-step rule" of listening, discriminating, persuading, making use, compromising, and making peace:

- listening, i.e., to listen to the statements of the two parties concerned, saying what is in their mind at court;
- discriminating, i.e., to interpret the law and make clear the facts, and discriminate right from wrong;
- persuading, i.e., to visit Six Feet Lane or Six Feet Lane Cultural Wall, listen to the story of Six Feet Lane for persuasion;
- making use, i.e., to narrate anecdotes of the past in alluding to the present and use this as a lever to mediate;

- compromising, i.e., the strong person compromises first and undertakes mutual understanding and compromise;
- making peace, i.e., to resolve disputes and shake hands for peace.

This is a typical case of the Chinese grass-roots court in making good use of local traditional cultural resources for mediation. In the practice of court mediation, we can see the influence of the traditional Confucian culture. From the viewpoint of the official coverage, such a mediation mode with the combination of tradition and modern law and sense has a remarkable effect. At Tongcheng Court, the withdrawal ratio of civil and commercial cases through mediation was up to 62 percent, indicating that of the civil and commercial cases appealed to the court, more than half were settled through mediation.

1.4 The Axiology of Mediation in China

Mediation and judicial judgment are both dispute resolution mechanisms, but mediation is a kind of consensus-oriented dispute resolution mechanism of convincing—being genuinely convinced, while judicial judgment is a kind of mandatory dispute resolution mechanism of confrontational judgment. Confrontation means that the two parties to a dispute undertake: a kind of competition through a series of attacking and defending means, such as appeal, counter-appeal, argument, claim, denial, producing evidence, and cross-examination, and strive to present to the judge the facts of the case favorable to them, while on the basis of the litigation materials provided by the two parties, the judge must make a mandatory judgment of black or white.[30] As Judge Wang Zuhui, in the Qing Dynasty, said:

> It is good to be diligent to hear and judge. However, where it is unnecessary to distinguish black and white excessively for amity, it is better to mediate through relatives and friends. Therefore, we hear and judge according to law, while mediate with emotions. Law must distinguish the clear and the muddy, while emotion allows somewhat mistakes in distinguishing the right or wrong.

Regarding the ideological difference between mediation and litigation, the author compared them on various occasions: the idea of litigation is to discover the case facts through the confrontation of interests between the parties, while the idea of mediation is to realize the consensus of the two parties to resolve a dispute by forming the community of interests between the parties. The litigation procedure upholds a static interest view: based on the litigation target, in the framework of disciplinary and adversarial authoritarianism, resolve the disputes within the dispute target of the parties and ignore the disputes outside the dispute target, while mediation maintains the diverse and dynamic interests, including the balance of material interest and spiritual interest, present interests and future interests, direct interests and indirect interests. Litigation is mainly looking backwards (recalling), while mediation is looking forward (prospective); litigation is the sliced formal thinking, while mediation is the comprehensive and overall thinking.[31] With the claims as the core, the litigation idea structures the logic of self-consistency and the seamless abstract "axiom system," while the basic value of mediation is the balance of interests. The idea of litigation states there is "only one correct answer" with positive law as the basis, while the value criterion of mediation is the diverse logic, with the compatibility and combination of sense, principle, and law; the idea of litigation pursues one-dimensional formalism, while the value pursued by mediation is a kind of "comprehensive justice" to balance diverse interests.[32] Based on the difference between the two forms of justice and thinking that the comparative advantage of mediation is shown as: mediation resolves a huge number of contradictions and disputes in a relatively relaxed way, as it favors repairing the relationship between the parties; mediation resolves a huge number of contradictions and disputes in a more thorough way, as it favors achieving closure of the case and reinstating harmony; mediation resolves a huge number of contradictions and disputes in a more flexible way, as it favors making up the defects and deficiencies in the type of judgment; mediation resolves a huge number of contradictions and disputes in a longer-term way, as it favors overall social harmony and stability of social relations; mediation resolves a huge number of contradictions and disputes in a more convenient and faster way, as it favors saving judicial resources, easing the pressure on the judicial system, and reducing the economic costs to the parties. Accordingly, some scholars have concluded there are eight comparative advantages of mediation over litigation:

1. voluntary use of mediation;
2. conciliation as the mediation purpose;
3. negotiability of the mediation process;
4. openness of the mediation contents;
5. confidentiality of the mediation information;
6. simplicity and efficiency of the mediation procedure;
7. flexibility and variety of mediation results;
8. the low cost of mediation.[33]

Such a comparative summary is comprehensive, but mainly describes the general features and common values of the Chinese and Western mediation institutions, and fails to display the unique value of Chinese mediation, which determines the vitality of the mediation institution in China. The author claims that the framework of the present "Grand Law Science" system and the "New Liberal Arts"[34] construction is the precondition for building the independent category of "mediation science" and thus forming the theory of an independent mediation discourse system to reinstate the value of mediation.

1.4.1 Mediation's View of the Person: Total Assurance of Human Dignity and Subject Value

Currently, dispute resolution theory centered on litigation ignores the subject value of the person. The mainstream research theory simplified the complete image of man as a utilitarian animal who only pursues the maximum material interests, and ignored the complete image of the person.[35] Modern litigation institution is a kind of highly formatted technique that transforms the statements and words of the parties into evidence and legal terms and cuts the facts of life up into legal facts. This process definitely filters out the emotional and moral narrative of the parties and forces the parties to take action according to the litigation procedure, while the two parties must try everything possible to attack and defend, and "swallow" the litigation results arising from their own conduct. Yet, the awarding result by the court can only make judgment of this or that for the right and wrong, grant the right to one party and the mistake to the other party, and try its best to transform the appeal of the parties into monetary compensation, which is extremely important in cases of infringement dispute and contractual dispute. During this process, the parties also have the right of disposition and space of free action, but eventually they must accept, in uncertainty, the mandatory awarding result of the court. Facing the highly complicated and specialized litigation procedure, like K in *The Trial*, the novel by Kafka, the parties are confined in the "legal fence" that they barely understand, resulting in the separation of the judicature and society. Therefore, modern law and its litigation institution strictly follow the formal rational logic in the Weberian sense, any political, emotion, moral, and other substantial factors will be deemed to be irrational factors to be excluded outside litigation. Such ice-cold formal rationality has resulted in the "differentiation" of man to some extent. It presets the person as an abstract and one-dimensional economically rational being, ignoring the spiritual pleasure, anger, sorrow, and joy felt and ignoring that during the course of the dispute occurrence and settlement, people experience such passive emotions as complaint, dissatisfaction, and anger as well as such positive emotions as sympathy, friendship, and honesty. It is important to transform such passive emotions into positive emotions. However, "Human beings are most emotional animals. We love and we hate; we fall into extreme depression and we experience happiness and pleasure; we also feel ashamed, guilty and lonely; we are sometimes righteous and sometimes also vengeful."[36] Due to the domination of rationalist thinking, for a long time, Western society has kept rationality and such irrational factors as emotion in binary opposition, ignoring the transformation of passive emotional factors into positive emotional factors so as to help the fundamental resolution of disputes, as is the fundamental reason why Qiu Ju showed a puzzled face when she faced the "explanation" given by the modern judicial procedure.[37]

It is just because of this, in the report to the 19th National Congress, as the ruling party, the CPC, was aware of, that China's major social contradictions have already been observed to undergo new changes, i.e., the change from the contradiction between the increasing demand of people for material culture and the backward social production to the contradiction between the increasing demand of people for a better life and the unbalanced and inadequate development of Chinese society.[38] This is actually the profound understanding of human development law. Social transformation is substantially the transformation of human beings, i.e., it is necessary to pay close attention to the "all-round development of human beings" and avoid the differentiation of human beings as "one dimensional man" in modern industrial society.[39] Human beings are different from birds and beasts because they not only have the material survival needs for clothing, food, accommodation, and travel as well as having, as a kind of social animal, such social contact needs, such as safety, security, and social justice as well as such mental spiritual needs such as ethics and morality, being respected and self-realization. The so-called "all-round development of human beings" should satisfy multi-level demands such as material, social, and spiritual demands, and also bring the better life humans are looking forward to. Faced with the diverse demands for a better life, dispute resolution mechanism should not follow only one road such as litigation, but should set up diversified dispute resolution mechanisms, enabling parties to be linked emotionally and complying with reason, as this is the essence of a diversified dispute resolution mechanism.[40] It is based on this understanding that the CPC promoted the construction of dispute resolution mechanisms at the level of state governance and encouraged the modernization of the governance system as an important part of the strategy of comprehensive legal governance. This is a major difference between the Chinese and the Western societies in the construction of legal governance.

In the diversified dispute resolution mechanism, mediation is placed in a prime position because mediation not only can respond to the appeal of the parties for the material interests, but also can encompass the spiritual appeals that are ignored by litigation but are essential for people. Mediation is actuated, undertaken, and completed, all with the free disposition or control of the parties as the principle, so that it is deeply felt that the dispute subjects decide by themselves and take their own responsibility. American scholar Lon Fuller defined the "central feature of mediation" as "making the parties to re-understand their own capability and such capability is not to force them to do so through regulation, but help them to change their own attitude and orientation."[41] German scholars pointed out that the basic principle of mediation is: "the dignity of man is respected and emphasized. The entirety composed of his body, soul and spirit is all sincerely treated … Mediation is just a kind of conflict resolution method for treating properly the entirety of man."[42] The mediator must show respect to the personal life and fortune of the parties, regard the emotion of the parties as a part of the mediation procedure, allowing the individual value of the parties to play a role in the mediation process. The mediator must take into consideration the reasons behind each dispute as a whole, the specific personal demands of the parties, the maintenance of future relations and other factors so as to seek a rational resolution of disputes. Therefore, mediation is essentially the comprehensive assurance of the dignity of man and a person's subject value, i.e., in the picture of mediation, man is emphasized, the particular, full and living existence rather than an abstract, isolated, and materialized individual. In terms of the final results, mediation ensures that all the parties can find the acceptable equilibrium point that is satisfactory to all the parties in the specific situation, i.e., "comprehensive justice," "situational justice," and "co-existential justice" in the field of diverse interests.[43]

1.4.2 Mediation and the "Polycentric Task": How Mediation Dissolves Judicial Difficulties

Generally speaking, the disputes that judicial procedure can handle must have the legal contentiousness or justifiability. Such justifiability requires the following conditions: disputes must be the particular and definite disputes of rights and obligations between the parties in opposition, and must be the matured and non-previous disputes rather than disputes that possibly won't happen, are imagined or already resolved.[44] American jurist Fuller discussed this in more details.[45] According to Fuller, the disputes that judicial judgment can resolve must be as follows: (1) the dispute subject is not beyond the technical capacity of the judge, lawyer and the parties; (2) the disputes include the contentious points of confrontation between the two parties and the parties can smoothly provide evidence in these cases for these contentious points; (3) the facts of the disputes have already happened; (4) the principle as a basis can be obtained for judgment; (5) the disputes must be ones for which definite judgment of right and wrong can be made; and (6) the disputes must be ones for which adequate confrontation argument can be accommodated. On the contrary, the judicial process is unsuited tor resolving the following disputes: (1) the judicial process cannot carry the new reform target and judges cannot act like politicians; (2) the judicial process cannot resolve the indefinite contentious points put forward by the parties and judges cannot act like legislators; (3) where society is changing rapidly and the social order is being severely restructured, the function of a judicial trial will be greatly discounted; (4) if disputes cannot make a definite differentiation between right or wrong, it is hard for judicial trial procedure to act, e.g., the internal relationship of couples; (5) there is a continued relation between the two parties, who must still collaborate with each other after the judgment, it is unsuitable for judicial judgment to resolve; (6) it is unsuitable for judicial judgment to make institutional arrangements; and (7) it is unsuitable for judicial judgment to handle the "polycentric task." Of these seven types of disputes unsuitable for judicial judgment to resolve, the first six types can all be easily understood, and it is especially required to point out what he "polycentric task" is. In *The Forms and Limits of Adjudication*, a famous thesis extensively cited, Fuller gave an example to expound this concept:

In New York, one rich old lady Timken died and left behind a very valuable famous art collections. Her will was to donate these famous paintings to two museums, but the will had no particular distribution program. Then, the two museum beneficiaries argued over how to distribute these famous paintings. In the opinion of Fuller, this was just a "polycentric task." Since the distribution of any famous painting will affect the distribution of other famous paintings and each beneficiary had different preference for the works and relied mutually, the judge could not assess the value of these paintings before making an equal distribution. In Fuller's opinion, such disputes were just like a spider web, with different factors involving one another, and the pulling of any single one thread of the cobweb will result in the complex change of the whole web.

Therefore, such disputes cannot be resolved through judicial judgment on right and wrong or black and white, or by declaring simply the rights and obligations of the parties. They are better resolved through market mechanism or administration.[46] Fuller had not expressively proposed to resolve such disputes through mediation, but actually implied the meaning of resolution through consultation.

In the cases brought to court, many disputes will involve the "polycentric task," only to different extents. Of these disputes, some are in the category of continued contact between the parties to some extent (e.g., neighborhood) and some are types of disputes for which the existential scope of rights between the parties can be judged in terms of right and wrong (e.g., property disputes between clans and families). For all such disputes, it is suitable to seek, through mediation, the equilibrium point of interest acceptable to both parties. In China, many disputes observed during the transformation period are, in a certain sense, the "polycentric task." When involving such issues as rural land, housing removal and relocation, enterprise restructuring, employment disputes, illegal financing, "realistic conflicts," resulting from the surface rights and interests, and "non-realistic conflicts," resulting from the imbalance in the social structure, co-existed. In order to maintain social stability, the state expected courts could realize the combination of political effect, legal effect, and social effect when handling such disputes, but it was obviously a task that the judicial judgment could hardly complete. For a good effect, mediation became a flexible and effective option.

1.4.3 Mediation and Social Governance: Litigation as Source Governance and the Maintenance of Stability

Since the reform and opening up, China has achieved the rapid development attracting worldwide attention, but also has experienced the sharp social transformation. Now the social structure is in a state of "break" and "imbalance," thus resulting in the high and frequent occurrence of social contradictions. If these contradictions are not properly handled, they may affect the stability of the social order, and the stable social environment is the precondition for economic development. Therefore, the social governance idea of the Chinese government especially emphasizes the stability of social order. "Maintaining stability is of top priority" has become a popular slogan. Since mediation can often fundamentally resolve the disputes between the parties and repair damaged social relation, mediation is expected to play a role in maintaining social stability. The Chinese people generally are aware of hardship and lay stress on taking precautions against a possible danger and saving for a rainy day. According to *The Medical Classic of the Yellow Emperor*, a classical ancient book of Traditional Chinese Medicine, "the Saint does not treat after one becomes sick, but prevents when one is not sick." The understanding of the state for dispute resolution is also the same, eliminating the contradictions in an expanding state to prevent them from becoming public security cases, criminal cases, and even group events. Some Western scholars have sharply captured the function of social governance offered by Chinese mediation, i.e., mediators are there not only to resolve disputes, but also to prevent contradictions from happening, prevent contradictions from developing and avoid contradictions from arising.[47] Because "mediation can reduce a big trouble into a small one and a small one into nothing and can avoid a trifle from becoming a major trouble." This point is significantly reflected in the work experiences of local people's mediation committees. The national model mediator has engaged in people's mediation for nearly three decades, Wu Qiangzhong concluded the people's mediation work as the "seven-word method" of "quick, dare, stable, careful, accurate, close, and visiting." This experience was officially promoted in Zhejiang Province as[48]:

"Quick" means to go straight to the site, take quick action and prevent the development of the situation.

"Dare" means that facing the danger of possible intensification, the people's mediator should carry forward the dauntless heroism, facing dangers fearlessly, stepping forward bravely, eliminating risks calmly, preventing the expansion of the event, and creating conditions and winning the time for further proper persuasion.

"Stable" means to keep stable the parties and prevent the parties from making a reckless move and committing physical assault or murder.

"Careful" means persuading the parties patiently and carefully, moving them with emotions, convincing them with reasons, and reasoning with law so that the two parties will understand the cardinal principles, discern the overall situation, and eliminate the misunderstanding.

"Accurate" means finding accurately the crux, applying the medicine according to indications, opening different locks with different keys, facilitating the parties to change their thoughts and eliminate the trend toward intensification.

"Close" means collaborating closely, coordinating mutually and controlling jointly with all relevant departments, and especially for the group disputes, cooperating energetically with the relevant departments, deploying various means for the work, and preventing the intensification of contradictions and disputes.

"Visiting" is to make timely return visits after mediation of disputes, undertake the work in a timely manner in case of discovering any trend of re-occurrence, and consolidating the mediation achievements.

In view of the mediator's work experiences, mediation in China is not a simple alternative to litigation, but is a kind of means for social comprehensive governance and a part of the modernization of social governance. Currently, the CPC is proposing to persist in systematic governance, legal governance, comprehensive governance, and source governance and insisting upon pushing forward the alternative dispute resolution. Therefore, China's mediation institutional system is a kind of "grand mediation" system, i.e., with the respect to the status of continually emerging social in-depth contradictions, under the guidance of the policy of "combination of mediation and visit, precaution is crucial, by multiple means, and using cooperation" and under the leadership of the CPC committees and the domination of the government, we understand multiple forces and use multiple means to jointly mediate in the people's internal contradictions.[49] From the perspective of the state's political governance, by bringing into the vision of mediation research such prominent social issues of governance as petition letters, public order, maintaining stability and law enforcement, it is possible to understand more profoundly the political social significance implied in the present mediation process in Chinese society.[50]

1.5 Regularization of Mediation in China

Before the mediation institution in China adopted the important function of maintaining social stability, mediation in China once was driven by the judicial policy to come in fits and starts, i.e., depreciating and excluding mediation for the purpose of intensifying the judicial function or advocating the active judiciary of pursuing "zero judgment." To a certain extent, it led to the randomness of mediation and affected the legalization and institutionalization of mediation. The fundamental reason for the abnormal operation of the mediation institution was the dominance of the logic of Chinese-style stability. The core task of stability is to control different social interest disputes, calm down different social unsuitable emotions and effectively maintain the social order. The CPC's understanding of stability saw the changing and developing process from a unitary emphasis on "stability is of the top priority" to correct treatment of the relations between reform, development, and stability and then to the unification of stability, i.e., maintaining and safeguarding rights.[51] This is actually also a changing process from an outlook of rigid stability to an outlook of tenacious stability. Based on observation of the Chinese local governments in maintaining social stability, Professor Yu Jianrong proposed the concepts of "rigid stability" and "tenacious stability." "Rigid stability" means that society lacks the necessary tenacity and extendibility, and has no buffer zone and the government is always in a state of high tension, regarding the public interest expressed as damaging to the social control and order and the state attempts to deploy all resources to maintain stability. On the contrary, "tenacious stability" is an outlook of order that is decentralized and open, dynamic, peaceful and orderly and able to self-repair.[52] An "outlook of rigid stability" is actually a product of the pressurized system, i.e., a package of work mechanisms structured by the party committees and governments at all levels for the purpose of accelerating the local social and economic development and completing all the orders and tasks allocated by the superior, combining the administrative orders with material interests and with the incentive of promotion in the job.[53] In such a pressurized system, in order to complete the tasks of maintaining stability imposed by the superior and even central government, the local governments at all levels may actually often take the easy way to maintain stability, i.e., simply equaling "maintaining stability" to "settling is just the stability, treating fairly is just the level, having no trouble is just the capability, compromising is just the harmony."[54] This is especially reflected prominently in administrative mediation, i.e., the parties to disputes urged by the government, by approaching Beijing for petition, to compromise and grant the material interests surpassing the law, thus consuming a huge amount of public resources, increasing the governance cost of local governments and weakening the authority of grass-roots governments.[55] In such a pressurized system, the logic of dispute resolution was also distorted, thus leading to such consequences as ignoring the procedure and regulation, violating the law to force mediation, exchanging justice for harmony, and damaging the judicial function.

Since the 18th National Congress, the Communist Party of China has continually summarized the experiences and lessons of social governance since the reform and opening up and attached more importance to the comprehensive structuring of interest coordination mechanisms, appealing to the expression mechanism, the contradiction mediation and disposal mechanism, the rights and interest safeguarding mechanism. On January 7, 2014, at the Meeting of the Central Political and Legal Work, General Secretary Xi Jinping stated: "Treat correctly the relation of stability with right-safeguarding, vitality and order, adequately motivate all positive factors to ensure the society is full of life and vitality as well as keeping the peace and order." This indicated that the Communist Party of China was aware of the defects with rigid stability and established the people-centric scientific outlook of social stability, and the systematic governance, legal governance, comprehensive governance, and source governance of society, and all have the aim of safeguarding the basic rights of the citizens. Under the guidance of such an outlook of social stability, mediation can be normalized, institutionalized, and legalized and can become the dispute resolution mechanism for resolving properly the reasonable and legal interest appeals of citizens, rather than a tool of simply treating fairly and straightening out. Within the strategic framework of comprehensive legal governance, the regularization of mediation in China is a systematic exercise. First of all, it is necessary to further perfect the mediation legislation. *The People's Mediation Law*, published in 2010 is excessively rough and cannot meet the present mediation practice. It is necessary to improve on it to integrate China's existing mediation institution and formulate the uniform mediation law. Regarding this issue, the author will discuss in detail hereinafter and here will mainly reveal the two basic issues that cannot be avoided in the regularization of the mediation institution in China:

First, mediation must resolve contradictions within the framework of legal governance. Modern mediation should intensify the social function of eliminating confrontation and settling and stopping disputes, abide by legal rationality and avoid legal nihilism in the process of dispute resolution. Mediation is not necessarily limited strictly to legal norms, as moral, custom, emotion, and other informal norms or folk law can all become factors for consideration, and policy, economy, administrative, and other means can all become the tactics of condensing a common view, but it must be undertaken on the premises of not violating the legal provisions and not damaging the principle of legal governance. Since under the previous rigid stability, some of the parties will make use of the pressurized stability system to seek economic interests exceeding the law and especially after the routine legal procedure is exhausted, they will still repeat a multiplicity of actions, bypassing petitions, going to Beijing for petition, and pressurizing by attending such important time segments as "Two Conferences," the local party committees and governments, or the courts to break through, due to the pressure of stability, the legal provisions and available policies to "break up, cover up and pay money for peace." But such short-sighted practice will again intensify, on the contrary, the public mentality of "big trouble getting big resolution, small trouble getting small resolution, and no trouble getting no resolution," "the crying baby has milk."[56] Therefore, the present grand mediation system must be operated pursuant to the bottom line of law, maintaining the authority of judicial final dispute resolution, providing the function of deploying the mode of legal governance and thinking of legal governance to resolve social contradictions and eliminate the public mindset of making trouble as the way to resolve disputes. This is the requirement for the dialectical unification of maintaining stability and safeguarding rights.

Another important reason for undertaking mediation under the framework of legal governance is to get rid of the mediation mode "mixing water into mud (blur the line between right and wrong)." "Mixing water into mud" is one common and prominent type of all interests criticizing and opposing mediation and also gives the impression of stigmatization of mediation that can hardly be eliminated. To support the name of mediation institution, it is necessary to stop the mediation mode of "mixing water into mud." "Mixing water into mud" is actually a figurative metaphor, while the more figurative expression is no discrimination of black and white and blaming both of the parties, i.e., the mediator fails to discriminate the right and wrong or the black and white and handles the dispute between the two parties in a simple middle-ground mode. The mediation result formed thereby is a kind of vague legal product that may result in discounting of rights or damage to interests. This is rather common in the local mediation in China. One "dispute over stealing a watermelon" that initiated the extensive public concern on the internet in 2019 is just the typical mediation of "mixing water into mud." The basic details of the case are as follows:

> A melon grower Pang lived in Qixian County, Hebi City of Henan Province, and contracted 200 Chinese *mu* of land for growing watermelons, but recently after the watermelons ripened, some people often came to steal the melons. On July 29, Song rode an electric bike with his daughter to the melon field to steal melons. When Pang discovered him, Song attempted to ride away but was caught by Pang. In the process as Pang stopped the melon thief, the electric bike was pulled down, and the three people fell over the bike. Song's knee was scratched and bleeding. Song first called the police. Upon arriving at the site, the policeman from Beiyang Police Station of Qixian County Bureau of Public Security asked Pang to compensate Song RMB 300, and Pang felt wronged: "Why have I to compensate the melon thief when my melon is stolen?" This event was reported by the local media, initiating a heated discussion. The netizens successively complained about the unfairness. With the event reported by the media, Qixian County Bureau of Public Security attached great importance and immediately organized its personnel for verification. Due to the patient education and advice of the policemen, Song and his daughter were aware that they had made a mistake first and voluntarily returned the compensated amount of RMB 300, and the two parties reached an understanding. In the meantime, the policemen of the Police State also helped Pang to take safety protection measures and set up the eye-catching slogans to prompt and warn against stealing melons.

In this case, the initial mediation of the policeman aroused dissatisfaction because he had not discriminated who was responsible for the crime and mistook the melon thief as the injured party. The melon grower justifiably defended his property from being stolen. By only considering the fact of the melon thief's injury, the policeman asked the melon grower to pay RMB 300, but obviously this neither complied with the legal provisions nor was the result that the melon grower was willing to accept. As early as in China's Ming Dynasty, the local administrative official Hairui made a penetrating self-examination of such mediation mode of "mixing water into mud":

> When asking those insiders, most of them said that litigation should be undertaken as per 40–60 so as to stop litigation. If the plaintiff is judged as 60% reasonable, the defendant must also be judged as 40% reasonable. The right and wrong of the two persons should not show much

> difference so as to avoid re-appealing due to engagement. Even though such judgment can prevent litigation for the time being, actually litigation will take place again afterwards due to disputes. If the person in the wrong and fond of going to court is judged as 50% right, he will tangle with the person framed as 50% guilty so that he becomes happy. When the subordinate guesses and knows the intention of the superior, litigation will thrive ... Can it be resolved in ambiguity because of fear of lawsuits? A gentleman holds the correct principle of his own for the rights and wrongs of the world. The 40–60 practice is a hypocritical approach that encourages lawsuits and causes disputes and thus is not feasible.

Modern mediation is mainly a kind of "judgment-type mediation," i.e., to "discover the legally correct solution" as the aim under the shadow of law.[57] On the basis of the legal mediation principle, Chinese law has also established in particular the principle of "facts are clear and right and wrong is distinguished" for the purpose of preventing the mediators from "mixing water into mud" in mediation. In terms of implementing the particular institutions, it is necessary to stimulate the special code of conduct for mediation to provide the parties with the adequate procedural assurance, including regulating the formulation of mediation notes to form the voluntary records and certification of the mediation process, providing the parties with judicial relief approaches for mandatory mediation in violation of the voluntary principle and establishing the accountability mechanism for illegal mediation. In the meantime, it is necessary to cancel completely the examination and incentive mechanism for mediation rate and prevent mediators (especially judges) from having a motive for forced mediation.

Second, it is necessary to treat correctly the relations between mediation and judgment. In terms of the relation between mediation and judgment, China has experienced basically the following policy adjustments in different periods: "mediation-focused" (1949–1981), "emphasis on mediation" (1982–1990), "voluntary and legal mediation" (1991–2002), "mediate as possible, judge as possible, combine mediation and judgment, and close cases for settlement" (2003–2008), and "mediation first, mediation-judgment combination" (2009–2013). Especially, at one time, in order to respond to the slogan for the local party committees and governments to maintain stability and serve the overall interests, it was once attempted to anxiously seek "zero judgment" and undertake the digital examination of the "mediation rate," but this violated the judicial law, deviated from the institutional original intention of mediation and damaged the independence of judgment. Consequently, court mediation deviated from the correct operating track severely, weakening the function of realizing, though the judicature, the "governance of rules" and establishing the sense of rules. Such a consequence was reflected most incisively in the Nanjing "Peng Yu Case" of 2006:

On November 20, 2006, Nanjing citizen Granny Xu got off the bus and then fell down at the bus stop. Seeing this, Peng Yu got off and collided with her. Upon the arrival of Granny Xu's relatives, together with her relatives, Peng Yu sent Granny Xu to hospital for treatment and paid, on the spot, RMB 200 for her. Granny Xu received surgery and was hospitalized for treatment, resulting in a series of expenses and losses. Afterwards, Granny Xu claimed Peng Yu for the medical expenses and he refused and after all types of mediation failed, submitted a civil lawsuit to Gulou District Court on January 4, 2007.

After the accident happened, upon receipt of the report, the police station treated the accident and prepared the interrogation record according to the law. With the case brought to court, the policeman in charge of the accident was present in court, stating the major process of the event and made a transcript of the conversation. The major content of talk was: a collision happened between Granny Xu and Peng Yu. Peng Yu viewed the minutes of talk reported in the interrogation record prepared by the policeman in charge of the accident on the day of incident, and the following day, for both of the parties, without checking with the interrogation record, its truth could not affirmed, and the son of Granny Xu worked at the Bureau of Public Security. Granny Xu stated that "at that time I personally saw him running into me!" and said "I and my husband both have the retirement pension and medical insurance and our son works at Bureau of Public Security. It does not mean that we cannot afford the medical expenses and we just want justice." Peng Yu denied that he ran into Granny Xu and insisted that he was doing boldly what was right. Upon the failure of mediation, the court of first instance affirmed Peng Yu had committed an infringement and ordered him to pay. But the following reasoning of the judge in the court verdict unexpectedly aroused a big dispute in society:

> By analyzing as by convention, the possibility for him to run into the plaintiff is relatively high. If the defendant were doing boldly what was right, the actual practice would be to catch the person running into the plaintiff rather than holding them up with a good intention; if the defendant was doing something good, according to social reason, upon arrival of the plaintiff's relatives, he could have completely made clear the facts and asked the relatives of the plaintiff to send the plaintiff to the hospital and leave at his own discretion, but the defendant had not done so and his conduct was obviously contrary to common sense.

After the judgment of first instance was made, Peng Yu expressed great annoyance, molding in the public opinion the image of "being accused falsely for saving someone with good intention" and "a hero sweats as well as bleeds," as he touched the vulnerable moral nerve of the public. In an environment where the moral manner of doing boldly what is right is rare, the public generally viewed that this judgment was a symbolic event of social moral decline.

Due to the high concerns and continual reporting of the media, facing such surging influence of public opinions, the parties including the plaintiff, the defendant, and the judge were all overwhelmed. Granny Xu was disabled due to her injury. When recuperating at home, she continually received abusive calls and attacks from strangers and journalists in interviews, censuring her for "framing a case against a good person." Facing one after another journalist and interrogation from all sides, Peng Yu also felt deeply worried. In this background, the court of second instance organized the two parties to meet for pre-court mediation, and the two parties reached a conciliation agreement and applied for the withdrawal of the appeal. The two parties requested the mediation content be kept confidential. Seven years after the case was closed, Peng Yu admitted the collision.

The mediation of the case was obviously due to the certain pressure of public opinion on the local party committee and government and the court. The case was eventually closed through mediation, resolving the dispute of the individual case and achieving the dispute settlement, but failed to fix the rights and duties. Since the basic facts of the case were observed as a major dispute, the mediation result could not form the significant rule guidance – what action people should take when seeing someone fall down in future, to avoid "being framed for saving someone with good intention." In such cases that need to establish the basic sense of rules and the idea of right and wrong, judgment is obviously required to be defined expressly. The basic function of the judicature should be to define right and duty for dispute settlement, rather than define a dispute for dispute settlement. Only through the definition of judicial judgment, the rational allocation of right and obligatory relations, and a clear classification of the limits of ownership, will it be possible to clarify the conduct limits of each person so as to rationally maintain individual free space and the scope of interests and ensure their conduct will not surpass the limit, thus preventing the dispute from happening and maintaining the safety of social order.[58]

In general, in terms of the relation between mediation and judgment, the official policy for "mediation first" is consistent. Article 14 of the *Provisions of the Supreme People's Court for Application of Summary Procedure in Trial of Civil Cases* (2003) provided: for the court trial of the following civil cases, the people's court should mediate first: (1) marriage and family disputes and inheritance disputes; (2) employment contract disputes; (3) disputes over damage compensation with relatively definite relation of rights and obligations resulting from traffic accidents and industrial injuries; (4) household and neighborhood disputes; (5) partnership agreement disputes; (6) dispute on small litigation target amount, except the disputes that cannot be mediated or are necessary for mediation according to the nature of cases and actual conditions of the parties. Such disputes are mostly the disputes between acquaintances and it is better to resolve the contradictions through mediation. Article 2 of the *Provisions of the Supreme People's Court on the Issues for Civil Mediation Work of People's Courts* (2004) provided:

> With respect to a civil case that may be settled through mediation, the people's court should mediate. But as for the cases applicable to special procedure, supervision and urging procedure, procedure of public summons for exhortation, and procedure of bankruptcy and liquidation, confirmation cases of marriage relationship and status relationship and other civil cases for which mediation cannot be undertaken as per nature of cases, the people's court will not mediate.[59]

In addition to continuing to emphasize "mediation-in-advance," the interpretation also defined the disputes not suitable for mediation. In 2010, *the Suggestions of the Supreme People's Court for Implementing Further the Work Principle of "Mediation first and Mediation-Judgment Combination"* proposed expressly the judicial work principle of "mediation first and mediation-judgment combination," laying stress on energetically carrying out properly the mediation work of the following civil cases: (1) cases related to people's life and group interest and requiring the government and relevant departments to collaborate; (2) group cases that may influence social harmony and stability; (3) group litigation cases and bankruptcy cases; (4) folk debt; (5) marriage, family and inheritance, and other civil dispute cases; (6) cases with complex details where evidence hard to find; (7) cases of serious confrontation of moods between the parties; (8) cases which the relevant law and regulations have not provided or have not provided clearly and for which it is somewhat difficult to apply the law; (9) cases hard to enforce upon judgment; (10) sensitive cases attracting the general concerns of the society; and (11) re-trials and petition cases with intensive moods and intensified contradictions of the parties. In the meantime, the document set forth the special interpretation of the connotation of "mediation first and mediation-judgment combination."

In the process of handling cases, first of all, it is necessary to consider the mode of mediation for handling; make sure to carry out rigidly mediation and judgment at the same time; either mediation or judgment must keep a foothold in effectively resolving contradictions and disputes, promoting social harmony, define right and duty for dispute settlement, and realize the organic unification of legal effect and social effect. According to the nature, particular conditions of each case and the appeals of the parties, scientifically hold and deploy the basis and conditions for handling the cases in the mode of mediation or judgment. Where it is possible for mediation, try the best to facilitate mediation; in the event of any case impossible for mediation and stipulated by law not for mediation, make a judgment at the earliest and give adequate play to the role of the two methods of mediation and judgment. It is necessary to pay attention to correct the practice of making judgment carelessly without caring for the case-handling effect, as well as pay attention to correct the practice of pursuing unilaterally mediation rate and forcing mediation without caring for the will of the parties.

In 2012, one of the most discussed amendments of the *Civil Procedure Law of the People's Republic of China* is the establishment of "mediation first" institution. Article 122 of the *Civil Procedure Law*, as amended, provided: "as for the civil disputes brought by the parties to the people's court and applicable for mediation, mediate first, except where the parties refuse mediation." In 2016, on the basis of "mediation first," the *Suggestions of the Supreme People's Court for People's Courts to Deepen Further the Reform of Diversified Dispute Resolution Mechanism* proposed officially to explore the establishment of mediation procedural prerequisite: as for the domestic disputes, neighborhood, small-amount debts, consumers' right protection, traffic accidents, medical disputes, property management and other disputes applicable for mediation, qualified grass-roots people's courts should, on the basis of obtaining the consent from the parties, guide the parties for mediation first by special mediation organizations or a special mediator before filing the case. Currently, the pilot work of legislation has been accelerated for China's mediation procedural prerequisite.[60] It is actually, under the idea of dispute gradation, to realize the distribution of mediation-trial cases, resolve the disputes suitable for mediation as much as possible before litigation procedure is actuated or outside litigation procedure so that the judges can concentrate their effort of court hearing in those cases for which mediation fails and which are in need of judgment to establish the rules. If a huge number of disputes are mediated before or outside litigation, the judgment can be relatively purified. Regarding the exploration of mediation procedural prerequisite, the author will discuss this further in detail hereinafter.

In the realistic circumstance of disputes rushing explosively to courts with prominent "more cases but fewer personnel," the policy of "mediation first" has always been insisted on and intensified to some extent, but academic circles have debated endlessly on the judicial policy of "mediation first."[61] In the opinion of the author, mediation and judgment are both modes of resolving social contradictions and both have their respective irreplaceable advantages as well as their respective defects. The golden mean is neither to fall into adoring the universal theory of judgment, nor to regard mediation as a perfect and intact approach for dispute resolution. Mediation and judgment should collaborate with each other, jointly advance dispute resolution, and try everything possible to achieve the dynamic balance of mediation and judgment under the constraint of such conditions as different regions, different court levels, different procedural stages, and social demands of different periods.[62] The policy expression of "mediation first and mediation-judgment combination" has appropriately reflected the thinking tradition of Chinese civil, judicial "practical moralism,"[63] and it practically requires that when handling the particular cases, the courts should flexibly apply the modes and means of mediation and judgment, according to the actual conditions of cases and should undertake mediation first where it is possible and suitable for mediation to realize the case to come to a settlement, and should make timely judgment where it is impossible or unnecessary for mediation so as to deliver the governance of rules. In this regard, the Vice President of the Supreme People's Court, Chief Judge Jiang Bixin emphasized specially, in a public speech, that it is necessary to avoid the wrong practices when using the mediation institution and he summarized it as "four-not" and "six-prevent." The "four-not" means: (1) not to regard mediation as the only approach for resolving contradictions and disputes; (2) not to deem mediation as the perfect and intact mode of dispute resolution; (3) not to exercise the principle of attaching more importance to mediation than to judgment for all the cases; and (4) not to exclude the necessity and importance of judging according to law. The "six-prevent" means: (1) to prevent deviation from the actual conditions in setting up the indicator of mediation rate; (2) to prevent mediation from covering false litigation; (3) to prevent any forced mediation in violation of the will of the parties; (4) to prevent forcing the parties to accept the mediation by delaying a settlement; (5) to prevent giving up the principle and the bottom line to encourage the trend of evil violation of regulations and treachery; and :(6) to prevent damaging the legal rights and interests of the third party and public interests through mediation.[64]

1.6 Conclusion: Make Mild Mediation a Mainstream Attitude in Dispute Resolution

Only by expounding the legal principle of mediation in China can the story of mediation in China be told properly. Currently, we should get rid of the restraint of litigation centralism discourse, establish, with the "legal relation of mediation"[65] as the link, the basic criterion of mediation science, structure the independent mediation law science, and intensify, in terms of legal principle, the experience summary and advantage and disadvantage analysis of the mediation activities, so as to advance the development and perfection of the mediation institution. It is a hard task and is primarily tried herein.

Everyone hopes to live in a warm, good, polite, thrifty and tolerant social environment rather than a social environment of looking at each other with angry eyes and fighting each other. However, even in a harmonious society, there are many grievances, conflicts, and disputes. Especially in the period of transformation, society is full of disharmony, fighting over disagreements, violent language, and physical violence can be seen everywhere and the relations between states are also similar to confronting each other with daggers. Just as the scholar He Huaihong said:

> It is still our present heavy burden to resolve problems by struggling rather than resolve by compromising, negotiating, talking, and tolerating … the society will definitely have kinds of people at both ends. At one end are the fierce persons and violent persons. At the other end are the complete quitters and submissive persons. It is best for the intermediaries to share the most, defending their rights and interests mildly and rationally but firmly, as well as caring for the rights and interests of others. When such force is the mainstay, the "new moral principles" (of maintaining Chinese social order) are also established.[66]

A kind society of legal governance should not only have competitive confrontation of either this or that, either black or white, either you die or I live, and either you lose or I win, and should not restore the order only through ice-cold mandatory judgment, but should have a flexible dispute resolution mechanism for repairing damaged social relations through consultation and consensus and create opportunities for the production of rationality and tolerance, as is the dispute resolution institution with human beings as the central subjects, as well as the real value for the existence of mediation. In the present environment of tight international relations with the theory of "China as a threat" fabricated by some Western politicians and Cold War thinking, we expect the mild mediation is not only the mainstream attitude to resolve disputes between individuals, and expect more for the Chinese mediation culture "harmony as most precious," "harmony in diversity," and "seeking common ground while reserving differences" to provide the enlightenment for the peaceful contact between states.

Notes

1 Su Li: *Legal Governance and Its Native Resources* (Beijing: China University of Political Science and Law Press, 1996), pp. 23–36.

2 Feng Xiang: Puzzles of Qiu Ju and Civilization of Vega, *Reading*, 1997 (11); Wang Liming: "Ask for an Explanation": Start with *The Story of Qiu Ju, Contemporary Guizhou*, 2015 (18); Chen Baifeng: Qiu Ju's "Anger" and the Village Head's "Face": Re-interpretation of *The Story of Qiu Ju*, *Journal of Shandong University (Philosophy and Social Sciences)*, 2010 (3); Chen Qi: Puzzles of Qiu Ju and Doubt Resolution : Studies of "Law and Literature" in China, *Open Times*, 2019 (1); Zhao Xiaoli: Fatal Part: Re-interpretation of *The Story of Qiu Ju*, *Peking University Law Review*, 2005, 6 (2), 707–718; Lin Bin: Law Popularization, Legal Illiteracy and Legal Governance, *Law and Social Development*, 2004 (2).

3 Chen Baifeng: Qiu Ju's "Anger" and the Village Head's "Face" – Re-interpretation of *The Story of Qiu Ju*, op. cit.

4 In the Western context, "right" originally referred to "a kind of proper or legal requirement," which has no corresponding expression in Chinese. Yuan Dehui, the translator of Lin Zexu translated it as "*daoli* (truth)" and later an American preacher William Alexander made a new word "*quanli*" for it. Mr. Wu Si considered this translation lost the humane factor of the traditional history and culture and it is more proper to translate it as "*quanfen.*" Wu Si: *Hidden Rules: Real Game in the Chinese History* (Shanghai: Fudan University Press, 2015), pp. 270–272.

5 For studies on transplanting and transfer of the right concept in China, see Li Laifan: History of Transplanting and Exchange of Right Concept, *Peking University Law Journal*, 2020 (2), 410–416.

6 Ying Xing: *Emotions and Contentious Politics in Contemporary Rural China* (Beijing: Social Sciences Academic Press, 2016), p. 4.

7 Chen Baifeng: Society of Acquaintance: Study on Ideal Village Order Mechanism, *Society* 2011 (1).

8 Zhang Wenxian: Legal Principle: Centric Subjects of Jurisprudence and Common Concerns of Law, *Tsinghua University Law Journal* 2017 (4). After this article was published, an upsurge of research on "legal principle" arose in China, and law scholars in different sectors were also active in responding, but up to now, no scholars have specialized in research on the legal principle of mediation.

9 Liao Yongan: *Mediation Course* (Beijing: China Renmin University Press, 2019), p. 30.

10 Hu Qian: Studies on the Folk Mediation of Civil Disputes in the Qing Dynasty, Doctoral thesis, China University of Political Science and Law, 2007, pp. 34–35.

11 Wang Chunzi: Development and Evolution of Civil Mediation Institution in Modern Times of China – With the Civil Mediation Law (1930) as the Keynote, *Nanjing University Law Review*, 2016 (2).

12 Such "convincing and educating" not only exist in the trial procedure, but also even extend into the enforcement. Wang Yaxin: Analysis of Enforcement and Convincing and Educating, *Social Sciences in China*, 2000 (2).

13 The extensive suitability of the law regulation system of generalization and formalism and mandatory judgment in terms of social psychology is the key to the formation of dispute resolution mechanism centered on litigation. Chen Hangping: Social Transformation, Legalization and Court Mediation, *Law and Social Development*, 2010 (2).

14 Takamieawa Osamu: *Disputes and Law in Modern China*, translated by H.E. Qinghua, et al. (Beijing: Law Press, 2003), p. 1 (in Japanese).

15 Zhao Xudong: Self-Criticism and Self-examination of Formation Mechanism in Civil Dispute Resolution – with the Consensus in the Perspective of the Parties as the Center, *The Jurist*, 2014 (1).

16 Simon Roberts and Michael Palmer: *Dispute Processes: ADR and the Primary Forms of Decision-making*, translated by Liu Zhewei, et al. (Beijing: Peking University Press, 2011), pp. 207–248.

17 With reference to the theoretical model of the Japanese scholar Tanase Takao, Professor Ji Weidong considered as equal the intermediary mediation as facilitatory mediation and arbitration mediation as evaluative mediation. Ji Weidong: Legal Development Mechanism of Mediation Institution, in Qiang Shigong (Chief Ed.): *Mediation, Legal System and Modernization: A Study of Chinese Mediation Institution* (Beijing: China Legal Publishing House, 2001), p. 46.

18 Fan Yu: Restructuring of Mediation – with Reform of Court Mediation as the Keynote (I), *Law and Social Development*, 2004 (2).

19 Wang Cong: Mediation-Judgment Separation or Mediation-Judgment Combination: Re-exploration on China's Prospects of Court Mediation, *Hebei Law Science*, 2019 (9).

20 Zhai Tongzu: *Chinese Law and Chinese Society* (Beijing: China Publishing House, 1981), pp. 1–328.

21 Liang Zhiping: *Searching for Harmony in the Natural Order* (Shanghai: Shanghai People's Publishing House, 1991), p. 188.

22 Chen Hongyi: Mediation, Litigation and Justice – Thinking of Confucianism in Modern Free Society, *Jin Ling Law Review*, 2001 (1).

23 Fei Xiaotong: *From the Soil: the Foundations of Chinese Society* (Beijing: People's Publishing House, 2008), pp. 25–34.

24 Liang Shuming: *The Substance of Chinese Culture* (Shanghai: Shanghai People's Publishing House, 2011), pp. 76–91.

25 Li Xia: Characteristic Analysis of Chinese Mediation Culture and Significance of Cross-culture Communication, *Journal of Huaihai University of Technology (Humanities and Social Sciences)*, 2018 (6).
26 Zhai Xuewei: Sensibility, Face and Reproduction of Power, *Sociology Study*, 2004 (5).
27 Roscoe Pound, Comparative Law and History as Bases for Chinese Law, 61 *Harvard Law Review*, 749, trans. Xiong Binwan, *Law and Economy*, 2019 (1).
28 For the particular coverage, see With "Six Feet Lane," Resolve People's "Puzzles"– Record of Tongcheng Court Anhui Province in Deploying Traditional Culture to Resolve Contradictions and Disputes, *People's Court Daily*, July 14, 2017, Edition 1.
29 The Zhang family in Tongcheng, Anhui Province, were prime ministers for two generations. Zhang Ying was a senior official during the reign of Emperor Kangxi of the Qing Dynasty, and his son Zhang Tingyu was a senior official of Emperor Kangxi and Emperor Yongzheng. During the reign of Emperor Kangxi, the Zhang family had a homestead dispute with their neighbors, the Wu family. Zhang Ying, a college scholar, received a letter from his family in the capital, asking him to use his position to intervene. He replied with a poem: "A letter to me is only for the wall, so what difference will it make if we give him three feet? The Great Wall is still there even today, but where is the powerful Qin Shi Huang?" The family immediately withdrew three feet when receiving the reply. The Wu family was deeply moved and gave up three feet, too, forming an alley six feet wide. The story of the two families' friendship and the Zhang family did not rely on the power to bully others has been circulating for more than 300 years. The allusion to "Six Feet Lane" clearly reflects the harmonious cultural values advocated by Confucianism.
30 Wang Yaxin: *Confrontation and Judgment: Basic Structure of Japanese Civil Procedure* (Beijing: Tsinghua University Press, 2002), p. 57.
31 Liao Yongan: New Idea and New Thinking of Contemporary Mediation, *People's Court Daily*, June 16, 2017, Edition 2.
32 Liao Yongan: Understand Scientifically Mediation Value and Promote the Innovation of Social Governance, *Chinese Social Sciences Today*, March 26, 2020, Edition 01.
33 Li Hao: Comparative Advantages of Mediation and Reform of Court Mediation Institution, *Journal of Nanjing Normal University (Social Sciences)*, 2002 (4).
34 The discipline classification of China in a modern sense is transplanted from the West, and especially such a discipline as law has basically been copied from the West. Since 2018, the Ministry of Education of China has proposed to promote energetically the construction of "New Engineering," "New Agricultural Science," "New Medical Science," and "New Liberal Arts" in the field of higher education. The so-called "New Liberal Arts" are actually the liberal arts based on the Chinese experiences and Chinese characteristics. "New Liberal Arts" are actually to replace, with the philosophy and social sciences with Chinese characteristics, those disciplines transplanted and copied directly from the West, and are mainly to resolve the issue of Chinese characteristics of philosophy and social sciences. Wang Xueding: What Is "New Liberal Arts"?, *China Reading Weekly*, June 3, 2020, Edition 05.
35 Regarding the criticism and self-examination of this issue, refer to Liu Wenhui: *Self-examining and Surpassing of Legal Philosophical Basis for Present*

Dispute Resolution Theory: Between Rights and Utilities (Beijing: China University of Political Science and Law Press, 2013).

36 Liao Yi: Dispute Resolution Oriented for a Better Life, *Law Science*, 2016 (6).

37 Some scholars pointed out that at the end of the movie *The Story of Qiu Ju*, seeing the police car driving away in the dust, Qiu Ju became puzzled. The content implied in her puzzled eyes is one of the major objects that the dispute resolution theory should be adequately concerned about. See Liu Wenhui: *Self-examining and Surpassing of Legal Philosophical Basis for Present Dispute Resolution Theory: Between Rights and Utilities* (Beijing: China University of Political Science and Law Press, 2013), p. 19.

38 See the Report to the 19th CPC National Congress: *Decide to Build Comprehensively to Better Society and Achieve the Great Victory of Socialism with Chinese Characteristics in the New Era.*

39 "One-dimensional man" is borrowed from the work of Marcuse, the famous scholar of the Frankfurt School. See Herbert Marcuse: *One-Dimensional Man: Studies in the Ideology of Advanced industrial Society*, trans. Liu Ji (Shanghai: Translation Publishing House, 2008).

40 Liao Yi: Dispute Resolution Oriented for a Better Life, *Law Science*, 2016 (6).

41 Lon L. Fuller, Collective Bargaining and the Arbitration, 38, *Wisconsin Law Review*, 1963 (39).

42 Lei Lei: German Mediation Concept and its Enlightenment, *Studies in Law and Business*, 2014 (2).

43 The term "co-existential justice" is borrowed from the concept proposed by the famous Italian comparative jurist, Mauro Cappelletti when discussing alternative dispute resolution (ADR). In the opinion of Cappelletti, an alternative dispute resolution pursues a kind of "co-existential justice," while litigation pursues a kind of "contentious justice," see Mauro Cappelletti: Access to Justice as a Theoretical Approach to Law and a Practical Programme for Reform (1992) 109 *South African Law Journal* 22. Mauro Cappelletti: Alternative Dispute Resolution Processes Within the Framework of the Worldwide Access-To-Justice Movement (1995) 56 *The Modern Law Review* 287.

44 Wu Yingzi: Judicial Limits: Between Judicial Action and Judicial Restraint, *Chinese Journal of Law*, 2009 (5).

45 For the following discussion on Fuller, mainly refer to Robert S. Summers: *Lon L. Fuller* (Beijing: Law Press, 2010), pp. 167–173. Lon L. Fuller. The Forms and Limits of Adjudication. 92 *Harvard Law Review* (1978): 353–409.

46 Lon L. Fuller. The Forms and Limits of Adjudication. 92 *Harvard Law Review* (1978): 353–409.

47 M. Palmer. The Revival of Mediation in the People's Republic of China: Extra-Judicial Mediation. In W. E. Butler (Ed.) *Yearbook on Socialist Legal Systems* (New York: Transnational Books, 1987), pp. 244–352.

48 Wu Qiangzhong was originally the Chief of Zhejiang Province Qingyuan County City Area Central Office of Justice and upon retirement, has been engaged in people's mediation for a long time, winning the National Judicial Administration Second-class Hero Model, National Model People's Mediator – "Busy Body" title. As for the report about his mediation experiences, see http://news.qingdaozaixian.com/newsshow-90583.html#p=1

49 Hu Jieren: *Perfect Social Contradiction and Dispute Mediation Mechanism: Contemporary Chinese "Grand Mediation"* (Shanghai: Shanghai Jiao Tong University Press, 2017), p. 25.

50 Wei Chenglin and Qi Haibin: New Paradigm of Chinese Mediation Research – with Political Governance Theory as the Basis, *Science of Law*, 2015 (6).

51 Rong Zhi and Chen Qixing: "Stable Politics": Political Thinking of Dilemma with Chinese Stability Maintenance, *CASS Journal of Political Science*, 2011 (5).

52 Yu Jianrong: *Contentious Politics: Fundamental Issues in Chinese Political Sociology* (Beijing: People's Publishing House, 2010), pp. 38–39.

53 Tang Huangfeng: "Chinese-style" Stability: Dilemma and Surpassing, *Journal of Wuhan University (Philosophy and Social Science)*, 2012 (5).

54 Huang Huo, et al.: Risk of "Systematic Retardation," *Outlook*, 2007 (24).

55 Some scholars called such mediation differentiation "profit-seeking" mediation, see Wei Chenglin and Qi Haibin: New Paradigm of Chinese Mediation Research – with Political Governance Theory as the Basis, *Science of Law*, 2015 (6).

56 Regarding the outstanding research on this issue, refer to Ying Xing: *Emotions and Contentious Politics in Contemporary Rural China* (Beijing: Social Sciences Academic Press, 2016).

57 Surely, mediation is not at all to seek a "legally correct solution," Tanase Takao classified the types of mediation as judgment, negotiation, education, and treatment. Tanase Takao: *Dispute Resolution and Trial System*, trans. Wang Yaxin (Beijing: China University of Political Science and Law Press, 1994), pp. 53–67.

58 Wang Liming: Define Right and Duty for Dispute Settlement and Define Dispute for Dispute Settlement, *Contemporary Guizhou*, 2015 (31).

59 Some scholars also pointed out that the cases with major disputes between the confirmed lawsuit and basic facts of cases should also be included in the cases not suitable for mediation. Refer to Li Hao: A Study on Mediation-in-Advance Institution, *Jianghai Academic Journal*, 2013 (3).

60 For instance, Shanghai Municipal Higher People's Court and Shanghai Municipal Bureau of Justice jointly issued, on August 13, 2020, *The (Trial) Suggestions for Exploring Mediation First and Promoting Litigation Source Governance.*

61 Wu Yingzi: "Mediation-first": Reform Pattern and Legal Interpretation, *Chinese and Foreign Law*, 2013 (3).

62 Wang Chong: Re-exploration of China's Prospects of Court Mediation, *Hebei Law Science*, 2019 (9).

63 Philip C.C. Huang: *The Past and the Present: Chinese Civil Justice in Practice* (Beijing: Law Press, 2009), pp. 8–11.

64 Jian Bixin: Don't Regard Mediation as a Perfect and Intact Dispute Resolution Mode, available at the official website of the Supreme People's Court: www.court.gov.cn/zixun-xiangqing-4780.html

65 So-called "legal relation of mediation" refers to the relation of rights and obligations formed between the mediation organization and mediator and the parties to disputes and other participants and between the parties to disputes and other participants, as regulated by the mediation law and regulations guiding the mediation conduct of mediation subjects and regulating the mediation organization, the mediator, and the parties to disputes in dispute resolution. This research is almost in a theoretical bank, with few scholars undertaking the systematic analysis on the difference between "legal relation of litigation" and "legal relation of mediation." Qiu Xingmei and Wang Qiulan carried out the primary study on this issue. Qiu Xingmei and Wang Qiulan: *Mediation Law* (Xiamen: Xiamen University Press, 2010), pp. 82–83.

66 He Huaihong: Make Mildness the Mainstream Attitude, *Global People*, 2013 (24).

References

Anon.: "Six Feet Lane," Resolve People's "Puzzles" – Record of Tongcheng Court Anhui Province in Deploying Traditional Culture to Resolve Contradictions and Disputes, People's Court Daily, July 14, 2017, Edition 1.

Cappelletti, Mauro, Access to Justice as a Theoretical Approach to Law and a Practical Programme for Reform (1992) 109 *South African Law Journal*, 22.

Chen Baifeng: Qiu Ju's "Anger" and the Village Head's "Face" – Re-interpretation of the Story of Qiu Ju, *Journal of Shandong University (Philosophy and Social Sciences)*, 2010 (3): 46–53.

Chen Baifeng: Society of Acquaintance: Study on Ideal Village Order Mechanism, *Society,* 2011 (1): 223–241.

Chen Hangping: Social Transformation, Legalization and Court Mediation, *Law and Social Development*, 2010 (2): 101–111.

Chen Hongyi: Mediation, Litigation and Justice – Thinking of Confucianism in Modern Free Society, *Jin Ling Law Review*, 2001 (1): 106–118.

Fan Yu: Restructuring of Mediation – with Reform of Court Mediation as the Keynote (I), *Law and Social Development*, 2004 (2): 113–125.

Fei Xiaotong: *From the Soil: the Foundations of Chinese Society*, Beijing: People's Publishing House, 2008.

Feng Xiang: Puzzles of Qiu Ju and Civilization of Vega, *Reading*, 1997 (11): 3–7.

Fuller, Lon L.: Collective Bargaining and the Arbitration, 38 *Wisconsin Law Review*, 1963 (39): 8–59.

Fuller, Lon L.: The Forms and Limits of Adjudication. 92 *Harvard Law Review*, 1978 (409): 353.

He Huaihong: Make Mildness as the Mainstream Attitude, *Global People*, 2013 (24).

Hu Jieren: *Perfect Social Contradiction and Dispute Mediation Mechanism: Contemporary Chinese "Grand Mediation,"* Shanghai: Shanghai Jiao Tong University Press, 2017.

Hu Qian: Studies on the Folk Mediation of Civil Disputes in the Qing Dynasty, Doctoral thesis, China University of Political Science and Law, 2007.

Huang Huo, et al.: Risk of "Systematic Retardation," *Outlook*, 2007 (24): 6–7.

Huang Philip C.C.: *The Past and the Present: Chinese Civil Justice in Practice*, Beijing: Law Press, 2009.

Ji Weidong: Legal Development Mechanism of Mediation Institution, in Qiang Shigong (Chief Ed.): *Mediation, Legal System and Modernization: A Study on Chinese Mediation Institution*, Beijing: Legal Publishing House, 2001, p. 46.

Jian Bixin: Don't Regard Mediation as a Perfect and Intact Dispute Resolution Mode, available at official website of the Supreme People's Court: www.court.gov.cn/zixun-xiangqing-4780.html

Lei Lei: German Mediation Concept and its Enlightenment, *Studies in Law and Business*, 2014 (2): 151–160.

Li Hao: A Study on Mediation-in-advance Institution, *Jianghai Academic Journal*, 2013 (3): 138–145.

Li Hao: Comparative Advantages of Mediation and Reform of Court Mediation Institution, *Journal of Nanjing Normal University (Social Sciences)*, 2002 (4): 19–27.

Li Laifan: History of Transplanting and Exchange of Right Concept, *Peking University Law Journal,* 2020 (2): 410–416.

Li Xia: Characteristic Analysis of Chinese Mediation Culture and Significance of Cross-culture Communication, *Journal of Huaihai University of Technology (Humanities and Social Sciences)*, 2018 (6): 74–77.

Liang Shuming: *The Substance of Chinese Culture*, Shanghai: Shanghai People's Publishing House, 2011.

Liang Zhiping: *Searching for Harmony in the Natural Order*, Shanghai: Shanghai People's Publishing House, 1991.

Liao Yi: Dispute Resolution Oriented for Better Life, *Law Science*, 2016 (6): 122–139.

Liao Yongan: *Mediation Course*, Beijing: China Renmin University Press, 2019.

Liao Yongan: New Idea and New Thinking of Contemporary Mediation, People's Court Daily, June 16, 2017, Edition 2.

Liao Yongan: Understand Scientifically Mediation Value and Promote the Innovation of Social Governance, *Chinese Social Sciences Today*, March 26, 202,0 Edition 1.

Liu Wenhui: *Self-examining and Surpassing of Legal Philosophical Basis for Present Dispute Resolution Theory–Between Rights and Utilities*, Beijing: China University of Political Science and Law Press, 2013.

Marcuse, Herbert: *One-Dimensional Man: Studies in the Ideology of Advanced Industrial Society*, trans. Liu Ji, Shanghai: Translation Publishing House, 2008.

Palmer, M.: The Revival of Mediation in the People' s Republic of China: Extra-Judicial Mediation. In W. E. Butler (Ed.) *Yearbook on Socialist Legal Systems*, New York: Transnational Books, 1987, pp. 244–352.

Pound, Roscoe: Comparative Law and History as Bases for Chinese Law, 61 *Harvard Law Review*, 749, trans. Xiong Binwan, Law and Economy, 2019 (1): 80–87.

Qi Haibin: New Paradigm of Chinese Mediation Research – with Political Governance Theory as the Basis, *Science of Law*, 2015 (6).

Qiu Xingmei and Wang Qiulan: *Mediation Law*, Xiamen: Xiamen University Press 2010.

Roberts, Simon and Palmer, Michael: *Dispute Processes: ADR and the Primary Forms of Decision-making*, trans. Liu Zhewei, et al., Beijing: Peking University Press, 2011.

Rong Zhi and Chen Qixing: "Stable Politics": Political Thinking of Dilemma with Chinese Stability Maintenance, *CASS Journal of Political Science*, 2011 (5): 87–96.

Shanghai Municipal Higher People's Court and Shanghai Municipal Bureau of Justice: *The (Trial) Suggestions for Exploring Mediation First and Promoting Litigation Source Governance*, 2020.

Su Li: *Legal Governance and Its Native Resources*, Beijing: China University of Political Science and Law Press, 1996.

Summers, Robert S.: *Lon L. Fuller*, Beijing: Law Press, 2010.

Takamieawa Osamu: *Disputes and Law in Modern China*, trans. H. E. Qinghua et al., Beijing: Law Press 2003.

Tanase Takao: *Dispute Resolution and Trial System*, trans. Wang Yaxin, Beijing: China University of Political Science and Law Press, 1994.

Tang Huangfeng: "Chinese-style" Stability: Dilemma and Surpassing, *Journal of Wuhan University (Philosophy and Social Science)*, 2012 (5): 17–25.

Wang Chong: Mediation-Judgment Separation or Mediation-Judgment Combination: Re-exploration on China's Prospects of Court Mediation, *Hebei Law Science*, 2019 (9): 184–200.

Wang Chunzi: Development and Evolution of Civil Mediation Institution in Modern Times of China – With the Civil Mediation Law (1930) as the Keynote, *Nanjing University Law Review*, 2016 (2): 169–185.

Wang Liming: Define Right and Duty for Dispute Settlement and Define Dispute for Dispute Settlement, *Contemporary Guizhou*, 2015 (31): 62.

Wang Xueding: What is "New Liberal Arts"?, *China Reading Weekly*, June 3, 2020 Edition 5.

Wang Yaxin: Analysis of Enforcement and Convincing and Educating, *Social Sciences in China*, 2000 (2): 110–119, 207.

Wang Yaxin: *Confrontation and Judgment: Basic Structure of Japanese Civil Procedure*, Beijing: Tsinghua University Press, 2002.

Wei Chenglin and Qi Haibin: New Paradigm of Chinese Mediation Research – with Political Governance Theory as the Basis, *Science of Law*, 2015 (6): 3–12.

Wu Si: *Hidden Rules: Real Game in the Chinese History*, Shanghai: Fudan University Press, 2015.

Wu Yingzi: "Mediation-first": Reform Pattern and Legal Interpretation, *Chinese and Foreign Law*, 2013 (3): 536–555.

Wu Yingzi: Judicial Limits: between Judicial Action and Judicial Restraint, *Chinese Journal of Law*, 2009 (5): 111–130.

Ying Xing: *Emotions and Contentious Politics in Contemporary Rural China*, Beijing: Social Sciences Academic Press, 2016.

Yu Jianrong: *Contentious Politics: Fundamental Issues in Chinese Political Sociology*, Beijing: People's Publishing House, 2010.

Zhai Tongzu: *Chinese Law and Chinese Society*, Beijing: China Publishing House, 1981.

Zhai Xuewei: Sensibility, Face and Reproduction of Power, *Sociology Study*, 2004 (5): 48–57.

Zhang Wenxian: Legal Principle: Centric Subjects of Jurisprudence and Common Concerns of Law, *Tsinghua University Law Journal* 2017 (4): 5–40.

Zhao Xudong: Self-criticism and Self-examination of Formation Mechanism in Civil Dispute Resolution – with the Consensus in the Perspective of the Parties as the Center, *The Jurist*, 2014 (1): 131–141, 178.

2 Transformation and Reshaping of China's Traditional Mediation Idea

Where there are people, there is a complicated human society, in which there are always disputes. The modes for dispute resolution are classified into three types: private relief, public relief, and social relief. Private relief takes conciliation or self-help as the main forms, emphasizing settlement by the parties themselves, without a neutral third party intervening. Public relief takes judicial and administrative resolution as the main forms, with the public power intervening. Social relief takes mediation and arbitration as the main forms, with the intermediary social forces intervening. Since the advent of states, they have banned, in principle, private relief, set up public relief and encouraged social relief.[1]

From the perspective of comparative law, since the period of Roman law, Western society has gradually formed the dispute resolution institution centered on the adversarial system, while China formed the dispute resolution institution centered on mediation. When studying Chinese law, the famous Japanese law historian Shiga Shuzu followed the ideas of American jurist Unger, placing the law of China and Europe at two opposite extremes and viewing China as having no "dominance of law" similar to the European adversarial system. In imperial China, the Confucian ideology advocated "when hearing a lawsuit case, I am like others (without any brilliance). It is important to prevent any lawsuit case from happening." The state classified disputes as "felony cases" and cases "under a magistrate's own jurisdiction," of which the latter were mainly deemed such "trifles" as land, debt, marriage, and heritage disputes. These disputes were generally resolved through folk mediation, rather than brought before the local government. Even if they were brought before the local government, when handling such cases, the magistrates also mainly followed the mode of mediation rather than giving judgment to settle the cases. Therefore, in the opinion of Shiga Shuzu, the civil judgment in imperial China was more "didactic-conciliation"[2] than "legal judgment." Without going into details, mediation became the most vital factor in the tradition of Chinese law and has survived till now as "change that has not happened for a thousand of years."

DOI: 10.4324/9781003385882-2

However, the social soil for the existence of traditional mediation institution was based on the self-sufficient, small-peasant economy, the patriarchal system, and the society of acquaintance,[3] and was a product of the centralized governance model of "imperial power not reaching below the level of the county," conforming to the "super-stable structure" of Chinese society. With the changing times, the present China has already stepped into modern society, in which the small-peasant economy has been replaced by the market economy, the patriarchal system has disintegrated, and the society of acquaintance has been replaced by the society of strangers. During this period of great transformation, what creative changes must mediation experience for the present vitality? In the age of legal governance, what is the difference between the ideas of traditional mediation and modern mediation? In the age of globalization, what contact is between the Chinese mediation and the Western mediation institutions? In an age of legal governance discourse of struggling for rights, what is the position of mediation in the whole dispute resolution system? Asking these questions is directly related to the modernity of mediation and even the modernity of Chinese legal governance. This chapter attempts to give a first answer to these questions.

Mediation as a product of the "harmony" culture and ethic value has a long history in China. In a vertical view of cultural history, as a traditional mode for the resolution of folk disputes in China, mediation has always received a lot of attention. In the meantime, as a dispute resolution mode and a mode of state governance, mediation is also internationally honored as an "oriental experience." However, during the process of modernization of the Chinese legal governance, mediation has been deemed the historical remnant "inconsistent with the spirit of modern legal governance" and, in practice, has also been abandoned. At the beginning of the twenty-first century, due to the frequency and variety of disputes, mediation has been re-evaluated and has formed, in the practical field, the pattern of "Grand Mediation." However, the present mediation is no longer the same as the past mediation. With the historical changes and social transformation, the mediation idea, the mediation institution, and even mediation methods must also follow historical evolution. In this chapter, the modern transformation of the traditional Chinese mediation idea is taken as the proposition, on the one hand, because the mediation idea has the directive function for the mediation institution and mediation methods are also favorable to the cultivation of a mediation culture; on the other hand, because China "still lacks a systematic, profound and objective exploration of mediation idea up to now."[4] With respect to the prospect of research, based on mediation as a practical art, this chapter places the "phase" of mediation idea at the level of the mediation method for discussion, in the hope of being more objective. With respect to the particular concept, starting the analysis with the specialty of traditional Chinese mediation, this chapter will analyze the modern dilemma of traditional mediation, and accordingly, discuss the need to establish the modern rational mediation idea and its major contents.

2.1 Specialty of Traditional Chinese Mediation

Disputes and the mediation of disputes have always accompanied human society, and any dispute resolution mechanism is closely related to the economy, politics, and culture of a specific society. In China, the earliest history of mediation can be traced back to the period of Yao and Shun, when mediation became a dispute resolution mode advocated by the ancient wise monarchs. *Han Feizi Difficulty I* of the Warring States Period recorded this story: the peasants around Lishan invaded and occupied the field where the boundary was unclear and Shun went there to farm. One year later, their respective field boundary was restored to normal. The fishermen on the Yellow River fought the men of the highlands for water and Shun went there to fish. One year later, they all showed courtesies to the elders. The quality of pottery made by the potters in Dongyi was poor and Shun went there to make pottery. One year later, the pottery made by all was very solid. Confucius sighed and said:

> Farming, fishing and making pottery were Shun's duties, but Shun went there to do the jobs with the aim of correcting the corrupt atmosphere. Shun was really honest and kind-hearted! He could really bear hardship and work hard so that all the people obeyed him. So, "the morality of the sage can move people!"

This ancient book recorded: when the field boundary of the peasants in Lishan was not clear, Shun went farming with the peasants and one year later, the boundary was made clear. When the fishermen of Leize argued over the fishing position, Shun went fishing with the fishermen and one year later, the fishermen vied with each other to leave the good position to the elders. When the art of making pottery in Dongyi was not good, Shun made pottery with the potters and one year later the pottery became solid.

The record of *Historical Records: Five Imperial Biographies* by historian Sima Qian in the Han Dynasty also verified this fact: when Shun was farming at Lishan, the people of Lishan let him farm by the river; when fishing in Leize, the people of Leize all allowed him to dwell; when making pottery on the riverside, the pottery there was all good. The place he lived became a gathering place one year after, became a small town two years after, and became a city three years after. These facts indicated that by leading by example in working, making himself an example and taking a lead, with noble morality, he moved the parties and facilitated the local people to form an atmosphere of mutual community with his "charisma" of charming personal authority. As per the viewpoint of modern mediation science, such a mode of dispute resolution or social governance is obviously the persuasive or example-type "mediation."

In the West Zhou Dynasty, the state specially set up the office of "Tiaoren (mediator)," "taking charge of mediating in the hatred of people,"[5] i.e., an official specially in charge of mediating in folk disputes. After the Qin and

Han dynasties, mediation of local government developed into governance by rural officials, Xiang (township), Ting (village), and Li (group) below a county set up "Fu (chief)," to mediate in folk disputes, and Lizheng (Group Head) in the Tang Dynasty and Baozhang and Jiazhang (local administrators on the basis of households) in the Song Dynasty both belonged in such a category. In the Song Dynasty, with the folk disputes increasing, mediation showed a trend of institutionalization. During the period of Ming and Qing dynasties, mediation was already at a perfect stage.[6] By the time of the Ming Dynasty, the township and village below the county level specially set up the "pavilion of statement," a place for the statement and education, where "Lilao (elders)" accepted and mediated folk disputes, and the decree of the Ming Dynasty stipulated expressively that folk trifles were banned from being brought directly to the local government, but must be first mediated at the township and village level, and criminal liability will be sought by "by-passing appeal."[7] It was not until the late Qing Dynasty that the state attached more importance to mediation and formed the dispute resolution model of "official approval and civil mediation," i.e., the prefecture or county officials would decide on the different considerations to send, in the form of "official approval and civil mediation," the cases back to the township or village for the clan elders, gentry, and leaders to mediate and settle.[8]

Mediation has been favored and continued for thousands of years, as determined by the cultural style and social structure of traditional Chinese society, and it has shown its unique specialty. In a nation like China with a long history, since Dong Zhongshu, the Confucian philosopher in the Han Dynasty, proposed "abandon all other thoughts and dedicate to Confucianism exclusively," Confucianism has always been the guide of mainstream culture of China. In the process of China's modernization, as the core value system of China, Confucianism has lost its legitimacy, but "in strong legal modernization discourse, modernity and tradition often bear a value choice and value orientation."[9] Therefore, at the level of legal institutions, the modern transformation of the state only reflects the transformation of the regulations, values, and culture of the will of the state, i.e., the "great tradition,"[10] while as a "little tradition" and folk regulation, the Confucian culture still exists in the spontaneous order, unconsciously influencing the value concept and conduct of the people. In the vision of mediation, state law and folk law and the "great tradition" and the "little tradition" affect each other and shape each other, and under their joint force, the mediation function, the mediation criterion, the mediation personnel composition, the mediation mode, and other elements have also changed and succeeded with the development of history. It is only the ideology and value orientation of the state that has been disrupted and replaced, while the ideology and conduct modes of people are somewhat conservative and stable and have been evolving slowly in the historical tide. Therefore, the traditional mediation mentioned here not only refers to the mediation in traditional Chinese society. In terms of mediation, all the mediation inherent in traditional Chinese rural society, reflecting traditional culture and bearing the traditional values can be called traditional mediation. In terms of time span, it includes the mediation of traditional society as well as the traditional mediation mode in modern society.

2.1.1 Cultural Origin: Outlook of "Harmony" between Man and Nature and between People

"Unity of man and nature" is a political and philosophical thought in ancient China, which originated in the Spring–Autumn and Warring States Period, expounded by such scholars as Dong Zhongshu, and summarized and proposed expressively by the Neo-Confucianism of Song and Ming dynasties. Its basic thought is that the political, ethical, and other social phenomena of mankind are the reflection of nature. "Unity of man and nature" has two meanings: one is that man and nature are consistent, cosmic nature is a great world, while man is a little world. The other is that man and nature correspond to each other, or man and nature communicate with each other. That is that man and nature are essentially identical, so all men and all things should comply with the natural law and achieve harmony between man and nature. Chapter 25 of Lao Zi's thoughts said: "Human should take their law from the Earth, the Earth follows the trail of Heaven, the Heaven follows the trail of Tao, and the law of the Tao is nature." This indicates the consistency and communication of man and nature. The concepts of the unity of man and nature in the Confucian philosophy of the Han and Song dynasties are

> All view that the universal foundation is the highest criterion of morals. Human morals are the discovery of the universal foundation. The basic reason is the normal reason of ethics. As for man, it is humanity; as for utensils, it is essence; as for things, it is moral principle. They are all the reflection of the universal foundation.[11]

Natural law is harmonious, so interpersonal relations should also be harmonious:

> The state and the population should be small. Though there are tools with the efficiency of ten or a hundred times, they are not used. The people look on death as a grievous thing, yet do not move away elsewhere. Though they have boats and carriages, they should have no occasion to use them; though they have helmets, armor and sharp weapons, they should have no occasion to show them. The people return to the use of knotted cords (instead of the written characters). They should think their (coarse) food delicious; their (plain) clothes beautiful; their (poor) dwellings places cozy; and their (simple) daily life valuable. There should be a neighboring state within sight, and the voices of the fowls and dogs should be heard all the way from it, but the people, even to death, will not have any contact.[12]

In the eyes of Lao Zi, the ideal society is "there should be a neighboring state within sight, and the voices of the fowls and dogs should be heard all the way from it, and the people, to the old age, even to death, will not have any contact," but what Confucius admired is a stateless world, *Da Tong*, with a commonwealth shared by all:

> When the Great Dao (Tao, perfect order) prevails, the world is for all, without a dictatorship. Virtuous, worthy, wise, and capable people are chosen as leaders. Honesty and trust are promoted, and harmony is sought. All people respect and love their own parents and children, as well as the parents and children of others. The aged are cared for until death, the strong adults are employed in jobs that make full use of their abilities and children are nourished, educated, and fostered. Widows and widowers, orphans, and the old without children, the disabled and the diseased are all well taken care of. Every man and woman has an appropriate role to play in society and in the family. They hate to see resources lying idle or cast away, yet they do not necessarily keep them for themselves. They hate not making use of their abilities, yet they do not necessarily work for their own self-interest. Thus intrigues and conspiracies do not arise, and theft and robbery do not occur, therefore doors need never be locked. This is the ideal world called "*Da Tong*."[13]

"The ancient Chinese people were seeking the order and harmony in the whole natural world and deemed it as the ideal of all human relations."[14] In order to reach the "harmony" between man and nature and between people, different ideological schools have different ideas of state governance and options to follow:

> Without fame, people shall not scheme and contend; without luxuries, people shall not steal; without desires, people's hearts shall not be disturbed. Therefore, in the government of the sage: he keeps his people calm with no greed, makes them well-fed, discourages their ambitions, strengthens their health, so that the people may be innocent of knowledge and desires. And the cunning ones shall not presume to get more. By the action without deeds may all live in peace.[15]

If Lao Zi claimed to abolish knowledge and wisdom, make people innocent and not desire and return to nature for the purpose of reaching the state of "all things and I are integrated," Confucian advocated rites and music to respond to heaven and fit with earth to achieve harmony between man and nature:

> The heaven is high above and the earth is low below, so all the things are different and thus the ritual institution can be applied. Air of heaven and earth circulates endlessly reconciling all things jointly for evolution, and

> thus music education rises. Planting in spring and growing in summer reflect the benevolence. Harvesting in autumn and storing in winter reflect the righteousness. The benevolence is close to music and the righteousness is close to rites.[16]

According to the ancient Chinese sage, disputes and conflicts damaged the existing order and reflected the disintegration of propriety, so the main purpose of mediating and settling disputes was to restore the norms of etiquette, stabilize social order and reach again the harmony between man and the natural order.

2.1.2 Sources of Authority: The Authority of Elders, Moral Authority, and State Authority

In ancient China, the law could be called the "integration of various laws without distinction between civil law and criminal law." The provisions of legal institution for civil affairs were simple and rough and all cases were punished with criminal measures only to different extents. Therefore, when mediating in such disputes as family, marriage, land, and debt, the legitimacy and authority of the mediation results relied on the personal authority of the mediators to a great extent. As a dispute mediation mode, mediation was first observed in the primitive society and later, with the state emerging, became a mode and measure for the rulers to govern the state. During the period of the West Zhou Dynasty, an office of the "Tiaoren (mediator)" was established, i.e., an official in charge of mediation and afterwards, in different periods, governmental mediation and folk mediation co-existed. In different periods, the rural mediators also had different names, e.g., "Xiangsefu" in the Qin and Han Dynasties, "Lizheng" and "Lizhang" of North Wei in the South and North Dynasties, "Shezhang" in the Yuan Dynasty, and "Lilao," "Jiazhang," and "Baozheng" in the Qing Dynasty. When studying the archive materials of the countryside in North China before 1949, American historian Professor Philip C.C. Huang discovered the mediation authority of folk disputes mainly included the following two types: the "middleman" in the affairs of formal lending, land lease, and land trade. As the intermediator facilitating the deal, the "middleman" also became, upon the occurrence of a dispute, the "conciliator," The other type was the person with prestige in the community and clan. When there was no "middleman" to help the marriage and family disputes and neighborhood disputes, the community and clan mediator became the third party with authority in dispute resolution. Generally, the virtuous elders of the community and clan trusted by the villagers and some principals of the grass-roots administrative organizations, such as Baozhang, Jiazhang, and village heads acted as the mediator.

Without exception, the officials in charge of governmental mediation all took the state coercion as back-up, and their authority was self-evident. "Lizhang," "Lilao" and others in charge of folk mediation were all elders of clans and people with high prestige, and their authority was sourced in their "seniority" or "virtues," as was determined by the social pattern of family-state integration in ancient China and the order of rite-governance it relied on. In China, the word "family" has an extremely high flexibility, referring to the family composed of parents and non-adult children as well as the "world." Just as Mr. Fei Xiaotong said:

> Our social structure itself is different from the Western pattern. Our pattern is not one bundle after another of firewood clearly bounded, but is like the circles of ripples pushed out by throwing a stone into water. Everyone is the center of the circle pushed out by his social influence. Pushing by the ripples of the circle results in contact ... The most important kinship in our society is just the nature of ripples of concentric circles formed by throwing a stone. Kinship is the social relation resulting according to the facts of procreation and marriage. From the network composed of procreation and marriage can push out the past, present, and future figures, including numerous people ... In our rural society, not only kinship is so, but the regional relation is also so ... Every family takes its own position as a center for drawing a circle around it, and this circle is just the "neighborhood."[17]

In such a social pattern composed by combining blood and regional relations, those with high seniority and older age are respected. This is because in the society of mainly small-peasant economy, people went out to work at sunrise, came back to rest at sunset, and were used to their dwelling place and unwilling to move, without the necessity for so much interpersonal contact and also without many changes of interpersonal relations. According to the experience of their predecessors, generation by generation, people could meet the demand of their present life and thus social development was also neglected in the human succession and cultural heritage, one generation after another. Therefore, in such a society, "tradition" was given an extremely important position, while the seniors and elders who well knew the "tradition" had an unchallenged authority.

The social pattern of traditional China was the relational network spreading out with "self" as the center. Such a relational network was just like the ripples of water pushed out circle by circle, the more it was pushed, the farther it went and the farther, the thinner. Hence, the "order" and the "push" became the basic features of the traditional social structure. The definition of the word "沦 (*Lun*, water ripple)," is, according to the "*Shiming*" [*Explanations of Appellations*]: "It is 伦 (*Lun*, order), a water wave sequence has order principle (ethics)." Order emphasizes discrimination, and order is the sequence of differences. In Confucianism, social ethics and morality were also integrated into the "rites" of "distinction of noble and humble and order of senior and junior."

> Be close to your relatives and respect the respectful, keep the order of elder and younger, the father shows love and sons show filial piety, the elder brother is kind and younger brother is friendly, the husband is righteous and the wife follows, and the senior favors and the junior is obedient.

This became the discipline of the interpersonal network. The word "push" is the "pushing oneself and others." In traditional China, social scope was "pushed" out from "self," while the process of this "push" was to apply different ethical guides and virtues to different relational networks. Additionally, in such a pattern of disparities "pushed" out from "self," the demarcation of family and state and the world, public and private was, relatively speaking, vague and unclear. What people can start with was particularly on "self" and hence, "self-restraint" became the most important virtue in society. Therefore, in Confucianism, the maintenance of such a pattern of disparities focused on individual self-regulation and cultivation of one's moral character. "Self-restraint and restoration of rites are benevolence," "that being established, all practical courses naturally develop," and those with "high virtue" naturally have "high prestige."

In traditional Chinese society with "imperial power not reaching below the level of the county," the maintenance of local communities (with villages as the main form) mainly relied on the Confucian concepts and its spokesmen, i.e., the elders and gentry. Therefore, the authority of disputes mediation was mainly sourced from the authority of the elders and the moral authority. In contemporary society in China, due to the decrease in state power and the penetration of law and policy, the binding force of folk regulations to maintain the rural communities was softened, the order of rite-governance was already damaged, and the maintenance of social order and mediation of disputes relied mostly on state authority. This is mainly reflected in: first, in terms of mediation subjects, the mediation subjects of judicial mediation and administrative mediation are the public power organs, and judicial mediation and administrative mediation are modes for exercising public power; the present people's mediation in China (the major form of folk mediation) is the government-promoted mediation, and mediation personnel composing the mediation organizations are also mostly the personnel of that system.[18] These personnel are not "formally" exercising state power when undertaking mediation, but their status of public servants or close contact with public power will be, without doubt, favorable to the promotion of mediation and the conclusion of mediation agreements. Second, in terms of the criterion of mediation, the legal principle of mediation implies the important position of the national law, regulations, and policies in mediation. Finally, in terms of mediation effects, in the process of mediation, the collaboration of public power organs is favorable to integrating the resources and ensuring the conclusion and performance of mediation agreements.

2.1.3 Basic Model: Mediator-Oriented Mediation

Mediator-oriented mediation refers to the mediation model where the mediators play a leading role in all such stages as actuation and advancing of the mediation, investigation of dispute facts and proposal of agreement solution. In traditional Chinese society, the mediator-oriented mediation originated in the pursuit of "non-litigation" and an attempt to "withdraw lawsuits" from the "outlook of harmony." In the Confucian outlook of harmony, the ideal society desired was that the monarch is considerate and kind to men of talent, the common people are honest and upright and everyone bears in mind the ethical order of "distinction of noble and humble and order of senior and junior." In order to achieve the ideal of "non-litigation," the rulers emphasized educating people with morality, convincing people with rites and making them "sick of litigation" and "ashamed of litigation." In the field of judicature, people were made to "fear litigation" through cruel torture and a crack-down on crimes of "instigating for litigation." What corresponded to the attempt to "withdraw lawsuits" was that the state encouraged the parties to disputes to start mediation. For instance, the *General Rules and Regulations* of the Yuan Dynasty stated:

> As for lawsuits on marriage, domestic properties, land and housing, and debts, if they are not major matters in violation of law, they should be resolved by the proprietor through reasoning to avoid interrupting and wasting farming work and disturbing the government.

The law of the Ming Dynasty stated: "All prefectures set up the pavilion of statement. In the event that people have any lawsuit, the elder and village head are allowed to accept and mediate at the pavilion." The "Official Instruction to People" promulgated in the year of 1328 stated: such civil cases as family, marriage, field land, debts, equal distribution of irrigation, private slaughtering of farm cattle and stealing of melons and fruits from orchards are all folk trifles and prohibited from being brought directly to the authority and must be adjudicated by the elder or the head of the village.

> Once this decree is issued, if any official dares to disobey, he will be sentenced to capital punishment. If any of the common people dare to disobey, he will be moved to the remote areas. The above provisions have been announced and the Ministry of Revenue should state it again.

In contemporary society in China, the motive for the state to attach importance to mediation and to positively intervene in dispute resolution is also based on the consideration of the following factors in addition to the pursuit of a "harmonious" society: due to the sharp contradictions in contemporary society, the increasing numbers of disputes and the increasing variety of dispute types, on the one hand, mediation is helpful to relax the pressure of litigation and increase the performing rate of cases; on the other hand, as a governance mode of the state, mediation can play a better role in preventing disputes and helping to achieve the governance target of "minor matters not beyond villages and major events not beyond township."

The uppermost feature of mediator-oriented mediation is the positive feature and activeness of the mediator in the process of mediation, i.e., the mediator does not assist the parties to resolve disputes by themselves, but guides and moderates the parties to resolve disputes. The positive feature of the mediator is mainly reflected as: first, the mediator positively intervenes in dispute resolution. "All the land under heaven belongs to the king; all the humans in the world are the king's people."[19] In the social pattern of family-state integration in ancient China, "state-family relationship and monarch-subject relationship are merely the extension of family relationship and father-son relationship,"[20] as determined by the natural rationality for the "family head" or "father-mother official" to intervene positively in the dispute resolution between "people" or "subjects." For historical and realistic reasons, in modern society in China, when any dispute happens, certain members of the common people will expect the "government" or the "superior" to intervene for a resolution, and the common people's acceptance constitutes the legal basis for mediators to intervene positively in dispute resolution. However, the traditional society of acquaintance and the prevailing people's mediation organization network distributed at the level of village or group have all ensured the feasibility of mediators positively intervening in disputes. Second, in the resolution of many disputes, mediators are active and positive when investigating the facts of disputes. In addition to the information obtained in "face-to-face" and "back-to-back" mediation, Chinese mediators would often collect evidence by themselves to understand comprehensively the facts of disputes, e.g., the reasons and historical background for the occurrence of disputes, the characters and features of the parties, the relationship between the parties and other facts. Third, no matter whether it is based on the facts of disputes found, Chinese mediators are all used to positively proposing the solutions according to the reasons or law. In traditional Chinese society and the period of the socialist planned economy, it was up to mediators to provide solutions directly, as was unavoidable to make mediation mandatory. In the present mediation practice, due to the emphasis on the voluntary will of mediation, after a mediator makes a judgment on the facts of a dispute and forms a mediation solution, it is generally up to the mediator to take charge of holding the consultation meeting, as this is a process of motivating all resources and forces to collectively "persuade" the parties to accept the mediation solution.

In terms of the mutual relations between the mediation subjects, there are two types of relations in the mediator-oriented mediation, i.e., the relations between the mediator and the parties and the relation between the parties. The role of the former is far greater than the latter and even the effective communication often fails between the parties, so that the relations between the parties tend to be nil (see Figure 2.1). Mutual relations between the mediator

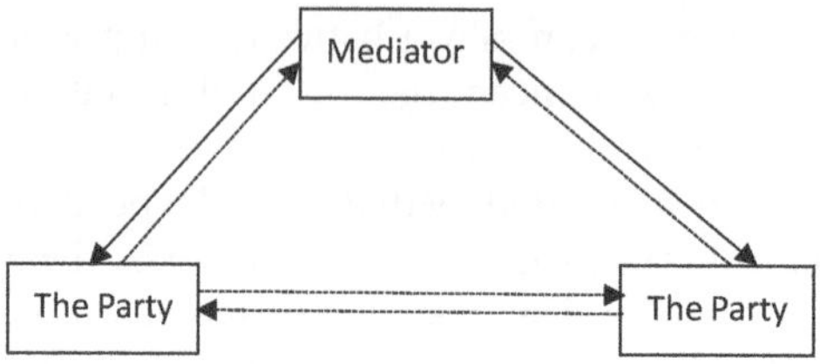

Figure 2.1 Mediation relations in mediator-oriented mediation.

and the parties are mainly reflected in lecturing and convincing from the top down, i.e., it is mainly the relations of the mediator with the parties, while the relations of the parties with the mediator also tend to be lacking (see Figure 2.1). The major topic of the mediator's lecture to the parties has differed per the times changing: in traditional society, the main topic was ethics and morality; after the People's Republic of China was established before the reform and opening-up was launched, the main topic was the national policy and communist morality; since the reform and opening-up, persuasion has been mainly pursuant to regulations, policies, and reasons. The mediation relational model of Chinese mediator-oriented mediation was the reflection of the Chinese "official standard" thought and the idea of "emphasizing entity and ignoring procedure" in mediation, and its direct consequence was the lack of the mediator's sense of service and sense of procedural assurance. Mediators were fond of reasoning and persuading based on their own judgment and were weak in the sense of assisting effective communication between the parties, not to say having the sense of assuring the procedural rights of the parties, granting the chance to the parties for adequate representation and patiently listening to and understanding the motives and interests behind the appeals of the parties. Simply put, the status of the parties in mediation was objectified and the relations between the mediator and the parties were subject-object relations.

2.1.4 Mediation Methods: Emotional Principle Prior to Legal Principle

In terms of mediation methods, the target of folk mediation is to maintain interpersonal harmony in the community of acquaintance and the main method of mediation is compromise and mutual accommodation. The famous sociologist Lin Duan generalized the continuity of the legal conduct of the Chinese in traditional society as the continuity from the informal folk mediation to the formal judgment of the government office, the process of its legal operation is gradually formalized, made official and complicated and the dispute resolution relies more on mediation, while the legal sense of mediation is the priority in "emotion–reason–law."[21] In the opinion of Professor Philip C.C. Huang, according to the official Confucian expression in the

Qing Dynasty, folk mediation should attach more importance than official judgment to human emotion and heavenly principle (emotional principle) and the function of state law in folk mediation is extremely slight, but in practical operation, state law, right and wrong in a common sense, and conciliation and compromise are the three principles guiding the operation of folk mediation. Compromise is the most important, but state law is always an important factor in folk mediation and provides a basic framework for conciliation and compromise, and the emotional principle in folk mediation is different from the heavenly principle and human emotion in the Confucian expression. In the actual operation of mediation; "emotion" refers to the compromise and mutual accommodation of maintaining harmonious interpersonal relations rather than the moral sympathy in Confucian theory; "reason" refers to the right and wrong sense of people in a common sense rather than the abstract heavenly principle in Confucian theory. Compromise, the concept of right and wrong, and state law operate jointly in the process of mediation to maintain community harmony.[22]

The application of these mediation methods in dispute resolution can mostly reveal the thinking and idea of traditional mediation. Hereafter, we will first see one case of official mediation. In the famous example from the Qing Dynasty, one of the mediation processes of "brothers fighting for fields" was recorded in the official motto book, *Complicated Legal Cases of Luzhou*:

> After their father died, the sons of Chen Zhi, Aming and Ading fell out for seven Chinese *mu* of farmland and sued the government office. Aming stated that the seven Chinese *mu* of farmland was left to him by his father and presented to the magistrate, Lan Dingyuan. the personal handwriting of his father, which clearly wrote: "After my death, the farmland property will belong to the eldest son." Ading said that before passing away, his father left an oral will to leave the farmland to him, with others witnessing. Seeing each side stuck to its own views, Lan Dingyuan said: "Both of you are right, but it means it is the responsibility of your father, why should he not have made it clear? What I can do is to open the coffin and ask him." The brothers looked at each other and felt ashamed. Lan Dingyuan said: "The farmland property is really a trifle compared with the brotherhood. Is it worth suing for such a trifle? It is so bitterly disappointing. Both of you have two sons. In the future, when your own sons grow up, it will be strange if they will not fight for the land like you. So, for the future peace, I can only take preventive measures and ask you to feed only one son respectively. Aming is the elder brother and keeps the elder son. Ading is the younger brother and keeps the younger son. It is decided to detain the two sons in the asylum and sell them to beggars as sons. The case is closed." Upon hearing this, Aming said: "I, the commoner, admit my guilt and am willing to give all the farmland properties to my younger brother, without any argument." The younger brother also repented thoroughly of his misdeeds. Lan Dingyuan wanted to know the

> opinion of their wives. The following day, the four people and the clan head came to the office, requesting conciliation regarding the farmland as the assets for a memorial ceremony for the father, collecting the rents in turns, without any dispute generation after generation of descendants.[23]

When summarizing the experiences of the case, Lan Dingyuan viewed that for this case, according to the general judgment method, they should be given 30 lashes respectively, and the farmland divided into two halves. The case can be closed with several words. Now, it has taken a lot of trouble, admonishing words and kind feelings, but after all, the effect is significant. "Then, the brothers and their wives become friendly and love each other, and the custom would last for more than three generations. Definitely, the official governance will become law-abiding."

From this official mediation, we see that the judge did not pursue the distinction of rights and status, but attempted to make the parties sincerely convinced, as the judgment was very educational. The official mediation was so, how about folk mediation? The famous sociologist Fei Xiaotong talked about his feelings when taking part in mediation in the countryside at the beginning of the twentieth century:

> In the countryside, the so-called mediation was actually a process of education ... Mediation was a new word, while the old word was reasoning. Almost every time, one sociable squire started to talk. His formula was always to curse the two parties of the mediation. "It is really a shameful thing for our village! You should admit the mistake and go home." Then, he taught them a lesson. Sometimes, he banged the table and got angry. He told them what he considered "necessary." This was extremely effective and the two parties often reached "conciliation." Sometimes, he penalized them for a dinner.[24]

Especially by presenting an interesting case, Mr. Fei Xiaotong explained the nature of folk mediation:

> Mr. A got on in years and smoked opium. For the sake of the whole family, the elder son greatly opposed this hobby of his father, but could not interfere. The second son did not do honest work and smoked opium secretly and often encouraged his old father to smoke opium so that he could share some. Once, the elder son saw this and hit his younger brother, but the young brother blamed the father. The elder son became angry and cursed his father. The families kicked up a fuss and were sent to the village administrative office for reasoning. The squire first said as usual that it was a scandal of the whole village. Then, he deployed the whole ethic principle: the younger son was scum and did not look a good bet, he was the worst and should be driven out of the village. The elder son cursed his father and should be punished. The old father didn't know

> how to control the sons and also smoked opium and was given a lesson. In this way, everyone admitted the punishment and went home.[25]

From these discussions and the particular cases, we can conclude the basic features of the thinking mode of traditional mediation.

First, the main target of mediation is to maintain harmony. It means that mediation does not promote rights, does not distinguish right or wrong and does not seek fairness and justice in individual cases, but is devoted to maintaining the harmony and order of the social communities. This point was clearly expressed in the well-known saying of Wang Huizu, a famous servant in the Qing Dynasty, and he said:

> It is good to be diligent, to hear, and judge. However, where it is unnecessary to distinguish black and white excessively for amity, it is better to mediate through relatives and friends. Therefore, we should hear and judge according to law, while mediate with emotions. Law must distinguish the clear and the muddy, while emotion allows somewhat mistakes in distinguishing the right or wrong. The righteous ones know the affection of relatives and friends while the wrong ones may avoid legal proceedings of court. It is why mediators were set up in Zhou Guan (the Official System of Zhou).[26]

Second, traditional mediation was a mandatory educational feature. Since social harmony was most valued, the officials who followed the Confucian intellectuals deemed litigation to be a bad social phenomenon, disturbing the social and moral order. So, a mediator would often mediate not only to resolve disputes, but also mostly to educate. Mediation and settlement of disputes provided all the villagers with the opportunity to learn, and helped people to reaffirm their common moral value. In other words, to a certain extent, mediation provided examples using the "case method," telling people how to handle their interpersonal relationships.[27] The mediation method of Lan Dingyuan in handling the case of the "brothers fighting for farmland" seemed to move with emotion, but actually was mandatory but not in an obvious way.

Third, traditional mediation insisted on emotion and reason first. Dispute mediation considered first "emotion," then "reason," and finally "law."[28] The functions of emotion, reason, and law in mediation were regressive, as they also led to dispute resolutions that may be mixing water into mud. Therefore, the order shaped by traditional mediation was a Confucian rite-governance order, rather than a legal-governance order for rights. In the case of disputes, the correct attitude the mediator required of the parties to sort it out was to "self-examine, self-criticize, modestly decline or make a concession, accommodate or compromise to others, and should not insist on their own interests and claim for their own interests,"[29] In the official mediation case mentioned by Lan Dingyuan and the folk mediation case mentioned by Fei Xiaotong, we can see the legal sense of mediation of such a moral and ethical standard.

2.2 Dilemma of Traditional Mediation in the Period of Social Transformation

Social transformation means the change of social structure and social mechanisms from one form to another form. From the Opium War of 1840 to 1949, with the invasion of Western powers and Western culture reaching the East, Chinese society had been slowly changing. Since 1978, when China launched the reform and opening-up, Chinese society has been in a period of accelerated transformation. In the process of China's industrialization, urbanization, and modernization, with rapid economic development, the shares of social resources among people were observed as unequal; the diversity of interest subjects and the variety of interest appeals also led to the intensification of contradictions and conflicts and a variety of dispute types. Mediation rooted in the traditional society witnessed the great change of the times as well as unavoidably the challenges of the times.

2.2.1 Functional Decline of Traditional Mediation, with Differentiation of Social Classes as the Breakthrough Point

Institutional reform, upgrading of the industrial structure, and urbanization will definitely lead to changes in the social structure. In the field of sociology, the "social structure" is a concept with various interpretations, but, generally speaking, it refers to the location of people in society and their interrelations according to the different parameters. According to the share of social resources, people can be classified into different classes in terms of vertical structure. According to whether people had the means of production, Karl Marx classified the people into "proprietor" and "proletarian," but Western scholars, represented by Max Weber, generally stated there are three major standards for differentiation of social classes: power, fortune, and reputation.

Since the primitive society disappeared, mankind has been divided into different interest groups and different classes. In the feudal society of China with a long history, there were the professional classifications of "soldier, farmer, worker, and businessman" and the class classification of "landlord, bureaucrat, and peasant," but Chinese society in those days was, as a whole, a small-peasant society, with the peasants comprising most of the total population, and the turnover between different classes was also low. In China from 1949 to 1978, individuals did not hold any means of production, so Chinese society before the reform was basically a status society. After 1978, China undertook a relatively profound institutional reform, i.e., the change from the planned economic system to the market economic system. Afterwards, a series of institutional changes profoundly affected the class differentiation and restructuring of Chinese society. The distribution principle of market-allocated resources, the primacy of efficiency and consideration of fairness, not only promoted the differentiation and restructuring of social classes, but also aggravated the poverty gap between different classes. According to the fortune, power, and reputation possessed by individuals, if Chinese society is classified into five classes such as upper, medium-high, medium, medium-low, and lower, the upper class comprised about 1.5 percent of the total national economically active population;[30] the medium-low class comprised 68 percent of the total national economically active population; the lower class comprised 14 percent of the total national economically active population; the medium-high and medium classes comprised respectively 3.2 percent and 13.3 percent of the total national economically active population.[31] From the above data, we can see the features of China's present social classification: of the total national economically active population, the proportion of the upper class is the lowest, comprised about 1.5 percent; the proportion of the medium class is next, about 16.5 percent; the social medium-low and lower classes comprised about 82 percent. The social classes show a pyramid structure. The building with a pyramid structure is stable because its center of gravity is low; but the social structure of a pyramid shape is unstable, because the proportion of people in the social medium-low class is high, indicating a large number of people who want to change their present status. If the channel for them to move up to the social upper class is interrupted, they will feel dissatisfaction, resulting in contradictions and conflicts.

Where there is social stratification, there is social inequality, not only because of the difference in natural endowment and acquired efforts between people, but also mostly because of the impossibility of an absolutely equal society. In the society of absolute equality, due to lack of the competitive mechanism and incentive mechanism, such a society will eventually lead to general poverty due to a lack of activity. Hence, the concerns of people for fairness turned to the equality of opportunities, while the equality of opportunities is ensured by the social institution. In the process for China to change from the planned economy to the market economy, the administrative power played a critical role in the formation of the market and the flow and distribution of fortunes. Hence, in the process of seeking fortunes and social status, people may possibly encounter inequality of market access, educational inequality and inequality of law and policy, all in the category of institutional inequality.

Since the beginning of the twenty-first century, the primary problem faced by China is not the problem of economic development, but is the social problem. Due to the differentiation of social classes, different interest groups will have unavoidably different contradictions in the process of maintaining available interests and expected interests. Resolution of the disputes initiated by these contradictions is the challenge traditional Chinese mediation can hardly cope with. First, in terms of dispute subjects and their interrelations, due to the unitary structure of traditional Chinese society and less interpersonal contact, most of the disputes are disputes between peasants and the gap between dispute subjects is generally not big. In the modern period, with the differentiation of social classes, dispute subjects also show a trend of diversity. In the meantime, in many disputes, there is an extremely large gap between the parties in terms of social status, economic power, and cultural quality. Second, in terms of dispute types, traditional Chinese mediation mainly resolved "family, marriage, farmland, monetary and debt" disputes and non-serious criminal cases. With the economy developing and the times changing, in addition to the traditional disputes, the modern society also brought many new disputes, e.g., land circulation, land acquisition and relocation, environmental pollution, traffic accidents, employment disputes, and so on. Since many new disputes involve a large number of people and a wide regional scope, comprehensive knowledge is required to resolve such types of disputes and traditional local knowledge can hardly cope with these disputes. Third, in terms of the nature of disputes, the traditional disputes arising in the society of acquaintance were mixed with relatively many emotional factors, mostly about "winning honors" or "a matter of face." Yet, in the market economy, modern people are utilitarian and economically rational. Therefore, modern disputes often have a very high interest orientation. Traditional mediation resolved and settled disputes mainly through moral education and, if faced with such disputes with a relatively high interest orientation, its function will naturally be limited. Finally, in terms of the development of disputes, in traditional society, most of the traditional disputes had a unitary nature, and the parties in the society of acquaintance also preferred to choose compromise and accommodation for dispute resolution, so the disputes in traditional society had a relatively low diffusion and also generally would not intensify. In the modern period, with the modern media and communication technology developing, some disputes soon became the focused issues of social and public opinion and some contradictions and disputes may even be intensified as group events. In terms of procedure as well as the entity, the resolution of such disputes depends more on the standard of certain universality to some extent.

2.2.2 Disempowerment of the Authority of Traditional Mediation from the Perspective of Changes in People's Thought and Ideas

As mentioned above, the legitimacy and acceptability of traditional mediation often originated from the personal authority of the mediator or the attached state authority. In modern society, in a market economy, democratic politics and a diverse culture bring the disempowerment of authority, and the authority of the Chinese government in the period of social transformation can hardly avoid this, and the credibility of the government is facing a severe test. There are various reasons for such a situation. First, due to some institutional inequality in the process of reform and opening-up, the public has been dissatisfied. A market economy naturally makes interest subjects diversified and the contradictions between different interest groups also become increasingly prominent and sharp with the reform going deeper. Second, the deeply rooted "official standard" way of thinking weakened the service sense of the government, the transparency of the government work declines, or the mode of crisis disposal is improper, thus intangibly damaging the credibility of the government. Third, the corruption and misbehavior of some government officials severely damaged the image of government in the public's eyes. Fourth, due to developed modern communication technology and the popularization of the law, the ideas of "democracy" and "rights" go deep into the hearts of people and the public has a basic understanding of the fields of public rights and private rights respectively and will also refuse, on some occasions, the intervention of public power.[32]

In the contemporary period of the "information explosion," the elders who are well versed in tradition have different interests from the younger generation in such aspects as information possession, approaches for information capture, way of thinking, and even ways of living. Due to the rapid economic development and increasingly changing society, tradition has come, on various occasions, to mean the same as "backward" and "conservative." In the rural areas, except for such traditional ceremonies and activities such as sacrifice and worship that may leave a space for the elder authority, in the interest-oriented dispute resolution, the elders have lost the right to judge as a clan chief. Even if they still have the chance to express opinions, it is also only limited to "opinions." Another reflection of the weakening elder authority is the weakening of the binding force of folk norms such as customs and habits, and folk regulations. With national law and policies penetrating layer by layer and the right to decide on criminal punishment returned to the state, like the "opinions" of the elders, these norms also play only a minor role of guidance of conduct and public supervision.

Concurrent with the decline of the elder authority was also the moral weakness, as it was closely connected with the evolution of the nature of modern Chinese society and lack of public belief. Traditional Chinese society was a society of acquaintance composed of a combination of blood and regional relationships. In such a society, people were attached to their native land and unwilling to leave it. They were born here and grew up here. They watched over and helped each other; they shared a basic integrated value outlook and followed similar behavioral criteria: the three cardinal guides and five constant virtues and ethics and morality. Since the reform and opening-up, the household contract responsibility system has liberated the peasants from the land and the process of urbanization has made the rural surplus workforce surge into cities. According to data published by the National Bureau of Statistics in 2018, China's urban population already exceeded 59.58 percent of the total national population.[33] Therefore, modern Chinese society is a society of strangers and semi-acquaintances based on the urban-rural "binary" structure. Even in the present countryside, under the impact of the tide of the market economy, the rite-governance order was damaged, the rural community maintained by the ethic guides and virtues was basically dissolved, villagers also became the calculating economic men, and the past ethical relationship between people has also become an interest relationship.

> The belief system of the Chinese nation was established on the basis of traditional culture with Confucian orthodoxy as the core, and this orthodoxy has been running in a single line from Yao, Shun, Yu, Tang, Wen, Wu, Zhougong, Confucius, Meng Zi to Dong Zhongshu, Wen Zhongzi, Zhu Xi, and Wang Yangming.[34]

But, the New Culture Movement about one hundred years ago advocated, on the one hand, the historical subject of "save the nation so that it may survive" and, on the other hand, completely negated and abandoned the traditional value of Confucianism as the dregs of feudalism. Chaos caused by wars and especially the previous political movements after 1949 have eventually destroyed the Confucian orthodoxy and made it lose the right to be the authority. Due to the break-up of cultural tradition and the collapse of the belief system, public morality has lost its ethical resources.

With the reform and opening-up, China has moved down the road of developing a market economy. A market economy is the rational economy and its core is to maximize the interests with minimum cost; a market economy is also a secular economy and between moral principle and practical benefits, it has chosen the latter; a market economy is more a this-worldly economy and does not believe in the future, but believes everyone wants this-worldly interests. A market economy is a well-performing engine. Once started, it will run at a high speed, creating huge material fortunes for society, but this engine itself is not provided with a system to limit its speed or a braking system and it needs to be controlled through other systems, including cultural value beliefs and morality and ethics. When mediating in only interest-oriented disputes, if the mediator still holds to the rule of ethics and morality, due to the lack of value acceptance, it is not only hard to reach consensus, but even the consensus will evolve to become "reckless."

2.3 Modernity Reshapes the Mediation Idea: Rational Mediation

In the contemporary human social sciences, modernity is a concept with a general interpretation. It is because it has spread extensively due to the force of its discourse that its influence is prominent but also vague. Even so, modernity still has several basic elements: a market economy, democratic politics, and scientific reason. Hence,

> Market economy implies the theory of a strong value target (the efficiency concept) and universal rationality (the economic reason concept); democratic politics expressed the so-called political rationality or legality and the rational arrangement of social and political institutions were the result therefrom or social universal order. Scientific reason represented the universal rationality based on the technical rationality or outlook of universal truths.[35]

Scientific reason rebelled against the "worship of gods" and "hero worship" during the eras of ancient Greek and Rome and the Middle Ages, and the authoritative view of knowledge it established replaced all the value beliefs surpassing the objects or forces of human rationality. The truth concept of such scientific reason upholds that only the knowledge that can be proved by mankind is scientific, and knowledge such as morality, religion, and arts that cannot be proved with scientific logic or verified by universal empirical facts, thus, is deemed to be non-scientific knowledge without intellectual legality and logical rationality, while "knowledge is power" is the expression of such a concept. However, when turning the objects of belief from the external world to the knowledge discovered, created, and invented by human beings, human beings also unconsciously fell into the morass of one-dimensional "human egocentrism." Hence, lack of belief is deemed a crisis of modern society. "God is dead" (as Nietzsche said). Politics requires democracy to ensure its legitimacy and legality. Then, in the field of mediation, when the authority that traditional mediation relied on is already disempowered, modern mediation maybe only can seek rational resources to make the parties recognize and accept a resolution, i.e., facilitating the parties to form consensus through rational mediation so that mediation returns to the "voluntary" origin.

With respect to the understanding of reason, different scholars in different periods had different viewpoints, such is the self-reflection of human reason. As a whole, the ancient reason pursued the rational and orderly order of the whole world and thus was a kind of overall reason. In modern times, people have understood the world with the self as the center, and thus promoted the development of subject independence. "*Je pense, donc je suis* (I think, therefore I am" of Descartes is just the evidence. Kant also deemed reason to be an innate understanding ability of man, and "reason is the ability of providing various principles of innate knowledge"[36] and is classified into knowledge reason and practical reason, according to the different objects. Hegel viewed the world as an entirety, i.e., "absolute spirit" or "absolute idea," and hence reason eventually became "absolute." Modern reason is basically a kind of rebuilding reason. Mr. Han Zheng summarized the viewpoints of reason rebuilding since the nineteenth century as the following types. The first type is the outlook of reason of "from reason to rationality" represented by Weber and the Frankfurt School. The second type is the "reason concept from ideal reason to instrumental reason" proposed by the modern pragmatists represented by Russell, the earlier Wittgenstein and Carnap. The third type is the reason concept of "from arbitrary reason to critical reason" represented by Popper. The fourth type is the reason concept of "from transcendental reason to practical reason" represented by Taylor and Macintyre.[37]

Traditional mediation lasted for thousands of years in China as well as the ADR (alternative dispute resolution) movement surging forward in the Western countries in modern times, called by scholars "the Third Wave"—both followed practical reason in development. In the modern society, due to the decline of traditional authority, people tending to be rational recognize and accept only the result of human rationality, therefore we should respond to people's demand for modern rationality through the rationalization of mediation. Here, authority comes from reason, but not on the contrary. In our opinion, mediation rationality can be understood as the abstract thinking capability of people about mediation and a series of mediation rules and modes reflecting such thinking capability, recognized and accepted by the public, including the rationality of the mediation process and the mediation results. Additionally, if the mediation rationality is defined only from the perspective of mediation subjects, due to the one-dimensional value, it may result in the use of unscrupulous divisive tactics to achieve the purpose, and in order to overcome the situation of slipping from purpose rationality to the "cage of instrumental reason," it is necessary to inject ethical and moral factors into the field of mediation. Therefore, mediation rationality should at least reflect the inherent requirement of procedural rationality, economic rationality, and moral rationality.

2.3.1 Procedural Rationality

Procedural rationality is the rationality of the procedure. As for the characteristic standard of procedural rationality, different scholars have different, criss-crossed, similar or same summaries. In terms of mediation of different countries in different periods, the universal feature is the activity of a neutral third person, according to the interests and demand of the parties to a dispute, to assist or moderate the parties in voluntary consultation on the dispute so as to resolve the dispute. The mediation process is essentially an activity of negotiation between the mediator and the parties and between all the parties to resolve disputes and prevent conflicts so as to reach a common view. Therefore, Habermas' theory of communicative rationality may provide some enlightenment in constructing the procedural rationality of mediation. Habermas' communicative rationality is essentially dialogue-oriented and reflected in the communication behavior. The characteristics of such a concept of rationality can briefly be summarized as follows. First, communicative rationality is language-oriented and communication itself takes language as the medium. In the opinion of Habermas, language is the condition for subjects to communicate effectively and reach a common view. Second, communicative rationality is also the inter-subjectivity and it replaces the traditional subject-object relation with the subject-subject relation. In the process of communication, all the subjects participating in the communication pursue their own purposes, but they all abide by such premise so as they coordinate their action plan as defined jointly. Third, communicative rationality is procedural. The participants in communication achieve mutual understanding through language and discussion. Fourth, communicative rationality is also an approach for democracy and peace. Habermas claimed that in the practice of communication, the communicators should, through the idealized language communication, reach a common view, eliminate disputes, and resolve conflicts so as to realize the rationalization of the life-world and achieve the target of freedom and liberation.[38] Habermas criticized traditional rationality, but he did not fundamentally negate and destroy rationality, and included modern instrumental reason in the communicative rationality, hence, communicative rationality is an open and inclusive theory. According to Habermas' theory of communicative rationality, the procedural rationality of mediation needs to restrict the arbitrary and reckless act in the process of reaching consensus, thus resolving the tension between procedural instrumentalism and procedural departmentalism and realizing the unification of formal rationality and substantial rationality. In particular, the procedural reason of mediation includes at least the following:

1 *Assure the basic procedural justice*. This is the precondition for the parties to recognize the mediation procedure and consult willingly so as to accept the mediation result. The basic procedural justice includes: first, the mediator is neutral, i.e., the mediator has no stake in the dispute. In the meantime, the mediator also has to act in such a way for the parties to believe he is neutral. It requires the mediator to remain objective, neutral, and impartial in the process of mediation and will not favor or decide whether any party is right or wrong and will patiently hear the opinions of the parties.[39] Second, adequately inform the parties of the matters concerning the mediation procedure, so that all the subjects reach a basic common view of the mediation procedure itself. These matters generally include: basic principle of mediation; the role and function of the mediator; major procedures of mediation; rights entitlement of the parties in mediation. Finally, ensure equally the procedural rights of the parties. For instance, stipulate that the two parties speak in turns so that they can adequately represent and can be patiently heard; any party has the equal decision right about the mediation procedure and contents of the mediation agreement.
2 *Assure the procedural subjectivity of the parties*. The subjectivity of the parties in the mediation procedure is mainly reflected as the voluntary principle of the parties, i.e., the parties decide, at their own discretion, whether to undertake mediation, whether to suspend the mediation procedure, whether to conclude a mediation agreement and the particular contents of the mediation agreement. In China's present mediation practice, upon finding out the facts, many mediators will directly propose their own mediation solution, and, with all types of implied or potential deterrent force, make the parties accept the mediation solution. But, in the modern society, on the one hand, due to enhanced individualism, rationality, and people's awareness of their rights, it may be relatively hard for the parties to willingly accept the solution which is short of legitimacy and rationality for them. Therefore, if the parties refuse to conclude an agreement, such a practice of the mediator to judge the facts and

directly present the mediation solution not only fails to close the case for settlement, but also, on the contrary, will disparage the mediation procedure and the mediator's credibility and authority. On the other hand, even when the parties accept the mediation solution, since they are not completely willing to do so, they may possibly go back on their word, fail to perform the mediation agreement, and turn to other approaches of dispute resolution, litigation or petition, as will result in a big waste of national resources and social resources. Therefore, when proposing a resolution solution, the mediator should obtain the authorization from the parties or propose at the request of the parties, as this is the assurance of the legitimacy of the mediation solution.

3 *Unification of the regularity and purpose of the mediation procedure.* Compared with the litigation procedure, the mediation procedure is better as it is flexible and inexpensive. The combination of regularity and the purpose of the mediation procedure means that the mediator can choose different mediation models, according to the types of dispute, the characters of the parties and the relations between the parties, to respond to the interests and demands of the parties and thus resolve the disputes properly and preferentially. When talking about the mediation models, Tanase Takao classified them according to two functional differentiation axes:

> As for the mediator, one axis reflects which is more important, the cost of dispute resolution or the nature of resolution content as the functional nature. The other differentiation axis reflects the basic target of mediation is to discover whether it is the legally correct resolution or the resolution the parties choose as they prefer.[40]

According to one coordinate composed of these two axes, mediation can be functionally classified into different types: judgment, education, negotiation, and treatment. Judgment-oriented mediation is a type of mediation with the target of discovering a legally correct judgment, giving adequate play to the advantage of mediation, to reduce cost in the process of discovering this target. Education-oriented mediation is a process of restoring the lost balance to resolve, according to the law, and restoring social solidarity by discovering the justice with mediation or so-called alternative correct resolution rather than seeking the reappearance of judgment. Negotiation-oriented mediation refers to the type of mediation to achieve dispute resolution by negotiating with the opposite party based on the lower limit of the resolution possibly obtained and cost required through judgment, as the parties estimate. Treatment-oriented mediation is, in the view of Tanase Takao, a functional type of mediation that is the most difficult to implement. This model deems disputes as a pathological phenomenon of interpersonal relation and for such pathology, it is necessary to achieve the resolution of disputes by restoring the mental state. In the opinion of Tanase Takao, every model has its unique advantages and disadvantages in terms of legitimacy or effectiveness in reaching the consensus and any one single model may lead to "pauperization of consensus."[41] Mediation is an art and also a practical rationality. Therefore, in the opinion of this author, mediators can choose different models according to the particular cases, and can apply comprehensively different models according to the changes in situation so as to ensure the legitimacy and appropriateness of consensus.

2.3.2 Economic Rationality

Economic rationality refers to the motive of any participant in economic activities to pursue the maximum material interests. For consumers, it is to pursue maximum utility and for producers, it is to pursue the maximum profits. The economic rationality of mediation means that mediation does not satisfy the distribution of available interests between the parties, but is meant to expand and create interests. If litigation is a kind of "zero-sum game," the economic rationality of mediation requires mediation is mechanism to realize a "win-win" situation. Therefore, in the process of assisting the parties in communication and negotiation, mediators should change the concept and lay stress on meeting the requirements of the parties for economic rationality.

To magnify interests, first of all, it is necessary to identify the stand and interests. In negotiation, the stand refers to the target one party expects to reach through negotiation; interest refers to the reason hidden behind the stand. For example, in negotiation, one party demands an annual salary of RMB 100,000, as is an issue of stand. But, why does the negotiator face such a demand? Is it meant to show his actual value? Or is it a general standard of income for his friends and classmates? Is it the general annual salary of a company? Or is it the amount the negotiator must have to maintain his family expenses? These are all the fundamental interests of the negotiator and also the matters concerned most by the negotiator. In mediation, the mediator should avoid the endless disputes on stand between the parties. If negotiation only focuses on the issue of stand, the negotiators will often take the extreme stand, or persist in a stubborn attitude, or will be unwilling to disclose his real intention, or make little compromise for the purpose of continuing with the negotiation and expecting to achieve a favorable result . It will not only make the negotiation become a seesaw battle and lower the efficiency of negotiation, but also it will easily make the negotiation fall into a deadlock and even break up. Therefore, the wise option of the mediator and negotiators is to bypass the conflict of the parties in terms of stand and focus on the interest demand of the parties so as to efficiently facilitate the conclusion of an agreement.

For example, in a case of divorce dispute, the couple both want to reach a divorce mediation agreement. They are now still living together, but will soon depart. They have two children. The husband agrees that the children can live with the mother, but insists that the distance of their dwelling place to his residence should be less than 30-minutes drive, while the wife does not agree.

It is an issue of stand about whether the wife must live somewhere within a 30-minue drive from the home of the husband. Similarly, if mediation takes only their stands as the basic point of negotiation, the negotiation will definitely fall into deadlock, but if starting to coordinate on their interests, it will break through the deadlock and achieve the effect to satisfy both parties. The interests behind their stands are respectively: the husband hopes to visit frequently the children for the relationship of the father with the children is extremely important and he does not want the children to become strange to him. The wife does not want to be under the control of the husband and she wants to freely choose a home convenient for work as well as for the children to go to school. Through negotiation, the mediation agreement eventually concluded is: the husband no longer insists on his claim, and upon divorce, the wife can move to a home farther away, but the wife has to promise to allow the husband to see the children frequently, and when he wants to see the children, send the children to a place nearer to his home for meeting. In this way, the wife can stay with her mother, and when she goes to work, her mother can help to take care of the children.[42]

The stand of the parties in negotiation is often particular and definite, but the interests hidden behind the stand are usually not particular and not definite and sometimes may be inconsistent with each other, thus requires the mediator to be good at discovering the interests of the parties. In face-to-face mediation, mediators need to listen carefully; in back-to-back mediation, mediators may make the parties present their case by asking some open questions and discover as much information as possible and probe into the real intention and interests of the parties. When coordinating the interests, it is required to take into consideration some basic demands of the parties, e.g., some issues appear to be a matter of money, but actually one party expects to be respected or fairly treated. Additionally, in mediation, it is required to creatively work out different possible solutions that can meet the interests of both parties, to avoid coordinating one aspect to make the parties choose between this or that. Creative optional solutions need to be proposed. It is required to first work out as many solutions as possible for the sake of screening one by one; strive to seek the common interests, and try the best to make different interests into complementary interests.

In addition to the distinction of stand and interests, in some commercial disputes, it is also required to help the parties to look forward to the future. Litigation is concerned with the facts of what occurred in the past and decomposes legally the facts into different legal relations and relevant legal elements before defining, according to law, the right and obligation relation of the parties and their liabilities to be undertaken. Being influenced by "state-centrism" and "legal monism" thought, the present Chinese mediation in practice also pursues the effect similar to judgment in terms of mediation functions, and also applies judgment-oriented mediation in the mediation model. However, such judgment-oriented dispute resolution mode will not create interests, but will only redistribute the available interests. Therefore, in mediation, it is required to turn the focus of concerns from "what happened in the past" to "what the parties actually want," i.e., to guide the parties to keep in mind the future and create the opportunities for the parties to cooperate, so as create more interests. For instance, in the contractual disputes, according to the interests and demands of the parties, it is unnecessary to rigidly adhere to probing into which party defaults and what default liabilities the defaulting party should undertake, but it is to creatively present the possibility for the future cooperation of the two parties, thus resolving not only the present disputes, but also creating the expected interests for the two parties.

2.3.3 Moral Rationality

A human being is the unity of spirit and body. In addition to material and physiological needs, human beings also need emotional pleasure and spiritual sustenance. In interpersonal contact, people require safety, trust and stable expectations. As a species in nature, man needs "correspondence between man and the universe," so "nature-man unification" is required. However, in the modern society of individualism, interest-first and value diversity, the ideal and pursuit of people has also become utilitarian and materialistic, high and holy moral ideals are lacking, abandoned and even mocked, and the moral norms have also lost the necessary binding force. The development of science and technology made the ability of human beings to understand the nature and the universe expand rapidly, but while revealing the secret veil of nature, the rational knowledge also caused man to lose reverence for nature and the unknown world. Due to the lack of faith, cold and detached interpersonal relations, environmental pollution, and exhausted energy resources, man has unconsciously lost his freedom in the process of pursuing freedom. Therefore, it is extremely important in modern society to take good care of one's heart, advocate moral rationality, and respect nature. As an important social activity and process, mediation must also meet the requirement of moral rationality.

> Moral rationality refers to the rational capability of moral subjects to analyze the moral circumstances, undertake the moral inference and establish their standard of conduct. The results of moral rational capability eventually settle as moral norms and moral principles.[43]

Through moral cognition, moral inference, and moral judgment, moral subjects form moral norms and moral principles as their standard of conduct, but also analyze the moral circumstances according to the formed moral norms and moral principles so as to form new moral norms. This is a process for unification of understanding and regulating practices and it is also a process for moral norms and criteria to overcome negation and self-abandonment. "Moral rationality is not equal to morality. Moral rationality is a kind of reason, a kind of perspective and vision, a kind of thinking and a kind of moral consciousness."[44] Moral rationality is individual as well as collective. It directs to and appeals for goodness and it is a kind of mental order, life order, and social order. Therefore, one of the bases for the legitimacy of mediation will naturally entail the mediation procedure and result will satisfy the moral rationality of the parties and social communities.

The morality of mediation first requires that mediation should respect the parties, i.e., make the parties feel respected in the process of mediation and emphasize the independence and dominance of the parties. It requires: (1) the mediator should give the parties the chance to represent their views adequately and allow the parties to air grievances, the mediator should listen patiently and in the back-to-back mediation, can also express appropriately his empathy so as to draw closer the mental distance of the parties. (2) In the process of mediation, the mediator also undertakes, through his moral rationality, the moral inference and moral judgment on the conduct of the parties, but the mediator should better not make moral assessment directly on whether the conduct of the parties is right or wrong. The moral assessment of the mediator will not only fail to make the parties examine their conduct, but will cause the parties to suspect the neutrality of the mediator and even will intensify the contradiction. (3) The mediator should keep the objective rationality, look at the case from the viewpoint of the parties, and actively work out a creative solution, on the premises of obtaining the authorization of the parties to maximize the interests of the parties. (4) It is necessary to keep confidential the information obtained in the process of mediation. This respects the parties as well as encourages the parties to disclose the information without any worries. Only in this way, can the mediator obtain as much information as possible and understand the common point in the interests of the parties so as to facilitate the conciliation.

The morality of mediation also implies that as a social activity of resolving disputes, mediation should also function as a bearer of community norms and good customs. This requires: (1) mediation is the "negotiation under the shadow of the law" and should, without violating the prohibitive provisions of the law, respect the local rules and regulations, the moral tradition and other local knowledge and folk norms so as to realize the organic combination of emotion, reason, and law and resolve the disputes properly and practically. (2) Generally speaking, the information obtained by the mediator in the process of mediation should be disclosed only upon obtaining the authorization of the parties, but when the information involves public interest, the mediator should disclose such information. (3) Mediation should not only resolve disputes, but also should "make the subsequent rationality of customs clear." In modern society, mediators better not undertake moral education directly and should better move the soul of the parties and make them self-examine by asking questions or quoting some old maxims or well-known philosophical sayings about life at the place of mediation. They must lay stress on the cultivation of the mediation culture, using the indirect education of "moistening everything quietly and softly" is more acceptable.

In a word, procedural rationality, economic rationality, and moral rationality of mediation are concerned with different levels and dimensions of mediation and the three have their respective emphases: procedural rationality emphasizes the instrumental value of mediation; economic rationality emphasizes the economic value; moral rationality emphasizes the ethical value. In the meantime, the three also have the relation of mutuality and overlap and support and affect each other. For example, procedural rationality and economic rationality of mediation imply the requirement of moral rationality. The morality of procedure and result of morality have the function of intensifying each other. Additionally, there is also the tension among the three. For instance, in certain circumstances, there may be mutual conflict between the instrumental value and the ethical value of the mediation procedure and between the economic value and the ethical value of mediation. It requires mediators to choose from the three rational choices emphatically according to the different types of cases. For example, mediation in marriage and family disputes requires moral rationality, while for the disputes with relatively high orientation of economic interests, the mediation require economic rationality.

2.4 Conclusion

Traditional Chinese mediation was born in traditional Chinese society of acquaintance and corresponded highly to its social structure and cultural pattern. It mainly featured "harmony" as the gist; reliance on the mediators' personal authority or attached state authority; and the mediator-oriented model as the basic model of mediation. Since the reform and opening-up, due to the advent of the market economic system, China's economy has developed rapidly, but with the social strata differentiating and new interest groups emerging, contradictions and conflicts unavoidably have occurred between different interest groups as they maintain their respective available interests and expected interests. Additionally, such problems as unfair distribution and the gap between the rich and the poor have also aggravated the social contradictions. The traditional mediation model eventually failed to cope with the intensified social contradictions and frequent and various disputes. Besides, modernization of people's thought also disempowered the authority of traditional mediation and the acceptability and legitimacy of traditional mediation was severely tested. Therefore, in the modern transformation of China's mediation institution, first of all, it is necessary to seek ideologically the sources of legitimacy and authority of mediation. In the modern society pursuing economic rationalism and following the outlook of human rational truth and lack of faith, the legitimacy of mediation in China should also be established on the basis of rational recognition. Therefore, in the opinion of this author, modern mediation ideas can be remolded as procedural rationality, economic rationality, and moral rationality. But, the reshaping is only the transformation of guiding thought, while the functional play of China' mediation institution not only depends on the perfection of mediation mechanism and mediation institution, cultivation of mediation culture and training of mediation talents, but is also required to correspond to the national economy, politics and social culture. Only in this way can the function of Mediation in China realize the modern transformation, i.e., turning from state-governance to community-autonomy and from judgment complementary to dispute resolution mode with independent value.

Notes

1 Xu Xin: *On Private Relief* (Beijing: China University of Political Science and Law Press, 2005), pp. 321–322.

2 Shiga Shuzo, Hiroaki Terada, Kishimoto Mio, and Susumu Fuma: *Civil Trial and Civil Contract of the Ming and Qing Dynasties* (Beijing: Law Press, 1998), pp. 1–17. Professor Philip C.C. Huang proposed a different opinion, viewing the civil judgment of the Qing Dynasty as advocating mediation in terms of expression, but insisted on judgment according to law in practice. Philip C.C. Huang: *Law, Society and Culture of the Qing Dynasty: Expression and Practice of Civil Law* (Beijing: Law Press, 2014).

3 Liu Min: On Traditional Mediation Institution and Its Creative Transformation, *Social Science Research*, 1999 (1).

4 Chang Yi: Chinese Mediation Idea Changes, *Research on Rule of Law*, 2013 (2).

5 *The Chou Rituals:·Local Official Mediator.*

6 Zhang Jinpan: *Tradition of Chinese Law and Transformation in Modern Times* (Beijing: Law Press, 1997), p. 283.

7 Huang Yuansheng: *Introduction to Chinese Law History* (Guilin: Guangxi Normal University Press, 2014), p. 302.

8 Zeng Lingjian: "Official Approval and Civil Mediation" in Prefecture/County Judicature of the Late Qing Dynasty, *Contemporary Law Review*, 2018 (3).

9 Guo Xinghua: *Dispute Resolution in Social Transformation* (Beijing: China Renmin University Press, 2012), p. 51.

10 The two categories of "great tradition" and "little tradition" were first proposed by Professor Robert Redfield of the University of Chicago in 1956 in his book, *Peasant Society and Culture*, which are used to explain the two strata of cultural tradition in a relatively complex civilization, i.e., the cultural tradition mastered by the social elites with literary records and the folk tradition mainly passed on orally and informally recorded.

11 Zhang Dainian: *Outline of the History of Chinese Philosophy* (Beijing: China Social Sciences Press, 1997), p. 177.

12 Translated and annotated by Rao Sangkuan: *Lao Zi* (Beijing: China Publishing House, 2007), p. 190.

13 [Qing] Sun Xidan (compiler): *Collective Interpretation of the Book of Rites*, collated by Shen Xiaohuan and Wang Xingxuan (Beijing: China Publishing House, 1989), p. 582.

14 Joseph Needham: *Collections of Joseph Needham* (Shenyang: Liaoning Science Press, 1986), p. 338.

15 Translated and noted by Rao Sangkuan: *Lao Zi* (Beijing: China Publishing House, 2007), p. 8.

16 [Qing] Sun Xidan (compiler): *Collective Interpretation of the Book of Rites*, op. cit., p. 992.
17 Fei Xiaotong: *From the Soil: The Foundations of Chinese Society* (Beijing: People's Publishing House, 2015), pp. 28–29.
18 In practice, China's present people's mediation organizations are mainly classified into three levels or four levels: village (community) people's mediation committees, township (sub-district) people's mediation committees and county/city people's mediation committees or federation of people's mediation. Except for the people's mediators at the level of the village (community), who are generally the village (residential) safety members, the members of the people's mediation committees at the levels of the township (sub-district) and the county/city are mainly the public servants with judicial and administrative personnel. Members of village (residential) committees are not the in-system members, but the "agents" of the state power, they are in close contact with "the system."
19 Translated and annotated by Wang Xiumei: *The Book of Songs* (Beijing: China Publishing House, 2006), p. 299.
20 Wu Shuchen: *Chinese Traditional Legal Culture* (Beijing: Peking University Press, 1994), p. 728.
21 Lin Duan: *Confucian Ethics and Legal Culture* (Beijing: China University of Political Science and Law Press, 2002), pp. 387–390.
22 Philip C.C. Huang: *Law, Society and Culture of the Qing Dynasty: Expression and Practice of Civil Law*, op. cit., pp. 44–57.
23 As for the translation of the case, see Liu Xin: *ABC of China Legal Science* (Guangzhou: Guangdong People's Publishing House, 1999), pp. 1–4.
24 Fei Xiaotong: *From the Soil: The Foundations of Chinese Society*, op. cit., p. 69.
25 Ibid.
26 (Qing) Wang Huizu: *Conjecture of Governance Study*, annotated by Zhao Ziguang: *Officialdom Scriptures of a Private Assistant* (Beijing: Jiuzhou Press, 1998), p. 111.
27 Chen Xingxiang: *Walk Out of the Country: Conversation on Fei Xiaotong's From the Soil: the Foundations of Chinese Society* (Beijing: Joint Publishing, 2017), p. 216.
28 Gu Peidong: *Social Conflicts and Litigation Mechanism* (Beijing: Law Press, 2004), p. 38.
29 Chen Hongyi: *The World of Jurisprudence* (2nd edn) (Beijing: China University of Political Science and Law Press, 2013), p. 193.
30 According to the statistical institution of China, the economically active population refers to all the population aged above 16 years and providing, within a certain period of time, the labor supply for different kinds of economic production and service activities. These people are deemed to be the population participating actually and requiring to participate in social economic activities and are also called the realistic human resources. They are in a state of employment or unemployment and are the sum of employed population and unemployed population.
31 Yang Jisheng: *Analysis of Chinese Contemporary Social Strata* (Nanchang: Jiangxi Higher Education Press, 2011), pp. 346–356.
32 When we interviewed the head of one township office of justice, the head talked about such a case: two villagers in one village had a dispute due to the problem of neighborhood rights. Upon receipt of the report from the village information handler, the office head of justice immediately took two policemen to the village

for mediation. Upon seeing the arrival of "government persons," the disputing villagers did not present the facts to them, but said: "you should come only after we injure others."

33 Data are from *2018 Statistical Bulletin of National Economic and Social Development of National Bureau of Statistics*.

34 Luo Haobo: Philosophical Self-examination of a Century of Deficiency of Chinese Social Core Value System, *Probe*, 2011 (5).

35 Wan Junren: Modernity Source of Belief Crisis and Iits Cultural Interpretation, *Journal of Tsinghua University (Philosophy and Social Sciences*, 2001 (1).

36 I. Kant: *Critique of Pure Reason*, trans. Deng Xiaomang (Beijing: People's Publishing House, 2004), p.18.

37 Han Zheng: *Rebuilding of Rationalist Belief* (Beijing: Beijing Publishing House, 1998), pp. 32–36.

38 Tian Runfeng: Research on Habermas' Rationality, Doctoral thesis, Shaanxi: Normal , 2010, pp. 78–79.

39 Chen Lijun and Chen Limin: Basis for Generation of Judicial Credibility, *Journal of Hunan University of Science and Technology (Social Sciences)*, 2011 (4).

40 Tanase Takao: *Dispute Resolution and Trial System*, trans. Wang Yaxin (Beijing: China University of Political Science and Law Press, 2004), p. 53.

41 Ibid., pp. 52–73.

42 Liao Yongan: *How to Be a Good Mediator: Enlightenment of China-America Mediation Training* (Xiangtan: Xiangtan University Press, 2012), pp. 16–17.

43 Yang Zongyuan: On the Connotations of Moral Reason, *Journal of China Renmin University*, 2007 (1).

44 Xu Guiquan: *Philosophical Inquiry and Meditation on the Value World* (Beijing: China Social Sciences Press, 2012), p. 72.

References

Chang Yi: Chinese Mediation Idea Changes, *Research on Rule of Law*, 2013 (2): 3–10.

Chen Hongyi: *The World of Jurisprudence* (2nd edn), Beijing: China University of Political Science and Law Press, 2013.

Chen Lijun and Chen Limin: Basis for Generation of Judicial Credibility, *Journal of Hunan University of Science and Technology (Social Sciences)*, 2011 (4): 58–64.

Chen Xingxiang: *Walk Out of the Country: Conversation on Fei Xiaotong's From the Soil: the Foundations of Chinese Society*, Beijing: Joint Publishing, 2017.

Fei Xiaotong: *From the Soil: the Foundations of Chinese Society*, Beijing: People's Publishing House, 2015.

Gu Peidong: *Social Conflicts and Litigation Mechanism*, Beijing: Law Press, 2004.

Guo Xinghua: *Dispute Resolution in Social Transformation*, Beijing: China Renmin University Press, 2012.

Han Zheng: *Rebuilding of Rationalist Belief*, Beijing: Beijing Publishing House, 1998.

Huang Yuansheng: *Introduction to Chinese Law History*, Guilin: Guangxi Normal University Press, 2014.

Huang, Philip C.C.: *Law, Society and Culture of the Qing Dynasty: Expression and Practice of Civil Law*, Beijing: Law Press, 2014.

Kant, Immanuel.: *Critique of Pure Reason*, trans. Deng Xiaomang, Beijing: People's Publishing House, 2004.

Liao Yongan: *How to Be a Good Mediator: Enlightenment of China-America Mediation Training*, Xiangtan: Xiangtan University Press, 2012.

Lin Duan: *Confucian Ethics and Legal Culture*, Beijing: China University of Political Science and Law Press, 2002.

Liu Min: On Traditional Mediation Institution and its Creative Transformation, *Social Science Research*, 1999 (1): 6.

Liu Xin: *ABC of China Legal Science*, Guangzhou: Guangdong People's Publishing House, 1999.

Luo Haobo: Philosophical Self-examination of Century of Deficiency of Chinese Social Core Value System, *Probe*, 2011 (5): 106–111.

Needham, Joseph: *Collections of Joseph Needham*, Shenyang: Liaoning Science Press, 1986.

Rao Sangkuan trans. and annotated: *Lao Zi*, Beijing: China Publishing House, 2007.

Redfield, Robert: *Peasant Society and Culture*, Chicago: University of Chicago Press, 1956.

Shiga Shuzo, Hiroaki Terada, Kishimoto Mio, and Susumu Fuma: *Civil Trial and Civil Contract of the Ming and Qing Dynasties*, Beijing: Law Press, 1998.

Sun Xidan (compiler): *Collective Interpretation of the Book of Rites*, collated by Shen Xiaohuan and Wang Xingxuan, Beijing: China Publishing House, 1989.

Tanase Takao: *Dispute Resolution and Trial System*, trans. Wang Yaxin, Beijing: China University of Political Science and Law Press, 2004.

Tian Runfeng: Research on Habermas' Rationality, Doctoral thesis. Shaanxi Normal University, 2010.

Wan Junren: "Modernity Source of Belief Crisis and its Cultural Interpretation," *Journal of Tsinghua University (Philosophy and Social Sciences*, 2001 (1): 22–29.

Wang Huizu: *Conjecture of Governance Study*, annotated by Zhao Ziguang: *Officialdom Scriptures of a Private Assistant*, Beijing: Jiuzhou Press, 1998.

Wang Xiumei trans. and annotated: *The Book of Songs*, Beijing: China Publishing House, 2006.

Wu Shuchen: *Chinese Traditional Legal Culture*, Beijing: Peking University Press, 1994.

Xu Guiquan: *Philosophical Inquiry and Meditation on the Value World*, Beijing: China Social Sciences Press, 2012.

Xu Xin: *On Private Relief*, Beijing: China University of Political Science and Law Press, 2005.

Xu Zhengying, Chang Peiyu: *The Chou Rituals: Local Official·Mediator*, Beijing: ZhongHua Book Company, 2014.

Yang Jisheng: *Analysis of Chinese Contemporary Social Strata*, Nanchang: Jiangxi Higher Education Press, 2011.

Yang Zongyuan: On Connotations of Moral Reason, *Journal of China Renmin University*, 2007 (1): 85–90.

Zeng Lingjian: "Official Approval and Civil Mediation" in Prefecture/County Judicature of the Late Qing Dynasty, *Contemporary Law Review*, 2018 (3): 126–136.

Zhang Dainian: *Outline of the History of Chinese Philosophy*, Beijing: China Social Sciences Press, 1997.

Zhang Jinpan: *Tradition of Chinese Law and Transformation in Modern Times*, Beijing: Law Press, 1997.

3 New Ideas and New Thinking about China's Modern Mediation

Mediation as the common dispute resolution mode of China has lasted for thousands of years since ancient times, really because of its close connection to the traditional Confucian culture. With the non-litigation idea as the base and with maintenance of social harmony as the value aim, the traditional mediation corresponded to the social environment of acquaintance in a small peasant economy. However, since the People's Republic of China was founded, Chinese society has undergone a great change in the process of modernization: in terms of the economy, the self-sufficient small peasant economy has been replaced by the planned economy and the market economy; in terms of social structure, the society of acquaintance has changed into the society of strangers and rural China has changed to urban China. Due to such changes in the basic conditions of the social structure, the traditional mediation institution faced great challenges: on the one hand, the types of disputes that mediation coped with and the functional scope also changed accordingly and the function of the traditional mediation mechanism declined; on the other hand, the modern legal governance discourse with freedom, equality, and rights as the core became the mainstream discourse in China's legal governance system, and the traditional mediation institution was deemed to be lacking procedural justice, pressurizing individual just claims and damaging fairness and justice, so it was criticized. In the opinion of some scholars, mediation constituted an infringement of civic rights and damaged the basic value of legal governance and injured legal governance and fairness. Mediation was the backward culture in the society of human governance and it was necessary to choose the criticism-centric dispute resolution institution.[1] It cannot be denied that traditional mediation faced a legality crisis in modern society. Chapter 2 discussed the transformation of traditional Chinese mediation into modern mediation and this chapter will discuss further how to reshape the legality of mediation in the new market economy and society of strangers and how to realize the creative change of traditional mediation through idea innovation, practical innovation, and institutional innovation of mediation, so that it is integrated into the value idea of modern legal governance.

DOI: 10.4324/9781003385882-3

3.1 Three Transformations of Traditional Mediation

3.1.1 The First Transformation: Mediation during the Period of Collectivization

With the Qing Government of the last feudal dynasty going to its doom, from the late nineteenth century and the early twentieth century, facing domestic troubles and foreign invasions, China started down the hard path of exploring modernization. During its brief period of rule, the government of the Republic of China attempted to copy Western legal institution to reform the traditional dispute resolution institution. In terms of texts, it transplanted a huge number of Western modern acts, but in practice the dispute resolution remained unchanged. The real transformation of traditional mediation started in the period of the revolutionary base of the Communist Party of China (CPC). Since the 1940s, in the areas liberated by the revolution, the land revolution of the CPC removed the gentry and landlords in the vast countryside of old China and crushed the traditional gentry's power and clan power. The rural elite reproduction mechanism failed. In the process of dispute resolution, the CPC replaced the position of traditional rural elites with its own officials and activists. Scholars might easily interpret the mediation of the Communist Party as the extension of Confucian traditional culture and view it thus:

> [The] new Communist Party's local police elites, party members, youth league members, bureaucrats, trade union activists, members of mediation committees and other semi-official figures replaced the gentry and privileged persons of villages, clans and associations for most of disputes to become the new authority mediation.[2]

Actually, mediation during the period of the revolutionary base of the CPC can neither be defined as the successor of the old tradition, nor simply deemed an extension of the Confucian cultural tradition. American scholar Stanley Labman clearly expounded the difference between the mediation of the CPC and the traditional mediation. He emphatically stressed the "political function" of the mediation during the period of the revolutionary base of the CPC.[3] The revolution under Mao Zedong resulted in great changes in the national political, social, economic, and cultural environments, as the existence of traditional mediation and the traditional society were comprehensively reformed through collectivization. The main reflection on such a transformation is: traditional mediation considered mainly human emotions and was supported by the law and principle, while mediation in the period of collectivization[4] took policy and law as the mainstay and supported it with human emotions and principle. Mediators changed from the past primitive authority to a community person acceptable to the new political power. Mediators tended to be officials but worked informally. When involving the national policy and law, the principles and methods of mediation were more mandatory.[5] The famous "Ma Xiwu Trial Mode" and "Fengqiao Experience" were formed during this period.

3.1.2 The Second Transformation: Mediation in the Early Period of Reform and Opening-Up

The mediation idea in the period of collectivization lasted from the 1940s to the early period of reform and opening-up in the 1980s. It was not until the reform of the market economy was spreading that mediation underwent the second transformation. With the economic structure changing due to the reform of the market economy and the types and numbers of disputes sharply increasing, the political function of mediation had gradually weakened as the function of social governance, and mediation was mostly related to litigation pressures. With the reform and opening-up spreading, the rural society changed from a "society of acquaintance" to a "society of strangers," the litigation function of courts expanded and the function of community mediation withered. With the state power withdrawn from the countryside, the official-based mediation started to weaken. Such a change was mainly reflected in: first, the legal element in the mediation principle gradually increased, and the sermonizing factor of policy and reason declined. In the opinion of some scholars, the spirit of mediation under Mao Zedong was the philosophy of struggle, and the spirit of mediation under Deng Xiaoping was the prevention of disputes,[6] i.e., prior to intensification of disputes, emphasizing the use of folk mediation and upon intensification of disputes, encouraging the parties to go to court to "ask for an explanation." In other words, the political function of mediation for mobilizing and struggling was replaced by the social function of dispute resolution. The bigger picture for such change is that the social governance had gradually been transformed from the "individual charming ruling" under Mao Zedong to "legal-principle ruling." Second, the mediation institution was gradually legalized and institutionalized. China formulated a series of laws and regulations to ensure mediation, for example, publishing successively laws and regulations, such as *The People's Mediation Law*. The organizational forms of mediation became increasingly varied. In addition to people's mediation, the organizations for mediation, such as court mediation, administrative mediation, commercial mediation, industrial mediation, and lawyer mediation, were continually differentiated, and the function of the traditional people's mediation gradually withered in the social environment of acquaintance and the function of the new social mediation became increasingly prominent. With the right consciousness of the parties rising, the principle of court mediation changed from the previous "emphasis on mediation" to "voluntary and legal." and forced mediation and "mixing water into mud" were criticized and abandoned. Mediation moved from the previous "educational type" and "judgmental type," and from "conditional resolution" to "normative resolution."

Third, the driving force of public-welfare mediation was insufficient. Under collectivization, the work of people's mediation was undertaken mainly by the village and commune officials and the mediation work was basically free of charge, "but the honor and privilege as the officials or activists made them fond of mediation work." After the reform and opening-up were launched, the society of acquaintance was disassembled, the state administrative power retreated, the power of rural officials moved from management to service, the administrative authority of rural officials was weakened, being driven by the profit-seeking of the market economy, the basic assurance of funding was lacking for mediation, the people's mediator had neither the previous authority for mediation, nor the motive to do the "hard but with no-thanks" mediation work. Non-profit-making public welfare mediation can hardly motivate them.[7] As a result, people's mediation relied more on the mediation platform officially set up and the folk mediation mechanism that had formed spontaneously increasingly declined. Besides, the function of administrative mediation in preventing and resolving civil disputes also declined gradually and the litigation-centralized pattern of "strengthening litigation and weakening mediation" was gradually formed.[8]

3.1.3 The Third Transformation: Mediation in the New Era

Over the last four decades since 1978, with China's reform and social transformation entering the deep-water zone, different in-depth social contradictions and disputes have become prominent. On October 18, 2017, the report to the 19th National Congress of the Communist Party of China made the important political statement: "with the long-term efforts, the socialism with Chinese characteristics has entered into the new era." Before that, the contradiction between the increasingly material and cultural demands of the people and the backward social productivity was the major social contradiction. Upon entering the new era, the contradiction between the increasing demands of people for a better life and unbalanced and inadequate development had become the major social contradiction. People's lives were significantly improved, the desire for a better life became stronger, as it not only sets forth higher requirements for material and cultural life, but the requirement also grows increasingly for such aspects as democracy, legal governance, fairness, justice, safety, and protecting the environment. In the process of social legalization and modernization, the rapid expansion of disputes caused the state judiciary organs to suffer overload. In such a social scenario, the position of mediation in the system for the reform of diversified dispute resolution mechanisms became an important move to promote social fairness and justice and maintain social harmony and stability and constituted an important part of the modernization of the state governance system and the governance capability. The significant changes in mediation in the new era are: first, the mediation system has been greatly improved. On the basis of the traditional people's mediation, administrative mediation, judicial mediation, industrial mediation, and commercial mediation are mutually dependent, and new mediation forms, such as lawyer mediation and notary mediation are emerging continually, forming a more complete mediation system. Second, the regularity of mediation is intensified, traditional mediators of noble character and high prestige have disappeared and mediators with knowledge authority, with professional advantages have become the mainstay. Mediation procedure becomes more regular and attaches more importance to safeguarding the legal rights of the parties. Mediation results become closer to the provisions of the available laws and are relatively less concerned with the traditional code of conduct outside the laws.[9] Upon assessment as a whole, the traditional mediation is being or has already been replaced by modern mediation.

3.2 New Ideas and New Thought about Modern Mediation: Starting with the Substantial Dimension

From the perspective of the cultural value system, "modern" or "modernity" often corresponds to "tradition" or "pre-modern." According to the mainstream viewpoint, the two basic elements of modernity are the expansion of instrumental rationality and the rise of individual rights,[10] and the important sign of legal modernity is the esteem of instrumental rationality/formal rationality, and the protection of individual rights. Professor Ge Hongyi summarized the modernity of law in eight points: openness, autonomy, universality, hierarchy or morality, certainty, justice, rationality, and authority.[11] With freedom, equality, rights, justice, democracy, reason, and procedure as the discourse of modern legal governance, traditional mediation is burdened with various negative labels, such as "mixing water into mud," "second-class judicature," and "contrary to legal governance" and the voices opposing the traditional mediation are still heard even now. In the times of comprehensively deepening the reform of diversified dispute resolution mechanisms and in the Third Wave of the "Access to Justice" worldwide movement, how mediation ideas will move from traditional to modern and be established and how they will practice new ideas and new thinking so as to correspond to the modernity of legal governance, are critical for the new life of traditional mediation. Since the modern formal judicature is considered a remarkable symbol of legal governance modernity, by comparing mediation ideas with litigation ideas, it is possible to tap into the modernity of mediation.

3.2.1 From Conflicts of Interests to a Community of Interests

Disputes arise from the imbalance of interests between the parties, litigation indicates the conflict of interests between the parties and judgment indicates the balance of interests by judges. In recent years, China's civil procedure system has gradually changed to the model of an adversarial system, of which the core idea is to discover the facts of cases by making adequate use of the confrontation and competition of the parties. With the backbone of the civil procedure institution – the institution of evidence as an example – procedures such as providing evidence, cross-examination, and authentication are all based on the neutrality of judges and confrontation of the parties. This aims to tap adequately into the past facts of the cases by discovering the conflict of interests between the parties and making use of such confrontation. Conflicts of interests in litigation will often cause the parties to fall into the dilemma of a "zero-sum game," increasing the litigation costs and resulting in litigation delays, which are detrimental to the maintenance of transaction relationships and the growth of a market economy. Being different, the idea behind modern mediation is to strive to emphasize the common interests between the parties to disputes and actively make the community of interests rather than the confrontation of interests of the parties in contradictions and disputes. In practice, the core aim of mediators in the mediation process is to emphasize the common interests behind the opposing positions of the parties to disputes, thus creating a space for a win-win condition for the two parties and realizing accordingly the aim of resolving the disputes through consensus of the two parties. Furthermore, modern mediation corresponds to the spiritual connotation of a transaction encouraged by the civil and commercial laws, it is the process of regenerating the future expected interests, and can effectively promote the efficiency of market transactions. Therefore, if the idea of litigation is to form a conflict of interests between the parties to disputes, the idea of modern mediation is to form a community of interests between the parties. As an example, the classic case in one mediation course is as follows.

> A and B are roommates in a co-rented house, sharing one refrigerator. The left side of the refrigerator is used by A and the right side is used by B, but no separation is made in-between. Usually, the food and fruits they purchased respectively are placed on their own side in the refrigerator. One afternoon, only one orange was left in the refrigerators. A thought the orange was his, while B thought it was his, and two of them argued with each other. In this circumstance, the mediator first inquired what they wanted this orange for. Upon inquiring, he discovered that A needed to supplement his Vitamin C by drinking a glass of orange juice before going to the gym in the afternoon, and B had to go for a very important date in the afternoon, taking a cake, and he needed the orange peel to decorate the cake he made. Hence, through mediation, the two people shook hands and made peace.[12]

3.2.2 From an Outlook on Static Interests to an Outlook on Dynamic Interests

Civil procedure is undertaken on the basis of a litigation target and upholds an outlook on unitary static interest, while modern mediation advocates the outlook on diverse dynamic interests. According to the disposition principle and the adversary principle of civil procedure, litigation pays close attention to and resolves the disputed interests of the parties, and such interests are fixed and unitary. The outlook of such unitary static interests obviously cannot meet the demand of the parties to disputes for increasingly diversified interests. Modern mediation has the idea of maintaining diverse dynamic interests, with consideration not only of material interests, but also of non-material interests. It is concerned with disputed interests as well as non-disputed interests. It focuses on present interests as well as focusing more on future interests. In the interweaving of such diverse interest appeals, due to the limitations of legal principles and procedures of litigation, litigation is unable to meet the diverse interest appeals of the parties in real disputes. Comparatively, the principle and mode of modern mediation are relatively flexible and open and, while resolving the disputed interests, can take into consideration the maintenance of non-disputed interests, indirect interests, and long-term interests. As an example, here is one case from the grass-roots mediation practice.

> Li and Zhang were originally friendly neighbors. One day, Li dug a drainage ditch outside the courtyard wall of Zhang's house and consequently, the courtyard wall fell down, injuring Li. Li was hospitalized and spent RMB 3,500, while Zhang spent RMB 1,000 to repair the courtyard wall. After the incident, the relatives of Li approached Zhang looking for compensation for Li for her medical expenses, while Zhang considered that Li was injured because she had dug and caused the courtyard wall to fall, purely bringing the trouble on herself, and Zhang required Li to pay the RMB 1,000 for the damaged courtyard wall. The two parties disputed and the neighborhood broke up, thus going to the people's mediator for mediation. When mediating in the case, the mediator did not simply blame both sides and require the two parties to compromise in terms of the compensation amount. The mediator did not limit it to the material interests, but facilitated the parties to obtain other interests than money, with consideration to such indirect interests and long-term interests as emotion, face, and relations between the neighbors.[13]

3.2.3 From Divided Thought to Comprehensive Thought

The important difference between modern mediation and litigation in resolving disputes is the different approach in thinking. Due to the influence of litigation target theory, litigation applies divided thought in resolving disputes, i.e., slicing disputes into several factual pieces, and making the judgment of black or white on the past disputes by applying the rules of syllogism with legalism as the guidelines. In particular, the relationship of civil rights and obligations disputed by the parties is pulled away from the overall social facts involved in disputes and related other social interrelations, for the purpose of seeking the result of dispute resolution from the viewpoint of the established regulations. According to the traditional litigation target theory, the litigation target refers to the legal relations disputed by the parties to the dispute. The legal relations of one dispute constitute one lawsuit, the legal relations of several disputes constitute a number of lawsuits, and one independent lawsuit constitutes one independent case. Since civil procedure take "slicing" thought as the guideline, the judge can make the judgment only on the legal relations of each independent dispute, otherwise it will constitute a litigation surprise. Under the guidance of consensus, modern mediation uses a kind of comprehensive thought, combining the legal relations of several correlated disputes when thinking. In the process of resolving contradictions and disputes, the comprehensive thought is mainly reflected as: the dispute resolution is placed in the multidimensional viewpoint of economy, law, morality, habit, mentality, and society for a comprehensive investigation into such factors as the nature of disputes, the cause of disputes, and the extent of contradiction, emphasizing the multidimensional thought viewpoint, the variety of solution options, the flexibility of the application of the means and the comprehensiveness of interest adjustment, for the purpose of really settling a case. It is explained by one example as follows.

On the Tomb Sweeping Day of 2011, Yan led all the families to the ancestral grave for tomb sweeping and on arriving, they found more than half the enclosure of the ancestral grave were occupied by Zhou's family, building a fence of more than one meter to block the ancestral grave and resulting in the inconvenience of Yan's families when tomb sweeping. Then Yan went to Zhou's house to argue about it, but no one was at home. Hence, without obtaining Zhou's consent, Yan made an opening in the fence to gain access for tomb sweeping. Upon returning, Zhou found the opening and went to Yan angrily arguing for the gap in the fence to be restored. Since Yan was already unhappy about the fence and now Zhou had come over, the two parties angrily fought. Zhou said that if the fence was not repaired, he would dig out the ancestral grave of Yan's family, and Yan had to agree to repair it, but still accused Zhou. Zhou became angry and dug up the ancestral grave of Yan's family in the afternoon of the same day. Yan became extremely angry and asked his clansmen over for help in the argument. The two families stood facing each other and confronting each other with daggers. The clans' dispute could be triggered into violence at any moment. Then, a neighbor reported the incident to the police. Afterwards, the mediator from the Bureau of Justice came to intervene and mediate. Yan's family claimed compensation of RMB 1 million. If the case had been handled in the mode of litigation, simply as per a lawsuit of infringement, for compensation of mental damage, the case would not be closed. Upon learning of the reason for the argument, the mediator took into consideration the importance of the ancestral grave in the local area, especially the matter of face and social evaluation, with reference to the traditional customs and family habits of rural society, and started with the prestige figures of the clansmen of the two sides and worked repeatedly by applying comprehensively personal emotions and ethics and legal provisions and eventually made Zhou apologize to Yan face to face. When considering the actual condition and compensation capacity of Zhou's family, finally an amount of RMB 14,000 was paid as compensation. The case of the dispute between the two parties was closed for settlement and harmony was restored.[14]

3.2.4 From Looking Backward to Looking Forward

Another characteristic of modern mediation different from litigation is that it looks forward into the future, while litigation looks back to the past. Also with the evidence institution of civil procedure as an example, since judges discover the past case facts through evidence, litigation is actually a process of recalling the historic facts and is oriented to the objective facts of the case that has already occurred. Both the authority principle model and the adversarial system model aim to discover the legal facts through evidence and then make a judgment on the legal rights and obligations according to the past case facts, and look back to the past. Modern mediation is different. Traditional people's mediation as well as administrative mediation, industrial mediation, and commercial mediation all have a hidden forward-looking orientation to the future. With the folk disputes in the society of acquaintance as an example, the proverb says: "a far-off relative is not as helpful as a near neighbor," while the two words "near neighbor" imply various future interests. The harmonious neighborhood is favorable to the physical and mental health of all the parties and favorable to the harmony of social relationships. Therefore, the resolution of neighbors' disputes usually cannot be merely limited to the resolution of the existing interest disputes, but should also focus on the maintenance of the future relationship between the neighbors. Commercial mediation is all the more so. Since it is closely related to commercial activities, it must follow commercial law. The essence of commercial law is to pursue business interests. All commercial transactions aim to pursue the maximization of interests, while the maximization of interests relies, in turn, on the final achievement of future long-term interests and expected interests. The forward-looking thought of commercial mediation requires that the dispute resolution should not stop at the resolution of present disputes and recovery of current interests, but should be oriented to the future to follow the path of "making the cake bigger" rather than "cutting up and distributing the cake" to seek the point of growth of new interest of both parties to the dispute and facilitate a new solution of cooperation so that the disputes are prevented in the long-term cooperation of mutual benefit and it is a win-win situation. An example of this follows.

In one case of a restaurant lease dispute, Proprietor A had a commercial real estate property. The property was not rented out upon expiration of the last lease contract, Proprietor A lowered the rental rate to lease it out. One year after, Proprietor A found a tenant B. Tenant B planned to use the retail shop of Proprietor A for the franchise of a famous restaurant chain called the Big Red Dog. The lease agreement specified the monthly rental as RMB 1,000, plus 3 percent of the gross profit and a lease period of 5 years. The lease agreement provided that Proprietor A should decorate the shop according to the requirements of Tenant B, at the cost of Proprietor A. The agreement also provided that Tenant B should pay Proprietor A the deposit amount of RMB 2,000. Upon signing the contract, Tenant B immediately paid the deposit amount of RMB 2,000 and Proprietor A started to decorate the shop. It was just after Proprietor A had spent RMB 2,500 for decoration and Tenant B had purchased the new equipment for the shop that the news came that the Big Red Dog restaurant chain was close to bankruptcy. Tenant B wanted to terminate the lease agreement, but Proprietor A did not agree to that. Proprietor A required Tenant B to continue with the lease agreement or pay liquidation damage amounting to RMB 80,000. Tenant B did not agree to the demands of Proprietor A, so Proprietor A changed the shop lock. In the shop was the kitchen equipment Tenant B had purchased for the business opening. When mediating in the case, the mediator did not look to the past and was not limited to existing facts, such as who would compensate for whose losses and whose losses were big and whose losses were small, but looked to the future and focused on the future of the two parties, with consideration on how to make the cake bigger by cooperation. Proprietor A wanted to lease out the shop, while Tenant B already had made preliminary investments to open the restaurant but now faced bankruptcy. If the mode of litigation was chosen to resolve the dispute, even in the event of winning the lawsuit, Proprietor A could not obtain the amount of RMB 80,000 either. Therefore, it was favorable for both of the parties to continue the contract. As for Tenant B, the Big Red Dog restaurant chain he had wanted originally to join went bankrupt, but Tenant B could still open a Muslim restaurant. Tenant B had the planning and the capacity, but due to its economic status, Tenant B could not pay more rentals and also required a period of time to set up the business. Hence, through the mediation of the mediator, Proprietor A positively indicated he would accept payment of a low rental at the beginning and increase the rental gradually afterwards. After the particular negotiation on the mode of rental payment, the two parties concluded a new agreement, making the cake bigger, integrating the respective interests of the two parties and realizing the win-win situation.[15]

In a word, civil procedure builds the litigation model, the litigation structure, and the litigation procedure under the ideological guidance of forming the conflict of interests between the parties to disputes and resolving the "unitary static interests." Yet, modern mediation realizes the optimal dispute resolution by creating an "interest community" between the parties to disputes and resolving diverse dynamic interests. There is no distinction of advantage and disadvantage between litigation and mediation. Both have their respective space of action and functional advantages and both are important modes of building modern legal governance. As for the comprehensive deepening of judicial reform, while continually perfecting the litigation institution, shaping and development of modern mediation should not be ignored. Only by breaking down the constraint of old ideas will the future development mediation have a more solid basis of ideological theory and will the institutional design of mediation be more scientific and feasible.

3.3 New Ideas and New Thought about Modern Mediation: Starting with the Procedural Dimension

In terms of the substantial dimension, modern mediation has the advantage that cannot be matched by litigation. But modern legal governance not only pursues the substantial appropriateness, but also emphasizes the procedural modernity and procedural justice, i.e., the "inherent virtue of law." To purge the negative image of "mixing water with mud," pressuring, and the closed mode, traditional mediation must also be regularized in terms of the procedural dimension.

3.3.1 The Procedural Subjectivity Status of the Parties

The main idea of modern mediation is people-oriented and people-centric. Here, "man" refers to the parties to a dispute rather than a lawyer. The parties are the possessors of disputes as well as the terminators of disputes, like letting the mischief-maker undo the mischief. In the modern mediation idea, one of the value bases for mediation is that the dignity of the person is respected and is attached importance. Mediation is considered the overall dispute resolution method of treating people appropriately. Modern mediation should take the fundamental starting point of maintaining the legal rights and interests of both parties, and enhance, through the high-quality mediation service, the parties' sense of safety in the process of dispute resolution. In the litigation procedure, a judge has more initiative, because he removes from both parties the responsibility to make judgment. Yet, in mediation, the parties to disputes themselves are the "experts" to make a judgment of their position and only they can propose the solution most suitable for them.[16] Mediation is the best method for the parties to take their own responsibility. One of the methods of such a procedural subjectivity of the parties is voluntary mediation. American jurist Lon Fuller defined the "central characteristic of mediation" as "ability of making the parties to re-understand each other, and such ability does not force them to do so through regulation, but helps them to change the attitude and orientation between each other."[17] The parties handle their own matters by themselves, as reflects the disposition right of the parties regarding their own rights and obligations, and the exercising of the disposition right requires that it must be the real will of the parties. The mediator should notify the parties that mediation is not mandatory. As for the parties, whether to mediate and whether to conclude a mediation agreement, all should comply with the will of the parties, the mediator must undertake the mediation only when all the parties give their consent and the mediator cannot force, in any form, the parties to accept the mediation solution and sign the mediation agreement.

3.3.2 Impartiality of the Mediation Procedure

Procedural justice is tangible justice. Generally, procedural justice mainly reflects that, in the litigation procedure, the mediation procedure seems to have no relation to procedural justice. Actually, the procedural justice of "treating equally without discrimination" can have a positive influence on the mutual understanding between the parties to disputes, and help both parties clarify the facts properly, rationally face their dispute, and resolve dissatisfaction properly to mentally fix the dispute. Therefore, procedural justice is also considered one of the procedural values of mediation.[18] As for the understanding of the procedural impartiality of the mediation procedure, some scholars have stated that:

> whether to attach importance to procedural justice and whether to run the appropriate legal procedure idea throughout the process of mediation is the watershed of modern mediation and traditional mediation. It is the basic appeal of modern mediation institution to follow the procedural departmentalism and procedural priority principle.[19]

Being different from the litigation procedure of the adversarial system, mediation is in the category of non-litigation procedures and insists on non-antagonism, non-disclosure principle and the doctrine of authority.[20] The basic procedural principles of modern mediation mainly include:

- *equal status of the parties*, i.e., avoiding imbalance of forces and oppression of both parties of mediation, it is better not to use mediation to resolve disputes when there is any severe force imbalance between the parties;
- th*e neutrality of the mediator*, i.e., the mediator stands outside the parties' interests and in a structurally neutral position;
- *confidentiality of the mediation*, i.e., the facts disclosed in mediation should be kept confidential between both parties and between the parties and the mediator, for non-disclosure is the foundation of the mutual trust between the mediator and the parties as well as the key to promoting free and frank negotiation.

3.3.3 The Induction Mechanism of Mediation Consensus

The famous Japanese jurist Tanase Takao stated that the most fundamental environmental factor determining the realistic position and image of mediation, in the society of legalization, is the social mentality that many disputes cannot be handled by judgment, but mediation is expected to handle them using judgment. Therefore, there are two basic directions taken by mediation: one is to undertake the judgment-oriented treatment so that mediation maintains, as much as possible, the dispute resolution direction approximated to the mode of judgment, i.e., syntropic mediation; the other is to seek, as much as possible, the inherent treatment of mediation different from the judgment institution, i.e., heterotropic mediation. Accordingly, Tanase Takao classified mediation into four types: (1) judgment-oriented mediation; (2) negotiation-oriented mediation; (3) education-oriented mediation; and (4) treatment-oriented mediation. During this process, the "pauperization of consensus" may appear, as may be reflected in three aspects: first, in the judgment-oriented and education-oriented mediation, "consensus" may deteriorate to "consent," the judgment made by the mediator holds the central position in the mediation procedure and the "consensus" of the parties becomes the "consent" to the judgment. Second, in the education-oriented and treatment-oriented mediation, "consensus" may deteriorate to "kindness," adding the extra burden of "eliminating confrontation and restoring the friendship" on "consensus." Third, in the negotiation-oriented mediation, the parties may not be able to rationally control the consensus content and it may deteriorate from "consensus" to "willfulness."[21] Such "pauperization of consensus" indicates that consensus in the process of mediation cannot be completely purified, but is a uniform constant element from consensus to decision. One of the important approaches for overcoming the "pauperization of consensus" is to give adequate play to the guiding function and forecasting function of judicial precedents so that the parties can make a basic assessment of the judgment results according to similar cases. "High conciliation rate or mediation rate relies on high-quality precedent foundation, reflecting that the parties have the basic expectation for the possible litigation results,"[22] as is just the so-called "negotiation under the influence of law."

3.3.4 Openness of the Mediation Subjects

In Western society, modern mediation is endowed with the value of civic social autonomy, while in China, it is placed in the social governance context of "national co-construction, co-governance and sharing." To realize such a social governance idea, it will be naturally necessary to integrate all types of social resources and adequately motivate the actions of different subjects so as to realize the national, social, and individual participation, cooperation, and governance. The idea of "construction, governance, and sharing" adequately corresponds to the realistic demand for social dispute resolution in the new era. Realization of such a target by adequately absorbing other different social forces than the court will naturally call for diversity in mediation subjects. Individual mediation, social organization mediation, court mediation, lawyer mediation, notary mediation, and joint "grand mediation" all require that the mediation process is open to the whole society so as to form the open mediation system, including such forms as people's mediation, industrial mediation, commercial mediation, administrative mediation, judicial mediation, and lawyer mediation.

3.4 New Concept for the Future Development of Chinese Mediation: Mediation toward Modernization

With socialism with Chinese characteristics entering the new era, the major contradictions of Chinese society are observed with new changes, and people's need for fairness and justice has increased daily. In such a state of "three periods of control"—the shifting period of economic growth, the sudden and sharp painful period of structural adjustment, and the period of preliminary stimulus policy—all fields show numerous and complicated new features, which have, without doubt, brought new challenges to the resolution of disputes, and the traditional mediation institution is in urgent need of reform. The guiding, highly abstract and internalized idea in an institution has a critical influence on the operation of that institution. The reform of the Chinese mediation institution is first of all to guide the updating and reshaping of ideas. Based on the realistic national conditions in China, only by continually updating the mediation idea, promoting the professionalization of mediation and innovating the mediation mechanism and model will it be possible to ensure the modernization of the traditional Chinese mediation institution.

3.4.1 Update and Reshape the Mediation Idea

The new ideas of modern mediation have been expounded in detail with the substantial and procedural dimensions and these mediation ideas should be continually upheld. With respect to the present status of mediation in China, the following two mediation ideas should be specially emphasized again: first, make prominent the neutral idea of mediators, i.e., liberate mediators from the leading position of the mediation institution operation so that the subjective position of the parties in mediation can be restored. Due to the long-term influence of such historical factors as the Confucian culture and elder authority and the working mode of some public power organs, Chinese mediators often hold a leading position in the process of mediation and the subjectivity of the parties is weakened. Such a mediation system already has failed increasingly to fit the needs of Chinese society for dispute resolution. During the period of China's social transformation, the people's living pace increasingly accelerated and population migration is increasingly frequent, China has changed step by step from the "society of acquaintances" to the "society of semi-acquaintances" and the "society of strangers," the relationship between people is starting to change increasingly from a simple moral and ethical relationship to complex social relationships driven by economic interests, and this poses problems for dispute resolution. Additionally, in modern society, people's legal sense and ability to obtain information are promoted and the independent consciousness of the parties is continually enhanced. These factors have all placed a big question mark over the present mediation model of "the parties' weak will autonomy and shortage of subjective characteristics." If it is necessary to make mediation continue to play a role and realize the effective resolution of disputes, it is urgent to liberate mediators from the leading system so that they can really return to the status of a neutral third party.

In addition, the idea of mediation should be highlighted in order to look to the future. In modern society, the economic activities are becoming increasingly frequent, all the participants of any economic activity pursue the maximization of their interests, while the maximization of interests will definitely look to realizing the future long-term interests and expected interests, rather than stopping at the resolution of existing disputes and recovery of present interests. Therefore, in modern mediation, it is extremely important to emphasize the long-term interests and the idea of looking to the future. This point is very well reflected in the American commercial mediation process. When a deadlock appears, the mediator will often look from the viewpoint of the parties in negotiation to guide, by discovering the interests behind their position, finding the agreement point of the two parties, and draw for the two parties the blueprint of the long-term development, so that the two parties return to the dispute resolution. In the process of applying mediation to resolve disputes, China should not simply retain the treatment of present disputes to realize the return of harmony by completing a "zero-sum game," but should help the parties harmonize their interests and eventually realize a "win-win" situation.

3.4.2 Promote the Professionalization of Mediation

At present, in various Western countries, the professionalization of mediation is being accelerated, mediation has formed a complete operating chain from training to practice, and professional colleges of law have opened mediation courses to educate professional students. Mediators can have an independent identity and status in the same way as judges and lawyers. With respect to the operating status of the Chinese mediation institution, more still has to be done to advance the professionalization with relevant standards, regulations, and institutions. In particular:

1. *Create a special professional teaching and training system.* In view of standardization, regularization, and institutionalization, different professional types currently already in society all have their relevant system to cultivate talent. As a unique dispute resolution mechanism, in the United States, mediation has also formed its relevant systematic teaching system to cultivate the professional talents of mediation. Yet, the succession and development of mediation in China still remain, to a great extent, as the oral-teaching study and application of traditional mediation modes and methods, without any uniform standards. Therefore, to advance the professional development of mediation in China, it is required to start with the source of professional talent cultivation, opening relevant mediation majors and designing relevant courses to cultivate and train a large number of professional talents to compose a mediation team.
2. *Create complete and regular professional standards.* To realize the professionalization of mediation, it is not only required to have the special talents with the relevant special knowledge, but also required to form a systematic and complete professional standard. The so-called complete regularized professional standard includes particularly the following aspects: first, establish the uniform professional access mechanism. In particular, according to the types of disputes to be handled, practitioners can be screened, examined, enrolled, and selected so as to ensure the quality and professionalism of mediators. Second, set up relevant professional criteria and moral norms. By setting up relevant professional criteria and moral norms for mediators, it will help form effective industrial self-regulation and ensure mediators abide by the neutral and non-disclosure principles and adequately respect the subjective status of the parties so as to ensure the credibility and acceptability of this profession. Third, create a complete and systematic professional evaluation system. That is, form, with reference to such factors as mediators' moral quality, mediation level and mediation quality, the ranking and awarding and disciplinary system of mediators so that those engaged in mediation work can expect career prospects and promote their work to assure the stability and long-term development of the whole mediator team.

3.4.3 Innovate the Mediation Model

In view of China's present mediation types, mediation in China is mainly classified into court mediation, administrative mediation, and people's mediation. From different perspectives, these three types of mediation undertake the mission of resolving disputes and maintaining social stability. But, as society is developing and changing and due to some inherent defects with the institution, these three modes of mediation have already failed to meet the needs of Chinese society to develop. Only by injecting fresh blood into the mediation institution while consolidating and perfecting the existing types of mediation will it be possible to assist the continual effective operation and development of the Chinese mediation institution. With reference to the features of disputes and market demands in the present social transformation, it is necessary to reshape the Chinese mediation system and energetically develop modern social mediation. First, rely extensively on such social forces as chambers of commerce and industrial associations to increase the construction of commercial mediation organizations and industrial mediation organizations and highlight their neutrality and autonomy. Second, strengthen the commercial or industrial mediation services in such key fields as finance, securities and futures, real estate, e-commerce, intellectual property, and international trade, and adapt to the new demands of dispute resolution. Third, perfect the diverse mediation legal system, define the legal status of commercial mediation and industrial mediation, perfect the mediation rules and docking procedure, give adequate play to the special and professional advantages of mediation, promote the credibility of social mediation and realize the resource integration and functional connection of diversified dispute resolution mechanism.

In the meantime, the market mechanism has offered chances for innovation. After social subjects realize their interests are more balanced and manipulated by the market, with the market driving and guiding, social subjects will also act spontaneously in their own interests, and if disputes occur in this process, their resolution is also driven and affected by the market. While seeking their own interests, the subjects of disputes will try everything possible to find the least cost and the most efficient approach for dispute resolution. In order to develop modern new mediation models, it is necessary to energetically advance market-oriented social mediation mechanisms. In China's prevailing social mediation system, people's mediation belongs in the category of free public welfare, folk mediation, for which the state public finance provides the funding and assurance, but if commercial mediation, industrial mediation, and lawyer mediation are generalized as people's mediation, and all provided as a free dispute resolution service, without establishing the mediators' incentive mechanism, it will severely constrain the development of mediation in Chinese society. In this regard, differentiation must be adopted to develop mediation in Chinese society, and while insisting on the public welfare attribute of people's mediation, it is necessary to support and encourage the market-based operation of commercial mediation, industrial mediation, and lawyer mediation. The market mechanism is the best approach to guide social mediation toward its maturity. Since the legal relations involved in modern commercial disputes are complex and the litigation target amount is relatively large, as long as the mediation organizations can provide high-quality mediation services, the parties also have payment capacity and are willing to pay. Therefore, this complies with the market law of "who uses, who pays" to encourage the social mediation organizations to charge for mediation in specific fields. This can attract those with talents with special knowledge to participate in the services of dispute resolution and also can realize the survival of the fittest through market competition, enhance mediation quality and mediation effects, cultivate a high-quality and low-cost mediation service, and promote the supply-demand balance of the dispute resolution market. Surely, since China's social mediation service market is currently still at the stage of start-up, local governments should issue such preferential and supporting policies as simplification of procedures and tax reduction and exemption according to local conditions, encourage the social forces to participate in dispute resolution by actively purchasing dispute resolution services from the social mediation organizations, and push social mediation to change from government-led autonomy to society autonomy.

Notes

1 Zhou Yongkun: On the Impact of Mandatory Mediation on Legal Governance and Fairness, *Science of Law*, 2007 (3).

2 Jerome A. Cohen: Chinese Mediation on the Eve of Modernization, trans. Wang Xiaohong, in Qiang Shigong (Ed.), *Mediation, Legal System and Modernity* (Beijing: China Legal Publishing House, 2001), p. 116.

3 Stanley Labman: Mao and Mediation: Politics and Dispute Resolution in Communist China, trans. Xu Xu, in Qiang Shigong (Ed.), *Mediation, Legal System and Modernity* (Beijing: China Legal Publishing House, 20010, pp. 120–121.

4 The period of collectivization initiated by Mao Zedong lasted a relatively long time. The period from the revolutionary base when the CPC implemented the mutual-assistance group to the 1980s when the people's commune institution ended is generally deemed as the period of collectivization. Xing Long: Thinking and Practice of Research on the Countryside in the Period of Collectivization, *Journal of Hubei University (Philosophy)*, 2019 (6).

5 Philip C.C. Huang: *The Past and the Present: Chinese Civil Justice in Practice* (Beijing: Law Press, 2009), pp. 20–61.

6 Qiang Shigong: *Mediation, Legal System and Modernity* (Beijing: China Legal Publishing House, 2001), p. 7.

7 He Yongjun: Evolution of Rural Society and Changes in People's Mediation Institution, *Law and Social Development*, 2013 (1).

8 In the 1990s, the administrative departments for industry and commerce played a great role in servicing economic contract disputes, with the maximum annual settlement of 450,000 cases of disputes, but only 12,000 cases in 2009, with the contractual disputes already flowing mainly to courts. Zhu Jingwen: *Report on China Law Development 2011: Law Enforcing towards Pluralism* (Beijing: China Renmin University Press, 2011), pp. 377–378.

9 Lan Rongjie: People's Mediation: Recovery or Transformation, *Tsinghua University Law Journal*, 2018 (4).

10 Jin Guantao: *Giant Mirror of History* (Beijing: Law Press, 2015), p. 9.
11 Ge Hongyi: *Law and Reason: Interpretation of Modernity of Law* (Beijing: Law Press, 2001), p. 5.
12 Liao Yongan: *Chinese Mediation Course* (Xiangtan: Xiangtan University Press, 2016), p. 157.
13 Liu Daolong and Liao Yongan: *Analysis of Classical Cases of People's Mediators* (Xiangtan: Xiangtan University Press, 2016), pp. 73–101.
14 Ibid., pp. 155–162.
15 Liao Yongan, Qin Binwu, and Robert Smith: *How to Be a Good Mediator: Analysis on Classical Cases of American Mediation* (Xiangtan: Xiangtan University Press, 2013), p. 47.
16 Lei Lei: German Mediation Concept and its Enlightenment, *Studies in Law and Business*, 2014 (2).
17 Lon L. Fuller: Mediation: Its Forms and Functions, 44 *South California Law Review*, 325–326/ (1971).
18 Lei Lei: German Mediation Concept and its Enlightenment, *Studies in Law and Business*, 2014 (2).
19 Tang Weijian: On the Modern Transformation of China's Mediation Institution, *Journal of Justice*, 2010 (2).
20 Hao Zhengjiang: On the Separation of China's Court Mediation and Judgment Procedure, *Journal of Jinan University (Philosophy and Social Sciences)*, 2017 (9).
21 Tanase Takao: *Dispute Resolution and Trial System*, trans. Wang Yaxin and Liu Rongjun (Beijing: China University of Political Science and Law Press, 2004), pp. 55–73.
22 Tang Li: Induction Mechanism of Litigation Consensus, *Studies in Law and Business*, 2016 (4).

References

Cohen, Jerome A.: Chinese Mediation on the Eve of Modernization, trans. Wang Xiaohong, in Qiang Shigong (Ed.), *Mediation, Legal System and Modernity*, Beijing: China Legal Publishing House, 2001, p. 116.

Fuller, Lon L.: Mediation: Its Forms and Functions, *South California Law Review*, 1971 (44): 325–326.

Ge Hongyi: *Law and Reason: Interpretation of Modernity of Law*, Beijing: Law Press, 2001.

Hao Zhengjiang: On the Separation of China's Court Mediation and Judgment Procedure, *Journal of Jinan University (Philosophy and Social Sciences)*, 2017 (9): 28–37, 129.

He Yongjun: Evolution of Rural Society and Changes of People's Mediation Institution, *Law and Social Development*, 2013 (1): 76–30.

Huang, Philip C.C.: *The Past and the Present: Chinese Civil Justice in Practice*, Beijing: Law Press, 2009.

Jin Guantao: *Giant Mirror of History*, Beijing: Law Press, 2015

Labman, Stanley: Mao and Mediation: Politics and Dispute Resolution in Communist China, trans. Xu Xu, in Qiang Shigong (Ed.), *Mediation, Legal System and Modernity*, Beijing: China Legal Publishing House, 2001, pp. 120–121.

Lan Rongjie: People's Mediation: Recovery or Transformation, *Tsinghua University Law Journal*, 2018 (4): 111–127.

Lei Lei: German Mediation Concept and its Enlightenment, *Studies in Law and Business*, 2014 (2): 151–160.

Liao Yongan, Qin Binwu, and Robert Smith: *How to Be a Good Mediator: Analysis on Classical Cases of American Mediation*, Xiangtan: Xiangtan University Press, 2013.

Liao Yongan: *Chinese Mediation Course*, Xiangtan: Xiangtan University Press, 2016.

Liu Daolong and Liao Yongan: *Analysis of Classical Cases of People's Mediators*, Xiangtan: Xiangtan University Press, 2016

Qiang Shigong: *Mediation, Legal System and Modernity*, Beijing: China Legal Publishing House, 2001.

Takao, Tanase: *Dispute Resolution and Trial System*, trans. Wang Yaxin, and Liu Rongjun, Beijing: China University of Political Science and Law Press, 2004 .

Tang Li: Induction Mechanism of Litigation Consensus, *Studies in Law and Business*, 2016 (4): 121–130.

Tang Weijian: *On the Modern Transformation of China's Mediation Institution*, *Journal of Justice*, 2010 (2): 51–63.

Xing Long: Thinking and Practice of Research on the Countryside in the Period of Collectivization, *Journal of Hubei University (Philosophy)*, 2019 (6), 85–92, 173.

Zhou Yongkun: On the Impact of Mandatory Mediation on Legal Governance and Fairness, *Science of Law*, 2007 (3): 11–24.

Zhu Jingwen: *Report on China Law Development 2011: Law Enforcing towards Pluralism*, Beijing: China Renmin University Press, 2011.

4 Transformation and Changes in the Mediation Model in China

The mediation model is an important theoretical category in the field of mediation studies. On the one hand, the mediation model reflects the mediation culture and mediation idea of a state or region. On the other hand, the mediation model plays a role in the construction of the mediation institution and the mediation procedure. In the studies on mediation, as a terminology, the mediation model has been widely used, but as a method of theoretical analysis, it has not yet attracted the attention of Chinese academic circles, so research studies are limited and the available research studies are not profound or systematic either. Based on this, with the status and role of the mediators in mediation as the analytical vision, this chapter interprets the changes in the Chinese mediation model with the expectation of aiding the modernization of Chinese mediation institution reform.

4.1 The Chinese Traditional Mediation Model: Mediator-Oriented Mediation and Its Characteristics

Regarding the mediation model, academic circles have not provided a uniform definition, but analyzed the mediation methods or mediation institution at different levels by deploying a theoretical tool, such as a "mediation model." This book deems mediation to be a field, viewing the mediation model as an abstract style of mutual relationship between the mediator and the parties to disputes in the process of mediation. In China, mediation has been performed for thousands of years. In different historical periods of social development, the content of the mediation institution and the functions it undertook have changed to some extent, but the reflection of the mediation model in the field of mediation as the value concept and conduct mode has a certain stability. Therefore, the traditional Chinese mediation model is the same mediation model as has been used continually since ancient times to the present, and its main characteristic is mediator-oriented mediation. In particular, it mainly includes the following aspects.

DOI: 10.4324/9781003385882-4

4.1.1 The Initiative of the Intervention Mode

In terms of the intervention mode, mediators have the right to intervene in dispute resolution and actively instigate and advance the mediation procedure. In traditional Chinese mediation, the mediation procedure can be actuated at the request of the parties for mediation, but mediators also often intervene positively in disputes. Mediation always is based on the voluntary will of the parties, and on the specific cultural background and social mentality, so the legality of an intervention in the disputes of others for active mediation, performed with "enthusiasm" and from "public spirit," has not been questioned, but has relatively high social acceptance. For instance, "upon hearing, the members of the mediation committee arrived ... after severely criticizing and carefully educating the mediation director, the two parties agreed to resolve the dispute through the mediation committee."[1] Especially in recent years, in the building of China's "Grand Mediation" working system, the initiative of judicial mediation and administrative mediation has been intensified to some extent. In the meantime, with reference to the particular practical experiences, different places have explored many practices of increasing the effect of people's mediation and the innovation of the people's mediation institution emerged in an endless stream. As the "Investigation on the Operation of Hunan Grass-roots Mediation Institution," undertaken by this author in Chenzhou and Xiangtan of Hunan, shows, all the places actively implemented the hierarchical management model of people's mediation organizations. When discovering any dispute or a tendency to any dispute, the village or community mediator or information worker can mediate locally. If the mediator or information worker cannot mediate it successfully, the dispute is submitted to the mediation committee at the village level. When the village committee fails to resolve it, the dispute will be submitted to the mediation center at the township or sub-district level or even to the joint mediation center at the county or city level, in an attempt to ensure the rule is followed: "minor matters not beyond the village, major events not beyond the township, and difficult things not beyond the county." In the effective resolution of contradictions and disputes, the initiative begins through mediators and information workers, and one after another coordination meetings held by the mediation committees at all levels for difficult and complex disputes, all these have indicated the initiative and action of Chinese mediators in the mediation procedure.

4.1.2 Extent of the Intervention Scope

In terms of the intervention scope, in the process of mediation, the mediator usually actively investigates the facts of the case and proposes a mediation solution. In the traditional patriarchal society, it was originally the "duty" of the elders, the gentry, and the chief officials to maintain the rite-governance order and resolve disputes between people. In mediation, sometimes without the need to find out the facts of disputes and without the need to distinguish right and wrong between the parties, as the spokesperson of ethics and morality and value norms, the mediator directly lectured and educated and made a judgment on the dispute conduct of the parties.[2] During the period after the People's Republic of China was founded and the period of the socialist planned economy, in addition to the function of dispute resolution, mediation also undertook the function of political mobilization, ideological education, and social integration, so in mediation, mediators would also often directly provide the mediation solution for the parties to accept.[3] In recent years, with society changing, what is valued at the level of regulation is the voluntary will and autonomy of mediation, but under the pressure of maintaining social stability, through building a "Grand Mediation" system, the function of mediation for social governance has been intensified. In this context, the mediators' aim is to settle disputes, close the cases for settlement, and dissolve contradictions at the grass-roots level. Therefore, in the mediation procedure, mediators will usually actively and positively investigate the facts of disputes and, on the basis of the facts, usually propose a solution according to emotional reason or the law.

4.1.3 Inequality of the Relationship between Mediation Subjects

In terms of the relationship between the mediation subjects, between the mediator and the parties is the subject-object relationship and this is mainly reflected as lecturing and convincing the parties from the top down. In the mediator-oriented mediation, there are two types of relationship, i.e., the relationship between the mediator and the parties and the relationship between all the parties. The action of the former is far greater than that of the latter and the parties often cannot even communicate with each other effectively, so that the relationship between the parties tends to be nil. The mutual relationship between the mediator and the parties is mainly reflected as lecturing and convincing the parties from the top down, i.e., it is the mediator's job mainly to lecture the parties, while the parties' disclosure of emotions and expression of interest appeals are pressurized to different extents. The mediator's lecturing of the parties differs mainly with the changing times: in traditional society, the main focus of the lecture was ethics and morality; after the People's Republic of China was established and before the launch of the reform and opening-up, the main topic was the national policies and communist morality; since the reform and opening-up, mainly regulations, policies, and emotional reason to persuade the parties have been the topics.

4.2 The Basis and Realistic Dilemmas of the Mediator-Oriented Mediation Model

4.2.1 The Basis of the Mediator-Oriented Mediation Model

4.2.1.1 The Social-Economic Base: Society of "Rule by Man" and the Agricultural Economy

Mediator-oriented mediation originated in the society of "the rule by man."

> Generally speaking, the so-called rule by man means the state realizes the state function of governing society, not by relying on the normative legal documents with universal binding force formulated beforehand, according to the statutory procedures, but by relying on the will and authority of individuals.[4]

In the feudal society in China, the rite-governance esteemed by Confucianism was actually a kind of rule by man, i.e., emphasizing philosopher politics and governing the state not according to external, objective, legal norms, but by the "administration by the people." Chinese society after 1949 and before the launch of the reform and opening-up is summarized by some scholars as a "unit system."[5] This was a society with extremely high social integration in which, through the unit system, i.e., the household registration system and the archive system, all the members of society were fixed in certain social positions. The whole society was hierarchically managed and controlled, in which each subordinate was responsible to their superior and the power of each unit was centralized in the hands of one person or several people. Scholars call such a governance model the "rule of power" society.[6] The rule of power society is essentially different from the rite-governance society, but also belongs in the category of a "rule by man" society. The basic units of the rite-governance society are not individuals, but the social units where the individuals are found: families, clans, villages, and guilds;[7] the basic units of the rule of power society are not individuals either, but the units or production teams where the individuals are found. Therefore, the influence of the rule by man society on dispute mediation means: the rule by man society is a society of state standards and power standards, in which the character and dignity of individuals are buried in the rite-governance order or the rule of power order, and it is natural for the spokesperson of social ethics and morality or the controller of state power to actively intervene in the disputes of others and dominate the mediation procedure.

In the meantime, the agricultural economy of traditional society also promoted mediator-oriented mediation. In traditional Chinese society, agriculture occupied a major role in the social economy and the majority of the total national population lived in the countryside as the agricultural population. The profound influence of such an agricultural economy on dispute resolution is mainly reflected as: first, traditional society was mainly a self-sufficient, small peasant economy:

> In the circumstance with the necessity to pay the huge amount of taxes to the remote local authorities or off-site landlords or undertake other burdens, villages and peasant households could always develop and maintain basically abundant resources to meet the basic needs of the expanding population.[8]

Such a small peasant economy determined that the types of disputes in traditional society were relatively simple and there were no special requirements for dispute mediators either. Second, the self-sufficient, small peasant economy determined the low migration rate of people and the regional limitation on the scope of activity of peasants dwelling in the villages. Therefore, rural society was a society of acquaintance, without strangers. In the dispute resolution of the society of acquaintance, emotion, reason, and face were critical. In the meantime, the traditional society of acquaintance was also a society of etiquette and custom, in which people in the local communities watched over and helped each other and shared the same basically integrated value outlook. Upon the occurrence of any dispute, the mediation solution by mediators as the third person, on the basis of their common value outlook, was recognized.

4.2.1.2 Sources of Legality: Traditional Authority and Charisma-based Authority

Regarding the mediator's authority, that is why people believe in mediator's mediation in disputes, this is the mediators' "source of legality." Chapter 1 in this volume has already discussed in detail the types of mediator authority. Max Weber classified the proper social authority into three types: (1) traditional authority, i.e., "legality is required to be believed firmly by others owing to the long rules and the sanctity of the spectrum of power;" (2) charisma-based authority, i.e., authority is established "on the basis of the rare divinity, heroism or model characteristic of one individual;" and (3) legal principle authority, i.e., based on legal principles.[9] As a whole, Chinese mediators' traditional authority is mainly a kind of traditional and charisma-based authority, rather than a kind of legal principle authority. The authority of elders and moral authority are both based on deep conviction of traditional force or charm. The traditional state authority is not based on legal formal reason either. The authority of official mediation was mainly the state authority, while the authority of folk mediation was mainly the local authority, but the authority mediation relied on in different periods was not consistent. In traditional Chinese society with "imperial power not reaching below the level of the county," the maintenance of local communities (with villages as the main form) mainly relied on Confucian concepts and its spokespersons, i.e., the elders and the gentry. Therefore, the authority of folk mediation arose mainly from the authority of the elders and the moral authority. Elders, the gentry and others in charge of folk mediation were all the elders of clans and people of high prestige, and their authority was based on their seniority or virtues, as determined by the social pattern of family-state integration in ancient China and the order of rite-governance it relied on. From 1949 to the early period of the reform and the opening-up, the main change in folk mediation (mainly people's mediation) subjects was the "official-based" mediators:

> The previous spontaneous high-prestige person of communities changed to "officials" of the state. Certainly, their identity was at the same time as one of the members of the village and the community. During this period, disputes in villages were mostly handled by the production team leader, party branch member (including women officers), village security officer, brigade leader, brigade party branch secretary and other village officials.[10]

During the period of the communes, villagers interacted with each other frequently, but since the collective economy started, the disputes involving substantial interests were limited, and generally, they were mainly family quarrels, such as small affairs, gossip, and children fighting.

> Resolution of these disputes was very easy: some were resolved by the two parties themselves; some were mollified by other villagers on the spot; some other relatively major disputes were mediated successfully by the elders within the clan or production team officials, and extremely few disputes needed to be resolved at the level of the brigade.[11]

Obviously, the authority of the folk mediation during this period arose from the combination of folk authority and state authority.

4.2.2 Dilemma Faced by the Mediator-Oriented Mediation Model

From a historical view, mediator-oriented mediation had certain commonalities with the traditional rule by man society and the agricultural economy and was able to obtain its legitimacy by relying on elders' authority, moral authority, and state authority, and also actually played different functions in different historical periods. But since the reform and opening-up, the social basis for the generation and development of mediator-oriented mediation has changed and traditional authority has been disempowered. Against this background, the inherent defects of mediator-oriented mediation model became more prominent and thus restricted the functions of mediation.

4.2.2.1 Changes in the Social-Economic Bases

First of all, is the transformation from the society of rule by man to the society of legal governance. The essence of legal governance is to restrict power and safeguard rights and the transformation from the society of rule by man to the society of legal governance indicates the turning from state standards and power standards to individual standards and right standards. In this situation, for disputes involving the nature of private rights, the initiative intervention of the state lost its legality. In traditional society, individuals had no personality and value of their own, but in modern society, with the construction of the legal governance of the state being advanced, the independent sense of individuals has been greatly enhanced. In the mediation of disputes, the legitimacy of the subject-object relationship between the mediator and the parties is unavoidably questioned.

Second, the transformation from a planned economy to a market economy occurred. The reform of China's market economy system initiated profound changes in society and profound changes in people's ideology, and also made disputes have different features from the traditional disputes. For instance, the traditional disputes arising in the society of acquaintance were mixed with relatively many emotional factors, mostly winning honor or a matter of face. Yet, in the market economy, modern people are utilitarian and economically rational. Therefore, modern disputes often have a very high interest orientation. Traditional mediation resolved and settled disputes mainly through moral education and when now facing such disputes with a relatively high interest orientation, its function will naturally be limited.

4.2.2.2 Prominence of Inherent Defects

With the social-economic bases for the generation of the mediator-oriented mediation model and the basis of legitimacy changing, the inherent defects of such a model also become more prominent. These defects are mainly: deficient subjectivity of the parties and weakening procedural justice.

The subjectivity of the parties in the mediation procedure is, first of all, reflected as the voluntary principle of the parties, i.e., it is up to the parties to decide, at their own discretion, whether to undertake mediation, whether to suspend the mediation procedure, whether to conclude a mediation agreement, and decide on the particular contents of the mediation agreement. In the mediator-oriented mediation model, the relationship between the mediator and the parties is the subject-object relationship, and the parties are only the objects of the procedure, while the legitimacy of mediation comes from the personal authority of the mediator or attached state authority. With the background of China's present active judiciary and "Grand Mediation" system, in practice, upon finding out the facts, many mediators will directly propose their own mediation solution, and, using all kinds of implied or potential deterrent force, make the parties accept the mediation solution. But, in modern society, due to enhanced individualism, rationalism, and right consciousness of the social subjects, it is relatively hard for the parties to willingly accept the solution which is short of legitimacy and rationality for them. Therefore, on the one hand, if the parties refuse to conclude an agreement, such a practice of mediator to judge the facts and directly present the mediation solution not only fails to close the case for settlement, but also, on the contrary, will discredit the mediation procedure and damage the mediator's credibility and authority. On the other hand, even when the parties do accept the mediation solution, since they do not do so completely freely, they may possibly go back on their word, fail to perform the mediation agreement, and turn to the other approaches of dispute resolution, litigation, or petition, which will result in a huge waste of national and social resources.

In modern society with authority already disempowered, the precondition for the parties is to recognize the mediation procedure, be willing to consult, and thus accept the mediation results to assure basic procedural justice. Basic procedural justice includes: neutrality of the mediators and equal assurance of the parties' procedural rights. Under the present pressure of maintaining social stability, judges or administrative personnel as mediators have a strong tendency to close the case for settlement, and their status in the disputes mediation is not perfect. It not only confuses the neutral stand of the mediators, but also, due to the impact of the idea of "emphasizing the entity and ignoring procedure," when undertaking mediation, the mediator is vaguely aware of procedural assurance and sometimes even facilitates the conclusion of the mediation agreement by manipulating the information in the back-to-back mediation, which greatly damages procedural justice. In such circumstances, sometimes, even if the mediator rationally facilitates the conclusion of a mediation agreement, according to the facts of disputes, the parties may also possibly suspect the judgment; if the parties come to learn, afterward, the information of the two parties is not at all symmetrical, they will not only go back on their word, but the authority of the mediator and the mediation procedure are also questioned.

4.3 The Dual Construction of the Chinese Mediation Model in the Period of Social Transformation

In changing times, the social-economic bases for the traditional Chinese mediation model and the authority sources have already evolved and the new social-economic conditions require new mediation models to match them. But, history always advances on the basis of yesterday and China's traditional mediator-oriented mediation model will definitely still function within a certain scope. Therefore, in the opinion of this author, China's mediation model in the period of social transformation will be in the form of co-existence of the mediator-oriented mediation model and the mediator-assistant mediation model.

4.3.1 Limited Application of the Mediator-Oriented Mediation Model

4.3.1.1 The Necessity of Limited Application

First, legal modernity implies high formalization and rationalization of the law, but the law is also a kind of "local knowledge,"[12] this implies that the process of China's legal governance will be a natural process of mutual structuring and mutual shaping of modern law and traditional habits and morality. China is now in a period of accelerated social transformation with a profound reform of the economic system, a profound change in the social structures, a profound adjustment of interest patterns, and a profound change in ideology, but compared with other elements, the ideology and people's conduct must retain a certain stability. For instance, the previous "official standard" thought and common people's mentality of both admiring and fearing officials are still relatively general. This is also the reason why China's prevailing mediation model is still the mediator-oriented mediation model, and this also indicates that the mediator-oriented mediation model will definitely still function within a certain scope.

Second, at present, China's legal governance construction is still in the process of advancing gradually. In the meantime, China is currently in the critical period of reform, with social contradictions growing and numbers of disputes sharply increasing. Since the state controls relatively many social resources and it has a major influence in the specific public fields, the state plays a very important role and has an indispensable responsibility to build and maintain social order. In some disputes, the courts fail to cope or in some disputes for which the parties have insufficient autonomy, the state is objectively required to adopt more flexible and practical modes to intervene actively in the resolution of disputes between people, and provide the public with convenient and economic approaches for right relief so as to maintain social stability and order.

Third, the rite-governance order is damaged, but in some villages and communities, there are still some characteristics of the society of acquaintance, social members interact frequently and have close relationships, so they still have the mechanisms for the generation of common values and folk norms, and can spontaneously generate their own authority and elites. This also determines that mediator-oriented mediation still has certain applicability.

4.3.1.2 Scope of Limited Application

From the above, it can be seen that according to the characteristics of the mediator-oriented mediation model and its embedded social structure, the mediator-oriented model is applicable to the mediation of civil disputes in the society of acquaintance. Therefore, the mediator-oriented mediation is applicable to general civil disputes between individual villagers in rural areas, and the urban community mediation can also be dominated by mediators.

However, compared with rural residents, the sense of what is right and the independent sense of urban residents are generally stronger and the procedural requirements and regularity of mediation are even higher. Therefore, except for domestic disputes and neighborhood disputes, the mediator-oriented mediation model is not applicable to the mediation of other urban civil and commercial disputes.

Besides, in view of the special situation that China is now in the period of social transformation, in the opinion of this author, in the Grand Mediation work system, it is necessary for local mediation centers or mediation federations to actively intervene in the mediation and resolution of group emergency events. Group emergency events arise from social class differentiation, unequal distribution of interest, lack of regulations, and control failure, and have spontaneous, disorganized, irrational, and other features. If the group emergency events cannot be effectively coped with and treated in a timely manner, they will have a relatively large impact on social order. Based on the management function of the state, facing any group emergency event, the state should take effective measures to cope with them and actively intervene in the mediation and resolution of the contradictions and disputes, so as to meet the public's appeals for legal interest and maintain social stability and order.

4.3.2 The Structure of the New Mediation Model in the Market Economic Conditions in China: The Mediator-Assistant Mediation Model

A market economy is a liberal economy in which every social subject freely and equally accesses the market and undertakes economic activities; a market economy is a rational economy, with the aim of gaining maximum interest at the minimum cost; a market economy does not advocate authority, and in the view of the individual economic subjects, the maximization of their interest is the main purpose for undertaking economic activities, while all others are means. Therefore, what is complementary to a market economy are definitely political democracy and cultural diversity, authority disempowerment, and correct standards. As regards mediation, the authority and legitimacy of mediation come from the parties' recognition and liberal choice of mediation activities and mediation results. Therefore, in market economy conditions, the role of the mediator and the parties in the mediation, the goal of the mediator and the scope of intervention have become issues worthy of attention.

We define the new mediation model structure in the market economy in China as a mediator-assistant model, compared with the traditional Chinese mediation model, i.e., the mediator-oriented model. In the mediator-assistant mediation model, mediators play the role of assisting communication and can make assessments and proposals only upon obtaining permission or authorization from the parties. The limited application of mediator-oriented mediation is decided by the national condition that China is still in the period of transformation; while the mediator-assistant mediation is similar to the

American consultation-promoted mediation and expert evaluative mediation, but the difference is that China's assistant mediation has a narrow application scope and is only applicable to the mediation of urban civil disputes (except for community mediation), commercial mediation, and special mediation. In our opinion, the mediator-assistant mediation model has the following features.

First, the subjectivity of the parties. The subjectivity of the parties first of all implies that the parties are the leaders of the mediation procedure. The actuation and progress of the mediation procedure and the conclusion of a mediation agreement are all decided by the parties and mediation is the procedure for the autonomy and decision of the parties. This implies that the mediator is only the assistant of a mediation procedure. The scope of the role played by the mediator in mediation includes: helping the parties to establish contact, acting as the channel for information exchange, promoting communication and mutual assistance of the parties, evaluating information, providing proposals on the basis of special knowledge, and striving to convince the parties to accept the proposals. Since no matter what role is played and what action is taken in the mediation procedure, the mediator will undertake all only upon obtaining the consent or definite authorization from the parties, the mediator is only an assistant in the mediation procedure.

Second, procedural justice. Appropriate procedure is always an important principle of the dispute resolution procedure. In mediation, when no protection of appropriate procedure is provided, the opportunity and space for manipulating and pressurizing will be found. The justice of the mediation procedure first of all requires neutrality by the mediators. The neutrality of the mediators requires mediators to comply with one of the following two conditions, i.e., interest neutrality and structural neutrality. The so-called interest neutrality means that mediators are detached from mutually opposed interests and opinions and really not related to the interests. The so-called structural neutrality means that the mediator has an equal relation with both of the parties. The neutrality of a mediator not only requires the mediator not to be involved in the interests of any party, according to professional ethics and norms, but also to appear to make the parties believe he is neutral and can realize tangible fairness. It requires the mediator to keep, in the process of mediation, objective rationality and impartiality,[13] without favor or deciding on the right and wrong of any one party, to listen patiently to the opinions of the two sides, advise, support, encourage, and urge in turns all the parties, and make all the parties see that they have received equal treatment.

Third, the justice of the mediation procedure also requires the mediator to adequately notify the parties of the matters related to the mediation procedure, so that all the subjects reach a common view of the mediation procedure itself. These matters generally include: basic principles of mediation; the roles and acts of the mediator; the major process of mediation; the rights the parties in mediation are entitled to. Finally, it is necessary to safeguard equally the procedural rights of the parties. For instance, to stipulate that the two parties speak in turns so that they state adequately and are listened to patiently; each party has an equal decision right regarding the mediation procedure and the content of the mediation agreement.

Fourth, the confidentiality of mediation. The non-disclosure principle of mediation means that the information exchanged in the mediation procedure will not be disclosed to a court, lawyers, social workers, or any other persons without obtaining the definite consent from the parties or the court order.

> Confidentiality is an indispensable part in the relationship between the mediator and the parties ... is the foundation stone for the trusteeship that must exist between the mediator and the parties as well as the basis for free and frank disclosure necessary to overcome the obstacles faced by conciliation. In terms of the voluntary will of the parties to participate and the justice of the mediator, it is critical. The parties must be assured that they will not feel at a disadvantage due to any disclosure and it is necessary for them to understand that they will not suffer any loss in appealing for mediation.[14]

Confidentiality of mediation means any statement made by the parties and any information obtained by the mediator in the mediation procedure will not be disclosed to other subjects, as well as the information disclosed by one party to the mediator in the unilateral meeting can be disclosed to the opposite party only upon obtaining the consent or permission from the first party. The exception to the non-disclosure principle of mediation is when the information involves public interest or any danger to the life, health, or safety of any other persons, then the relevant information must be disclosed.

Fifth, it is the basic structural model for the relationship between the mediator and the parties. Different from the subject-object relationship between the mediator and the parties in the mediator-oriented model, in the mediator-assistant model, the relationship between the mediator and the parties is a subject-subject relationship. The mediator is the moderator of the mediation procedure and maintains order and provides cooperative proposals so as to advance the procedure and promote cooperation; the parties are the final determiners of the mediation procedure and the recognition of the parties determines the legality of the mediation procedure. In the event the parties grant their consent or authorization, the role of the mediator can also be extended and a more substantial information exchange can be undertaken between the mediator and the parties. For instance, mediators declare and restate the key points of an agreement and issue rules and standards in consultation; define information and attempt to provide proposals; guide the parties to turn their attention to their hidden interests; assess the information of the parties, and consider optional solutions and provide their own proposals and advice.

Notes

1 Chang Ming: *Stories of People's Mediation* (Beijing: Law Press, 1984), p. 1.
2 Fei Xiaotong: *From the Soil: The Foundations of Chinese Society* (Beijing: People's Publishing House, 2008), pp. 69–70.
3 Qiang Shigong: *Mediation, Legal System and Modernization: A Study of the Chinese Mediation Institution* (Beijing: China Legal Publishing House, 2005), pp. 117–203.
4 Yang Jianjun: *Compendium of Evolution of China's Modern Criminal Laws* (Beijing: China Legal Publishing House, 2011), p. 193.
5 Li Lulu: Changes and Studies of the "Unit System," *Journal of Jilin University (Social Sciences)*, 2013 (1).
6 Guo Xinghua: *Dispute Resolution in Social Transformation* (Beijing: China Renmin University Press, 2013), p. 262.
7 See Stanley Lubman, Mao and Mediation, Politics and Dispute Resolution in Communist China, 5 *California Law Review* (1967) 1294.
8 Gilbert Rozman: *The Modernization of China*, trans. "Comparative Modernization" Project Team under the National Social Sciences Fund of China (Nanjing: Jiangsu People's Publishing House, 2010), p. 90.
9 Raymond Wacks: *Understanding Jurisprudence*, trans. Yang Tianjiang (Guilin: Journal of Guangxi Normal University, 2016), pp. 289–290.
10 Philip C.C. Huang: *The Past and the Present: Chinese Civil Justice in Practice* (Beijing: Law Press, 2009), p. 40.
11 Dong Leiming: *Mediation of Song Village: Authority and Order in the Times of Great Changes* (Beijing: Law Press, 2008), p. 98.
12 Liang Zhiping: *Cultural Interpretation of Law* (Beijing: Joint Publishing, 1998), p. 73.
13 Chen Lijun and Chen Limin: Basis for Generation of Judicial Credibility, *Journal of Hunan University of Science and Technology (Social Sciences)* (2011) (4).
14 M. Roberts: *Mediation in Family Disputes: Principles of Practice* (Farnham: Ashgate Publishing, 2012), pp. 133–135.

References

Chang Ming: *Stories of People's Mediation*, Beijing: Law Press, 1984.
Chen Lijun and Chen Limin: Basis for Generation of Judicial Credibility, *Journal of Hunan University of Science and Technology (Social Sciences)*, 2011 (4): 58–62.
Dong Leiming: *Mediation of Song Village: Authority and Order in the Times of Great Changes*, Beijing: Law Press, 2008.
Fei Xiaotong: *From the Soil: The Foundations of Chinese Society*, Beijing: People's Publishing House, 2008.
Guo Xinghua: *Dispute Resolution in Social Transformation*, Beijing: China Renmin University Press, 2013.
Huang, Philip C.C.: *The Past and the Present: Chinese Civil Justice in Practice*, Beijing: Law Press, 2009.
Li Lulu: Changes and Studies of "Unit System," *Journal of Jilin University (Social Sciences)*, 2013 (1): 11–14.
Liang Zhiping: *Cultural Interpretation of Law*, Beijing: Joint Publishing, 1998.
Lubman, Stanley: Mao and Mediation, Politics and Dispute Resolution in Communist China, *California Law Review*, 1967 (5): 1294.

Qiang Shigong: *Mediation, Legal System and Modernization: A Study of Chinese Mediation Institution*, Beijing: China Legal Publishing House, 2005.

Roberts, M.: *Mediation in Family Disputes: Principles of Practice,* Farnham: Ashgate Publishing, 2012.

Rozman, Gilbert: *The Modernization of China*, trans. "Comparative Modernization" Project Team under the National Social Sciences Fund of China, Nanjing: Jiangsu People's Publishing House, 2010.

Wacks, Raymond: *Understanding Jurisprudence*, trans. Yang Tianjiang, Guilin: Journal of Guangxi Normal University, 2016.

Yang Jianjun: *Compendium of Evolution of China's Modern Criminal Laws*, Beijing: China Legal Publishing House, 2011.

5 The Road to Professionalization of Mediation in China

In the changing process of Chinese mediation models, the role orientation and authority source of mediators have also changed accordingly, and such change directly determined the effectiveness of mediation. As already discussed, the type of traditional Chinese mediation authority is mainly a traditional and charming type (based on charisma, as discussed by Weber) and the existence of mediators seems to make up for, as an "irregular force," the shortage of regular judicial professional teams. Indeed, these types of authority used to play an important role in the past, but with the advent of the market economy, and modern commercial work division in society being increasingly refined, "the disenchantment and secularization of culture in the process of modernization also continually dissolves the authority of traditional elites in mediation."[1] The legal resources of the traditional mediation authority have already been gradually lost, and the traditional authority of the mediator is no longer effective in dispute resolution.

Because of this, eight years ago, *The People's Mediation Law* was implemented, and people's mediation has also recovered to some extent after falling into disuse, but is facing the new challenges of social contradictions in the new era and the new expectations of people for fairness and justice. However, problems such as old age, low educational level, and limited legal knowledge of the people's mediators have become prominent when facing the new complex disputes. The specialization and professionalization of the people's mediator team are low, training is not systematic, and the ability to resolve contradictions and disputes needs to be enhanced. Building the special and industrial people's mediator team is advancing slowly; assurance of funding for people's mediation is difficult, and the incentive mechanism is imperfect, as all constrain the functioning of the people's mediation institution. In order to resolve the shortage of mediators in modern dispute resolution, since the beginning of the twenty-first century, China has started gradually to attach importance to the professionalization of mediators, and this started to attract attention in academic circles. However, regarding the professionalization practice of mediation in China, on the one hand, mediation is still in a state of scattered development, lacking uniform and feasible normative guidance and path design. On the other hand, the relevant studies

DOI: 10.4324/9781003385882-5

by academics mainly explored the professionalization issues of people's mediation and showed few concerns about the prospects for the professionalization of other types of mediation. Based on the systematic consideration of perfecting the mediation institution, with people's mediation, commercial mediation, industrial mediation as the objects,[2] this chapter discusses the dilemmas and offers a solution to advance the development of China's mediation professionalization.

5.1 Modern Social Governance and the Professionalization of Mediation

5.1.1 Mediation Professionalization Is the Inevitable Requirement for Modernization

Since the beginning of the twenty-first century, China has been in a critical period of modernization. Society has changed greatly, traditional lifestyles have been seriously impacted, individual value concepts have shown a trend of differentiation, and social contradictions and disputes have become increasingly complicated and varied. In the meantime, with the management of society changing to governance of society, the governmental functions have also changed accordingly, i.e., changing from "omnipotent" government to a "service-oriented" government, and they started to make use of folk wisdom and employ private forces to deal with public affairs, with a pattern of diversity and co-governance being gradually formed. Against such a background, the professionalization of the mediation institution emerged and rapidly showed a trend of developing.[3]

Professionalization of mediation is the inevitable requirement of the complication of social disputes as well as an important symbol and basic assurance of the development of mediation skills. In the process of modernization, with the workload of mediators increasing and the work difficulty being enhanced, the original knowledge structure and working skills can no longer satisfy the needs of society, and the traditional mode of dispute resolution, relying on moral authority, is in urgent need of change. Mediation in China is an urgent issue to be resolved, regarding how to establish the special authority and form the professional characteristics to cope with the complex and changing needs of social reality now. In this regard, professionalization is not only a reason for the self-reform of the mediation institution, but is also the inevitable requirement for the modernization of Chinese society.

Taking a global view, since the second half of the twentieth century, the mediation institution has developed rapidly in Western society and has realized a transformation from the spontaneous traditional mediation to the conscious modern mediation. Today, mediation in many Western countries has attracted multidisciplinary professionals in law, psychology, sociology, ethics, and business to join it, forming a diversified development model, so now mediation flexibly co-exists with different styles, and is developing as an approach for global professionalization of dispute resolution. Discussion on the professional development of mediation in China responds to the modernization of Chinese society, as well as echoing the development of global mediation professionalization.

5.1.2 Elements of Mediation Professionalization

For a discussion of the professionalization of mediation, it is necessary first of all to analyze the connotation of mediation professionalization. In our opinion, mediation can become a profession because it has the following characteristics: (1) the legality of mediation has gained an energetically theoretical defense; (2) the important role of mediation in dispute resolution cannot be replaced by other modes; (3) mediators take mediation as their main life skill and income source; and (4) a complete set of professional models, different from public conduct models and professional ethics, is formed for the mediation practitioners, thus cultivating a community of mediator careers. In other words, mediation professionalization refers to the process for the personnel engaged in mediation work to have a relevant special quality and service quality, undertake activities according to the universally acknowledged professional ethics and professional conduct norms, undertake all the risks arising from the profession, gain the remuneration deserving of their workload and contribution to society, form a stable career group, and enjoy a certain social status. In particular, mediation professionalization should include the following elements.

First, the special techniques and mediation attainments. Possession of special techniques refers to the special skills the mediators should have, different from other dispute resolution work. The work skills of mediators include both their language communication skills and non-language communication skills. The language communication skills of mediators mean the mediators should be convincing, effective, contextual, and technical, while the non-language communication skills require the mediators to be good at body language, through their eyes and their gestures, guiding the parties to disputes to express their viewpoints. The professional attainments of mediation refer to the professional morality and professional consciousness of a mediator. Professional morality is just the combination of moral criterion and moral quality closely related to mediation work or required by the features of mediation work. Generally, mediators should abide by the non-disclosure principle, the neutrality principle, and the justice principle. Professional consciousness is the sense of self-restraint the mediator must bear in mind, which is most basic for the work they are engaged in, involving in particular the mediators' sense of innovation, contribution, and cooperation.

Second, uniform professional conduct norms. The professional conduct norms imply the mediators' common value idea, through which the mode can be defined to share the responsibilities and grant honor among mediators. The professional conduct norms of mediators are a set of special technical rules with a binding force on the whole mediator team, constituting the major norms for assessing the conduct of mediators. The formation of uniform conduct norms is based on the collected experience of mediation work as well as on the policy influence of the professional administration.

Third, systematic career education and training. Career education and training are mainly to promote the professional techniques of mediators and aid the career development management of mediators. Since mediation is a recognized occupation in society, in addition to the necessary special knowledge of the law, mediators are also required to have knowledge of sociology, ethics, economics, psychology, and other special knowledge. As compound talents, mediators are required not only to have a solid knowledge base, but also to adapt to the needs of continual development by constantly updating their knowledge and expanding their work experience.

Fourth, the stable career group is a critical element in the development of professionalization. For professionalization, mediators must form a stable mediator career group. The formation of the mediator career group can promote the formation of a sense of an individual career for the mediators, and intensify the practitioners' sense of recognition, sense of pride, and sense of belonging to the mediation career. When this group becomes stable and gradually expands, mediators will form an outlook of common values and moral beliefs. Within the common institution, they will get to know each other well through long-term approach, intensify their mutual understanding and recognition, and generate a common view of career. Based on this, with the efforts made jointly by the career group, mediators gain a relatively high social status and enjoy the steady and rich material remuneration and spiritual returns.

5.2 Dilemmas Facing the Professionalization of Mediation in China

Currently, mediation in China has shown a tendency toward professionalization, but the professional group of mediation has not yet been formed, special professional techniques and attainments are not strong, uniform conduct norms are not perfect, and systematic career education and training are not mature. Professionalization of mediation faces difficulties and the progress of development is relatively slow.

5.2.1 Dilemmas Facing the Professionalization of People's Mediation

5.2.1.1 Lack of a Management Mechanism for Complete Career Development

A management system for complete career development should include such core contents as training, examinations, supervision and exit mechanisms. At present, China has not yet formed this management system. With respect to training, *China's People's Mediation Law* stipulated the provisions of training,[4] but the law has not stipulated the particular provisions of the content, frequency, and particular requirements of regular training. In practice, all local judicial and administrative organs have attached importance to undertaking training for people's mediators and devoted resources to help promote the level of legal knowledge and capability in dispute resolution, but the systematic specialty of relevant training is not strong and the contents of training are also those concerning the law, regulations, and policies or knowledge related to the mediation institution, with limited contents concerning the cultivation of the professional quality of mediators. Those personnel taking part in training also mostly held an attitude of enhancing the qualification by engaging in advanced studies and lacked understanding of the professionalization of mediation.

In terms of examinations, as one of the nine duties of the judicial offices, people's mediation is merely one part of the comprehensive legal examination and assessment. Currently, in terms of people's mediation in China, generally, the bureaus of justice undertake the examination of the people's mediation committees at the township level, and the township judicial offices undertake the examination of the mediation committees at the level of villages. Furthermore, such an examination is mainly undertaken with mediation committees as units, while no special examination and assessment are available for mediators individually. The examination results are only linked to the awards of the judicial offices, almost without any influence on the benefits of mediators individually. And the awarding mechanism of people's mediation currently remains at the level of legislation and is in a state of being ready but not yet deployed.

5.2.1.2 Lack of Full-Time People's Mediator Groups

A Chinese people's mediator team is generally composed of the staff of village committees, the staff of resident committees, the staff of the units, the staff of the township or sub-district offices, members of social groups and other organizations (women's federations, federations of disabled persons, consumers association, committee on care for children, trade unions, chambers of commerce, and property management associations), and experts and scholars in the relevant fields, lawyers, notaries, retired judges, and procurators. These mediation practitioners work mostly on a part-time basis and they do not see mediation as their main career. Even the retired judges and procurators do not depend on mediation of folk disputes to maintain their basic income.

5.2.1.3 Insufficient Assurance of Funding for People's Mediation

After *The People's Mediation Law* was promulgated in 2010, it still followed the tradition of "people's mediation charges no fees," but only provided extra funds when necessary, subsidies for loss of working time may be granted to people's mediators engaged in mediation work. Therefore, the sources of funding for people's mediation mainly depended on the state, but such funding from the top down was basically insufficient, causing the township mediation committees and township judicial offices to turn to the township administration and grass-roots legal service market for support.[5] As for the mediation committees at the level of villages, the assurance of mediation funds was even weaker. Such a financial status is still observed with a big gap from the requirement of professionalization.[6]

5.2.2 Dilemmas Facing the Professionalization of Industrial Mediation

5.2.2.1 Low Usage Rate of Industrial Mediation

Industrial mediation relies on trade unions and trade organizations. In the construction and development of China's market economy, in the theory of social composition as well as in the structural framework of the market, there were basically no trade union between the government and enterprises in the modern market economy.[7] Naturally as a result, China's trade unions had a very narrow space for survival and the relevant functions failed to be effective. Currently ,in China, a trade union has to be established subject to the approval and professional guidance of the government department, so many trade unions continued to use the old government habits in terms of ideas and style of action. Such a reality intensified the leading role of the government over the trade unions and also resulted in the narrow coverage of trade unions and a lack of industrial representatives. Against this background, the set-up of the complementary mediation institutions run by trade unions is insufficient. Trade unions have defined the function of dispute mediation in the industrial rules, but had not allocated the relevant mediation institutions and mediators, and the inherent motive for providing a mediation service was missing, and this has greatly constrained the realistic usage rate of industrial mediation.

5.2.2.2 Relatively Low Dispute Resolution Capability of Industrial Mediators

The advantage of industrial mediation is its special knowledge. However, currently, due to the interpersonal relations network, Chinese industrial mediator often cannot remain objective and neutral, thus greatly affecting the justice of mediation agreements. Besides, in the judicial practice, the special advantages of industrial mediators resulted in excessive reliance of industrial mediators on their special judgment and they were ignorant of the basic mediation principles and mediation skills. Furthermore, currently, China lacks definite provisions regarding the access conditions, qualification certification, and examination of the work of industrial mediators, and trade unions also fail to attach importance to the training and examination of special knowledge and special skills for industrial mediators. Consequently, industrial mediators have the industrial special knowledge, but their mediation skills are severely lacking, failing to form the development model of professionalization.

5.2.2.3 No Normative Assurance Is Defined and Practitioners Lack Awareness

Article 34 of *The People's Mediation Law* (2010) provided: "townships, subdistricts and social groups or other organizations may set up, as per needs and with reference to the relevant provisions hereof, a people's mediation committee to mediate in folk disputes." In 2011, the Ministry of Justice issued the *Suggestions for Strengthening the Establishment of Industrial and Special People's Mediation Committees*, pointing out further the basic requirements for social groups or other organizations to set up industrial and special people's mediation committees, but China is still at the stage of primary development of definite normative assurance and the relevant laws, having not yet made the particular provisions for the procedure, organization, operation rules, funding sources, and other critical issues of industrial mediation. Currently, except for the difference from the traditional people's mediation in terms of institution, industrial mediation is no different in other aspects. Its organizational funds are not assured either, mediators come and go frequently, and practitioners lack awareness.

5.2.3 Dilemmas Facing the Professionalization of Commercial Mediation

5.2.3.1 Delay of Legislation

Currently, the relevant laws have not yet stipulated any definite and systematic provisions for commercial mediation and the practice of commercial mediation is still lacking a direct legal base. Besides, as for the particulars of commercial mediation, academic circles have not yet reached a consistent view on them and the national law has not expressly defined them either. Therefore, judgment of whether one case of mediation is in the category of commercial mediation can only be made on the basis of whether the field involved is in the category of commercial disputes. Yet, such a judgment is simple and rough, resulting in frequent confusion and difficult discrimination of commercial mediation from other types of mediation. Therefore, the professionalization of commercial mediation is first faced with the normative dilemma of delayed legislation.

5.2.3.2 The Institutional Set-Up Lacks Regularity

Currently, China has various types of commercial mediation institutions and the institutions that can undertake commercial dispute mediation according to law include courts, commercial arbitration institutions, chambers of commerce, industrial mediation associations, and administrative organs (e.g., the administrative institutions mentioned in *The Trademark Law* and *The Patent Law*). Additionally, in practice, non-governmental non-enterprise units and other non-governmental commercial mediation institutions can also engage in commercial mediation. These institutions have different functions, powers, and provisions and the funding sources also differ, resulting in commercial mediators with different identities, thus, the mediation quality is also varied.

5.2.3.3 Lack of Public Credibility

China's prevailing commercial mediation institution is not recognized widely among the public, it is hard for public commercial mediation to step forward, and commercial mediation firms are still at the initial stages. Furthermore, due to a lack of market recognition, the particular operation of commercial mediation originally meant for market-based operations is in chaos. Besides, in commercial disputes, the parties prefer to firmly pursue their own interests and have relatively high requirements for profitability and efficiency. Furthermore, the parties in commercial disputes generally are relatively geographically distant from each other and cannot form a regional alliance and the application of the traditional face-to-face mediation method is obviously impossible. In a word, the complexity of commercial disputes increases the difficulty for mediators to mediate and the mediation success rate is relatively low, thus directly affecting the public credibility of commercial mediation.

5.3 Reasons for the Dilemma Facing the Professionalization of Mediation in China

5.3.1 Lack of Scientific Top-Level Design

Due to the complexity of modern social disputes and the rationalization of interpersonal relationships, the specialty of mediation becomes necessary, as it shows that it is necessary to set up certain access standards for mediators, to avoid the infinite expansion in their numbers and ensure the quality of the mediation. Therefore, the modernization of Chinese society needs to promote the professionalization of mediation, but currently the scientific top-level design and overall arrangement for the professionalization of mediation in China has not yet been developed. The various advantages of types of mediation are disregarded and different types of mediation act on their own and have their own systems, without uniform conduct norms and without uniform access standards, and the professional morality and professional spirit of mediation have not been properly cultivated. The social status and special authority of mediators have not been properly established.

5.3.2 Constraints of **The People's Mediation Law** *on the Professionalization of Mediation*

The promulgation of *The People's Mediation Law of the People's Republic of China* started a new stage in the Chinese diversified dispute resolution mechanism,[8] but the constraints of *The People's Mediation Law* on the professionalization of mediation have hindered the professionalization of mediation in China:

1 The mass character and autonomy of mediation organizations are corroded. The people's mediation institution in China is good because of its general character and autonomy. *The People's Mediation Law* provided that people's mediation organizations and people's mediators are now under the management of the judicial administrative departments. Thus, trade unions can set up a people's mediation committee, but if they are under the management of the judicial administrative departments, its organizational independence, autonomy and general character will be discounted, and the administrative tendency of mediation will be more serious, and it will be increasingly difficult for its professionalization to be achieved.
2 Lack of material assurance damages the actions of mediators. China's *People's Mediation Law* stipulated the provision of funds for people's mediation work, as can be considered as an advantage for people's mediation, assuring at the legal level the benefits of people's mediators. But Article 4 of *The People's Mediation Law* still continued to follow the tradition that people's mediation did not charge any fees, so the mediation work of the people's mediators is still obligatory work free of charge, and weakens the vitality of people's mediation. Lack of assurance of material benefit for mediators will naturally reduce the enthusiasm and actions of people's mediators in mediation work. Furthermore, the legal provision of no charge of fees will also naturally increase the reliance of people's mediation on the government funding and their independence is thus easily damaged.
3 To be a people's mediator, there is no particular specialization path. To follow a career as a people's mediator, the appointment qualification for this job is almost the same as the qualification of voters.[9] There is no quantitative standard and it focuses on the consideration of legal knowledge, but with folk disputes becoming complex, the special technical requirements for mediators must also be promoted accordingly. Therefore, if the requirement is set forth only for the legal attainments of people's mediators, the path for specialization is out of the question.

5.3.3 Industrial and Commercial Mediation Lack the Basis for Market-Based Operations

The basis for professionalization of industrial mediation and commercial mediation rests on the normative development of the mediation market.

However, there is only the brief range of the Chinese mediation institution on offer. Currently, China lacks the basis for market-based operation of mediation.[10]

First of all, in terms of charges, chargeable mediation will indicate the "beginning of the new era for mediation."[11] Whether a mediator is willing to or can remain in this career for a long period is closely related to whether he can obtain certain and even abundant financial rewards. Mediators will pursue their own interests, and if their interest demands are blindly ignored, only seeking their contribution spirit, the law of market economic development fails.. Traditional mediation charged no fees, and the public were used to enjoying such free public services. For them, it is acceptable to pay litigation fees to go to court, but usually they will not accept paying for mediation. Therefore, under the present system, it will take time for mediation to change from free to chargeable.

Second, the market structure of mediation needs to be perfected. Currently, the government dominates the supply of Chinese mediation resources and this fails to follow the market logic of equal rights and obligations.[12] Furthermore, Chinese public organizations, social groups, and individuals are weak, severely constraining the realization of the public and autonomous nature of mediation and hindering its market-based development. Besides, since there are good and bad mediators, the commodity of mediation on the market – a specialized mediation service – has not yet reached a state recognized by society.

Finally, the social credit system has not been established. Trust is the basis for concluding a mediation agreement. Currently, China's overall credit system has not been established or perfected, and this will definitely affect the professionalization of industrial mediation and commercial mediation. People lack good faith, the parties of mediation are mutually suspicious and jealous and are wary of mediators, and it is very hard to conduct mediation work. Moreover, due to the lack of trust and credit, even if an agreement is concluded, it is a mere scrap of paper and disputes are not thoroughly resolved, and it is impossible even to think about the professionalization prospect of mediation.

5.3.4 Lack of a Complementary Mechanism for Professionalization

Currently, China has neither established professional conduct norms for mediators, nor created a system for the uniform mediator qualification and certification. The subject of mediation is not part of the higher education curriculum, and only a few schools have set up a course in people's mediation,[13] in which the cultivation of talent is not prominent and direction is not definite. More importantly, mediator groups have not yet formed a common professional belief and professional sense of morality. During the course of professionalization, mediators often find that they are in the vortex of moral conflicts, and their professional view will often conflict with the public views as well as conflict with those of other legal professions.

5.4 Possible Ways to Solve the Dilemmas Facing the Professionalization of Mediation in China

Currently, socialism with Chinese characteristics has entered a new era and major social contradictions are also observed. The new era endowed mediation with a new mission and a new direction, and the mediator team and its capacity of dispute resolution must also adapt to the needs of the new era, so as to play their required role. *The People's Mediation Law* has been in force for more than eight years, but facing the new challenges of social contradictions in the new era and the new expectations of people for fairness and justice, it is noted that people's mediation still has many incompatible aspects. The special and professional level of the people's mediator team is not high, training is not systematic, and the ability to resolve contradictions and disputes needs to be promoted; the special and industrial people's mediator team building is advancing only slowly; funding for people's mediation is difficult to find and incentive mechanisms are imperfect; all this constrains the functioning of the people's mediation institution. Thus, on March 28, 2018, the first meeting of the Central Commission for Comprehensively Deepening the Reform reviewed and adopted *The Suggestions for Intensifying the Construction of People's Mediators Team*. Afterwards, the Political and Judiciary Commission under the CPC Central Committee, the Supreme People's Court, the Ministry of Justice, the Ministry of Civil Affairs, the Ministry of Finance, and the Ministry of Human Resources and Social Security jointly printed and distributed *The Suggestions for Intensifying the Construction of People's Mediators Team* (hereinafter referred to as *The Suggestions*), proposing to attempt to promote the quality of mediators, perfect the management institution, intensify the work assurance and strive to build a people's mediator team that is politically qualified, familiar with the services, enthusiastic about public welfare, fair and upright and neutral. One important concept is: "to insist on the full-time and part-time combination. While actively developing the part-time people's mediator team, energetically strengthen building the full-time people's mediator team, and constantly optimize the people's mediator team structure." It is important to promote the quality of people's mediation work, giving adequate play to the role of people's mediation as the first line of defense in maintaining social harmony and stability, advancing the construction of peace and legal governance in China, and realizing the modernization of the state governance system and governance capacity. The measures suggested in *The Suggestions* to advance the mediator team building include the following aspects.[14]

First, define the conditions for selection and appointment of people's mediators and increase the access to ways to become a people's mediator. The people's mediators should be adult citizens who are fair and upright, honest and autonomous, enthusiastic about people's medication work, and have a certain educational background, and have policy and legal knowledge. Members of people's mediation committees are appointed through elections, re-elected at the end of their term of office, with a second term allowed upon re-election. Lay stress on selecting and engaging people of noble character and high prestige as the grass-roots people's mediators and lay stress on selecting and engaging lawyers, notaries, arbitrators, local legal service workers, doctors, teachers, experts and scholars, and other social specialists and retired judges, procurators, policemen, judicial administrative officers and the retired personnel of the relevant industrial competent departments as people's mediators.

Second, strengthen professional training and management of people's mediators and promote the quality and capacity of the people's mediator team. In order to provide the disputing parties with quality mediation services, the judicial administrative department and the association of people's mediators should set up training courses, according to the features of local and industrial and special disputes, and emphatically undertake training in such aspects as social situations, legal policies, professional morality, special knowledge, and mediation techniques.

Third, propose to intensify the security of the work of people's mediators, and promote the work of the people's mediator team. According to the level of local economic and social development and financial position, the local village should support funding for people's mediation work and provide the working conditions, such as a place to work and facilities and the necessary funds for people's mediators to undertake the work. Through the government's purchase of services, advance the people's mediation work, implement a fair remuneration policy of people's mediators and strengthen the personal protection of people's mediators.

The foregoing *Suggestions* are meant to build the people's mediator team, but in the context of generalization of people's mediation. Generalization refers to China's legal documents, official policies, and academic discourses, which are all observed with serious "path dependence." This confuses, intentionally or unintentionally, the definitions of people's mediation, expanding infinitely the limits of people's mediation, including all such new mediation modes as industrial mediation, commercial mediation, and lawyer mediation under the discourse of people's mediation, while the original meaning of people's mediation is the general organization for dispute mediation set up under the village committee and resident committee, calling all new types of mediation organizations emerging in practice "people's mediation."

Such a generalization concept conceals the institutional characteristics of such diverse social mediation modes as commercial mediation, industrial mediation, and special mediation, resulting in unclear legal orientation of these non-official types of mediation and severely constraining the coordinated development of diverse mediation forms. This did not develop the professionalization road for mediation and was unfavorable to international exchange and cooperation in dispute resolution.[15] Because of this, the foregoing *Suggestions* have actually also covered the team building of commercial mediators and industrial mediators. *The Suggestions* provided enlightenment and opportunity to strengthen the professionalization of the Chinese mediator team, but the institutional arrangements are still required. In the long-term view, we should take the development road of differentiation and restore the original feature of people's mediation: on the one hand, insist on the "folk character" and "general character" of people's mediation, respect the common-sense operation of people's mediation, and keep the flexibility of people's mediation in such aspects as mediation mode, mediation method, and mediation procedure. In this regard, if "people's mediation" is defined in a narrow sense, *The People's Mediation Law* is obviously a waste of legislative resources, which was originally meant to endow the new mediation modes with legal status, and, as a result, not only failed to achieve the expected legislative purpose but, on the contrary, constrained the development of people's mediation and new mediation modes. If people's mediation is established on the basis of people's autonomy and self-management, self-education and self-service, it should be regarded as the endogenous institution or spontaneous order, without the need to regulate it in the legal institution. If the mediation procedure and mediation mode of people's mediation are stereotyped, they will, on the contrary, lose their vitality.[16] On the other hand, it is necessary to strengthen the professionalization, specialization, and marketization of industrial mediation, commercial mediation, lawyer mediation, and other new types of mediation, endow new mediation modes with a legal status, regulate the mediation procedure, intensify the institutional construction, and help all the mediation organizations to undertake the orderly arrangement of their mediation quality, so as to finally structure the diversified mediation system. In particular, with respect to the professionalization of new mediation modes, it is necessary to start with the following five aspects.

5.4.1 Perfect the Scientific System and Cultivate Professional Ethics

To advance the professional development of mediation in China, first of all, strengthen the state orientation and formulate a uniform mediation law or social mediation law applicable to different types of mediation conduct. This law should stipulate the general mediation norms, realizing the mature development of the third dispute resolution model other than litigation and arbitration. In the meantime, it is necessary to design the scientific mechanism system, define the access threshold, the appointment requirements, qualification certification, performance examinations, and professional ethics of a mediator and guide the healthy development of the professionalization of mediation. Most importantly, establish the mediator qualification certification or a practicing permit system, review the mediator qualification, training, and assessment and include only those who pass the mediator qualification standard as suitable to be on the list of names of mediators for the use of the parties in selecting a mediator.[17] Furthermore, innovate the mediation idea, refer to the development experiences of other legal professions, and lay stress on the cultivation of professional ethics and the morality of mediators.

Professional ethics and morality are the value criteria for mediators and are the moral responsibility and obligation to be undertaken by the industry to improve society. Professional ethics and morality are the foundation of mediators' work and are the inherent spiritual motives of mediators. Through rational control and balancing interests, the scientific complementary mechanism can make mediators dedicated, loyal, and enthusiastic and form, in practice, the professional conduct norms that are universally recognized.

5.4.2 Establish the Special Authority and Promote Professional Status

The professionalization of mediation is the result of specialization. Specialization emphasizes professional technology and knowledge and directly determines the professional status and special authority of mediators. Generally, the special cultivation of mediators involves two stages: one is the special education and the other is professional education. The former is the foundation of the latter and the latter is the extension of the former, while both are indispensable. On the one hand, the work objects of the mediators are the disputes in all kinds of fields, mediation has different special requirements for different types of disputes, and thus the mediation work requires the mediators to master the basic knowledge of law, know the principles of the people's mediation law well, and master the contents and institution of alternative dispute resolution as well as have knowledge of such aspects as commerce, psychology, sociology, and ethics, and possess good communication skills to face dispute resolution. On the other hand, the special education of mediators only helps the trainers to have the necessary theoretical accomplishment as a professional mediator. To achieve the professionalization in reality, the professional education should be undertaken. In our opinion, the professional training can be classified into pre-job training and on-the-job training. The pre-job training can be controlled by qualification certification. The uniform high-level national mediator qualification exam can be undertaken, like the national qualification exams for the legal profession, as a stepping stone to become a mediator. On-the-job training can be guided by people's courts, with the local judicial administrative organs taking the lead, in combination with the forces of grass-roots social organizations and groups, highlighting the special advantages of different schools of law, providing regular practice, probation, and training, and cultivating the mediator team that can apply the learned special knowledge in reality and stress the training of actual operating skills.

5.4.3 Highlight the Advantages of Industrial Mediation and Promote Professionalization with Industrialization

During the period of social transformation, different contradictions frequently occurred and showed a cross-regional development trend. Thus, the realistic need is to cope with the difficult problems of grass-roots social governance, in the period of deepening the reform, and show the advantages of industrial mediation, catalyze commercial mediation, and form a development mechanism for the professionalization of mediation with Chinese characteristics.

Modern society is a society with work divisions continually being classified and commodity exchange increasingly flourishing. An important breakthrough in advancing the professionalization of mediation in China would be to recognize the advantages of industrial mediation, attach importance to the influence of commercial mediation in commercial dispute resolution, break through the existing system of mediation types, and by spreading development, form the special advantages and professional characteristics of commercial mediation. To show the advantages of industrial and commercial mediation, the key point is to give priority to developing such types of social organizations as trade unions, science and technology organizations, chambers of commerce, public welfare and charity organizations, private non-enterprises units, and urban and rural community services, so that the social organizations and the public participate in governance in society, and social organizations undertake the task of building mediator teams so as to motivate adequately social subjects, form the two-way interaction model for the prevention and resolution of social contradictions jointly by the government and social organizations, and inject vitality into the professionalization of mediators.

5.4.4 Establish the Long-Term Mechanism and Strengthen the Management of Mediator Teams

In order to provide a good development space for mediators and increase their scope, initiative and creativity in the work of mediating in public disputes, it is especially required to establish the long-term management mechanism for mediator professionalization. The long-term management mechanism should include the test and assessment mechanism, the development mechanism, the exit mechanism, and the eliminating mechanism. Establishment of the test and assessing mechanism of mediators is the important basis for scientific decision-making. The system of relatively scientific and quantitative work examination and assessment standard can be formulated, according to the complexity of the public disputes, and the numbers of disputes. It is necessary to stipulate the uniform regulations and rules, set forth the definite requirements for duties, procedures, and discipline of mediators' work, establish the grading assessment institution,[18] and urge the mediators to positively undertake qualification development.

In the meantime, to stimulate the career vitality of mediators, it is necessary to carry out proper career development management. The mediator career development mainly depends on two aspects: one is the socialized professional qualification certification and maintenance mechanism. The particular measures are to structure the multilevel training network, formulate different types of training programs, and strive to promote the dispute resolution capacity of mediators by using experience exchange, on-the-spot observation, and remote visual teaching. The other is to select outstanding mediators for further refined and high-end development and realize the hierarchical training of basic talents and high-end talents of mediators, under the leadership of the judicial administrative organs and on the basis of comprehensive examination and assessing the special attainments of mediators. Finally, the exit mechanism of mediators should also be given adequate attention. According to the performance examination and assessment, some unsuitable or incompetent mediators can be eliminated. While implementing the optimal allocation of human resources, make sure to safeguard the legal rights of the eliminated mediators.

5.4.5 Strengthen Job Security and Stabilize the Personnel Structure

Currently, mediation has not yet formed an accepted independent professional group. Therefore, to advance the development of mediation professionalization, first of all, it is necessary to ensure mediators cannot be relieved of their duty and dismissed at random, ensure that they undertake the mediation work in an objective, independent, and just manner as well as ensure they have the relevant professional status and social honor. Second, whether a mediator is willing to stay in the industry on a long-term basis is closely related to whether he will receive the appropriate financial returns. Mismatch of expenditure and income will weaken the professional vitality of mediators. In the opinion of the author, in order to increase the benefits of mediators and ensure they have a good life-style and professional prospects, first of all, the local government and social groups jointly should support their funding. With the professional status of mediation being promoted, the reliance of mediators on government finance will gradually decline and eventually, a situation will be formed to safeguard the stable income of professional mediators through market selection and resource allocation. Finally, a mediator undertakes the work in a convincing and persuading mode, and his work objects are the different parties to disputes. Due to this feature, he will bear a bigger risk than other people, which includes personal safety as well as mental health. In this regard, it is necessary to attach importance to the personal safety and mental health of mediators and form a long-term, "normal," and "general" assurance institution and maintain the continuity and stability of the mediator group.

5.5 Remove the Misunderstanding about Chinese Mediator Professionalization: Between Professionalization and Socialization

In the process of advancing the professionalization of Chinese mediator teams, it is worth thinking sincerely about one question: whether the professionalization of mediators implies that all mediators should be versed in the law, or in other words, whether all mediators should have a legal professional background. Behind this question is actually a paradox between the professionalization and the socialization of mediators.

In Western countries, the ADR (alternative dispute resolution) movement was initially not promoted by lawyers, but such an autonomous movement in the field of dispute resolution was considered to be "threatening directly the monopoly position of legal professionals in the field of dispute resolution," Therefore, the ADR movement forced the practicing mode of lawyers to change, mediation became a new growth area in lawyers' legal affairs, and the mediation professionalization resulted from the mutual competition between lawyers and other non-legal careers in the mediation service market. In the United States, the lawyer mediation business expanded rapidly. In Germany, *The Legal Consultation Act* has stated that lawyers are the only professional group who are allowed to undertake mediation. The debate on legal professionalization and non-professionalization of mediation has been raging for a long time in Western society. Western legal circles claimed they were promoting the legitimacy of mediation by promoting the professional access standard of mediators, but the community mediation and non-judicial mediation, the non-legal profession were still the norm.[19] The American *Uniform Mediation Act* provided explicitly, "This act does not require mediators to have one special professional background or professional qualification."

Different from the mediation model of Western countries and the United States, that is led by lawyers, in China, most of the lawyers still limit their services to the traditional field of litigation, Chinese lawyers' traditional thought still remains resistant to mediation, and lawyers specializing in mediation are extremely rare. Chinese lawyers participate in mediation mainly on the request to participate in the mediation undertaken by the people's court, administrative organ and people's mediation organization, and the participation width, depth, and activeness of lawyers are somewhat limited and only the adequate play is given to their unique advantages in preventing and resolving contradictions and disputes. Therefore, the context of discussion on mediation professionalization in China is different from that in the Western countries. When Western society was debating the defects of mediation professionalization, China's mediation professionalization was just starting. Even so, the debate of the Western mediation professionalization movement is still of certain assistance to Chinese mediation professionalization. It at least reminded us in the professionalization of mediation, if only professional lawyers can undertake mediation, it will naturally result in the unitary judgment-oriented mediation, but in order to keep such natural advantages of mediation as flexibility and informality, it is necessary to mobilize more social forces for participation in mediation. On the one hand, we must recognize that mediation professionalization is the necessary requirement for coping with modern complex society. On the other hand, the mediator qualification and access institution needs to set a certain threshold for mediators to form the possibility of a professional monopoly. But we must see that just because

China is a huge country with inadequate and unequal development, with such factors mingled together as the east, central, west, urban and rural areas, types of disputes and demands of mediation will differ in thousands of ways. The types of mediation are also naturally different and the knowledge demands of mediators are also naturally different. If the mediator qualification access or practicing permit is affirmed by a uniform national standard, this may ease the demands of some specific fields for dispute resolution. In the realistic life in society, since mediation often has contextual characteristics, not only mediators with legal knowledge or a background in the legal profession can moderate mediation, but also some people of specific status can have the capability of dispute resolution even though they have no mediator qualification. In commercial disputes, only professional mediators with special knowledge and legal background can be competent. In community disputes, professional mediators do not necessarily have the advantage and in the remote and backward regions, professional mediators can hardly be found.

Therefore, we should not take the unitary thinking model to "deem the Chinese mediation practice as a uniform homogeneous entirety and consider mediation is the same in different regions of China as a kind of dispute resolution practice."[20] On the contrary, we must also pay close attention to the flexibility and diversity of mediation and cannot write off the vitality of the mediation institution with the unitary professional model. It is also because of this that the professional institution of mediators, first of all, does not imply the unitary legalization of a mediator qualification standard, but as long as they have basic legal knowledge, experts in all the trades and in walks of life can also become professional mediators. Second, the professionalization of mediators should not exclude the non-professional person from participating in dispute resolution, but lay stress on providing conduct guidance, assessment and regulation for mediation structure and mediators. From this point of view, *The Suggestions for Intensifying the Construction of People's Mediators Team* proposed "six ministries and commissions" (2018), that the team building of mediators should insist on the basic principle of "full-time and part-time combination" and "classified guidance," as complies with the dispute resolution law. In order to adapt the various features of contradictions and disputes, while strengthening the professionalization of the mediation team and optimizing the people's mediator team structure, it is necessary to promote the diversity of the people's mediator team, continuing to consolidate the community part-time people's mediator team, as it is the mainstay of the people's mediator team, as well as actively and energetically intensifying building the full-time people's mediator team in the industrial and special fields. For instance, in 2018, the All-China Federation of Industry and Commerce and Ministry of Justice jointly promulgated *The Suggestions for Advancing the People's Mediation Work of Chambers of Commerce*, indicating that the members of the chamber of commerce should become the new growth area for the people's mediator team building. It is worth noting that in September 2017, the Supreme People's Court and Ministry of Justice printed and distributed *The Suggestions for Undertaking the Pilot Work of Lawyer Mediation*, making the arrangements for undertaking the pilot work of lawyer mediation in a dozen provinces. Under the Chinese and Western different institutional contexts, lawyers became the mainstay of the Chinese professional mediator team and one should observe further whether Chinese lawyer mediation can become a new field of lawyer career, as happened in Western society and especially the United States.

Notes

1 Wang Fuhua: Dimensions for Transformation of Chinese Mediation System, *Legal Forum*, 2010 (6).
2 In China, court mediation and administrative mediation exercise the duties of mediation through the public power, and their mediation conduct is substantially the application of judgment rights and administration rights, and the mediators under the models of court mediation and administrative mediation are in the category of part-time workers. Yet, people's mediation, industrial mediation, and commercial mediation are the mediation institution with typical autonomous characteristics and it is feasible to talk about the professionalization of mediators under the existing pattern.
3 See Daniel Bowling and David Hoffman, Bringing Peace into the Room: The Personal Qualities of the Mediator and Their Impact on the Mediation, *Negotiation Journal*, 2000 (6).
4 Para. 2, Article 14 of *The People's Mediation Law* provided: "the judicial administrative departments at the level of county people's government should conduct the professional training of the people's mediators."
5 Fu Yulin: *Research on Rural Grass-roots Legal Service* (Beijing: China University of Political Science and Law Press, 2006), pp. 108–111.
6 Li Yuhua and Yang Junsheng: On Professionalization of People's Mediators, *Justice of China*, 2006 (6).
7 Zhang Xiaoru and Zhang Meijuan: Dilemma and Way Out of Industrial Mediation, *Arbitration of Beijing*, 2015 (2).
8 Ruan Jingchi: Appraisal and Perfection of People's Dispute Resolution Mechanism—Comments on the People's Mediation Law of the People's Republic of China, *People's Forum*, 2013 (35).
9 Para. 1, Article 14 of *The People's Mediation Law* provides: "people's mediators shall be the adult citizens who are fair and upright, enthusiastic about people's medication work and have a certain educational background, policy level and legal knowledge."
10 The marketization of mediation indicates the mediation resources and mediation institutions gradually participate in the market flow, introduce the competitive mechanism and provide chargeable services for society.
11 Zhou Jianhua: French Mediation: Comparison and Reference, *Study & Exploration*, 2012 (1).
12 Zhou Jianhua: On the Market-based Operation of Mediation, *Lanzhou Academic Journal*, 2016 (4).

13 In 2012, Shanghai University of Political Science and Law took the lead in opening the undergraduate major of law (oriented for people's mediation); in 2013 Xiangtan University tried for the first time the innovation of the mediation experimental program.

14 Liao Yongan: Strengthen People's Mediator Team Building and Reproduce New Glories of People's Mediation, *Legal Evening News*, April 6, 2018.

15 Regarding the criticism of this issue, see Liao Yongan and Wang Chong: Self-Examination on Generalization Phenomenon of People's Mediation and Remolding of Social Mediation System, *Law and Economy*, 2019 (5).

16 Liu Zhisong: *Authority Rule Model: Casual Discussion on Disputes and Dispute Resolution* (Xiamen: University Press, 2013), p. 165.

17 Wang Fuhua: Dimensions for Transformation of Chinese Mediation System, *Legal Forum*, 2010 (6).

18 For grading, reference can be made to the professional grading for judges and procurators to structure the echelon of special-class mediator, first-class mediator, second-class mediator, and third-class mediator and form a complete professional group of mediators.

19 Fan Yu, Shi Changqing, and Qiu Xingmei: *Mediation Institution and Mediator Conduct Norms: Comparison and Reference*)Beijing: Tsinghua University Press, 2010), pp. 97–100.

20 Xiong Hao: On the Transformation of Chinese Mediation Law Regulation Model, *Studies in Law and Business*, 2018 (3).

References

Bowling, Daniel and David Hoffman, Bringing Peace into the Room: The Personal Qualities of the Mediator and Their Impact on the Mediation, *Negotiation Journal*, 2000 (6): 5–28.

Fan Yu, Shi Changqing, and Qiu Xingmei: *Mediation Institution and Mediator Conduct Norms: Comparison and Reference*, Beijing: Tsinghua University Press, 2010.

Fu Yulin: *Research on Rural Grass-roots Legal Service*, Beijing: China University of Political Science and Law Press, 2006.

Li Yuhua and Yang Junsheng: On Professionalization of People's Mediators, *Justice of China*, 2006 (6): 67–69.

Liao Yongan and Wang Chong: Self-examination on Generalization Phenomenon of People's Mediation and Remolding of Social Mediation System, *Law and Economy*, 2019 (5): 67–80.

Liao Yongan: Strengthen People's Mediator Team Building and Reproduce New Glories of People's Mediation, *Legal Evening News*, April 6, 2018.

Liu Zhisong: *Authority Rule Model: Casual Discussion on Disputes and Dispute Resolution*, Xiamen: University Press, 2013.

Ruan Jingchi: Appraisal and Perfection of People's Dispute Resolution Mechanism: Comments on the People's Mediation Law of the People's Republic of China, *People's Forum*, 2013 (35): 59–61.

Wang Fuhua: Dimensions for Transformation of Chinese Mediation System, *Legal Forum*, 2010 (6): 31–37.

Xiong Hao: On Transformation of Chinese Mediation Law Regulation Model, *Studies in Law and Business*, 2018 (3): 115–125.

Zhang Xiaoru and Zhang Meijuan: Dilemma and Way Out of Industrial Mediation, *Arbitration of Beijing*, 2015 (2): 113–126.

Zhou Jianhua: French Mediation: Comparison and Reference, *Study & Exploration*, 2012 (1): 93–97.

Zhou Jianhua: On the Market-based Operation of Mediation, *Lanzhou Academic Journal*, 2016 (4): 132–138.

6 Practical Exploration of the Mediation Procedural Prerequisite in China

Since the reform and opening-up, Chinese society has been experiencing a sharp and profound transformation, showing an extremely complex intersection of benefits and defects in society, with social progress and social costs both displayed, including social coordination and social inequality, bringing feelings of being filled with hope and being full of pain.[1] The profound reform of the economic system and continual disturbance of interest patterns imitated the changes in social relations and values, thus causing people to choose lifestyles moving from unitary systems to diversity. Consequently, the contradictions and conflicts between people also suffered an explosive growth and in order to prevent contradictions from exceeding the limit of what society could bear, to limit and prevent bad events, the social control mechanism has also been continually intensified. Taking the long-term view, based on individuals and society inducing the conflicts, the numbers of contradictions will still tend to rapidly increase and the extent of these contradictions will be fierce.[2] However, the strength of the social control mechanism cannot be infinitely intensified, nor can the social resources infinitely favor the social control mechanism. Therefore, we must allocate rationally and make efficient use of the available social control resources and especially the dispute resolution resources. Thus, the dispute resolution value of mediation was tapped again. On June 28, 2016, the Supreme People's Court promulgated *The Suggestions for People's Courts to Deepen Further the Reform of Diversified Dispute Resolution Mechanism* (hereinafter referred to as *The Suggestions for the Reform of Diversified Dispute Resolution Mechanism*), officially proposing to explore the establishment of the mediation procedural prerequisite and defining a number of pilot courts nationwide to undertake the exploration to reform the diversified dispute resolution mechanism. At the level of the state, the mediation procedural prerequisite reallocates dispute resolution resources and is an important move to advance the modernization of the state governance system and its governance capacity. At the level of the judicature, the mediation procedural prerequisite is an important trial for courts to introduce the social resources to resolve disputes and relax the situation of "more cases but fewer personnel." At the level of individuals, the mediation procedural

DOI: 10.4324/9781003385882-6

prerequisite is an important approach to reduce dispute resolution costs and offer more access to justice.

However, up to now, due to the rough legislation, diverse theories, various practices, and the unique form of development of the two-way promotion of "bottom-up + top-down" justice in China's judicial reform,[3] the operation of the mediation procedural prerequisite still faces a series of problems: (1) it is not clearly defined, and further discussion is required on how to define the mediation procedural prerequisite and how it is connected with and distinguished from such concepts as mediation-first, mandatory mediation, and mediation-in-advance. (2) The theoretical base is weak and its scope of application is not comprehensive. As is well known, Article 27 of *The Suggestions for the Reform of Diversified Dispute Resolution Mechanism* stipulated the primary provisions of the scope of application of the mediation procedural prerequisite, but certain issues have not yet been defined, such as whether types of disputes without a definition in law and regulations are also suitable for the mediation procedural prerequisite and what the judgment standard is. (3) The procedure is not unified and the mechanism is not perfect. Regarding how to activate the mediation procedural prerequisite, how to mediate upon activation, and what to do when mediation succeeds or fails, currently, on these points, different pilot courts all have their own different practices, according to their own characteristics. This is good as it provides various references for refining legislation, but it is also raising the worrying possibility of damaging the unity of the procedure. Furthermore, the pilot courts attached inadequate importance to the complementary measures for the mediation procedural prerequisite, resulting in an imperfect relevant mechanism. In order to fundamentally resolve the aforementioned problems, we will seek to establish and perfect the mediation procedural prerequisite with the basic principle of civil procedures and the general law of institutions structured as the coordinator, and with the summary of innovative practices and law in judicial practices as the reference. After all, one of the important tasks for theoretical study is to provide rational guidance for practice, while with respect to the mediation institution, the "technical worker," who is unknown to the public may be more "reliable" than the fastidious but incompetent "designer."[4] Maybe it is a dose of good medicine to explore and establish the mediation procedural prerequisite, to promote it from the analysis of individual cases to type-oriented study and then to the abstraction of a set of universal rules.

6.1 The Basic Theory of the Mediation Procedural Prerequisite

6.1.1 Definition of Mediation Procedural Prerequisite

Since the mediation procedural prerequisite has not yet been defined, at the crossroads of history and reality, theory, and practice, we define it as "the institution for the court to assign to mediation, under the dual action of the consensus induction mechanism and mandatory activation, specific types of disputes that have not been filed to the corresponding specially invited mediator or specially invited mediation organization." In particular, it means that after the parties submit a civil dispute to the grass-roots people's court, the judge finds the dispute is the type of dispute suitable for resolution through mediation, and first advises, through the consensus induction mechanism, the parties to resolve the dispute through mediation, and only in the event that the parties refuse without giving any proper reason, will the judge activate mandatory mediation, assigning the dispute to the relevant special mediator or special mediation organization for mediation. Where the mediation succeeds, the parties may apply for withdrawal of the lawsuit or judicial confirmation, or may ask the people's court to issue the mediation statement upon filing the case. Where the mediation fails, the parties can ask the court to directly transfer the dispute to the procedure of case filing so as to resolve the problem through litigation. It is defined in this way, mainly based on the following reasons.

6.1.1.1 Historical Factor

Generally, the development of modern mediation has basically followed the path of "importance recovery – mediation-in-advance – mediation prerequisite." In 2004, the Supreme People's Court promulgated the relevant judicial interpretations, proposing the slogan of "mediate as possible, judge as possible and combine the mediation and judgment,"[5] and actively guided the litigation-mediation matchmaking by establishing the judicial conformation institution.[6] During this period, mediation recovered the importance it had lost, and people's mediators and people's mediation organizations rapidly developed and started to explore the approach for benign interaction with the judicature. In 2009, the Supreme People's Court promulgated *The Suggestions for Establishing and Perfecting the Resolution Mechanism of Contradictions and Disputes with the Linkage of Litigation and Non-litigation*, providing the legal basis for mediation to be assigned before case filing. In order to relax the pressure on courts of handling so many cases as well as to provide the legal basis for pre-litigation mediation institution, *The Civil Procedure Law*, as amended in 2012, officially established the mediation-in-advance institution on the basis of summarizing the practical experience.[7] However, afterwards, since the case filing registration system was established and new mediation institutions emerged, such as assigned mediation, trusted mediation, and special mediation,[8] the original mediation-in-advance failed to adequately adapt to the needs of judicial practice and it became necessary to explore the establishment of the mediation procedural prerequisite. Obviously, mediation-in-advance originated in the summary of the previous pre-litigation experiences, while the mediation procedural prerequisite carried on and developed the mediation-in-advance institution. Therefore, the mediation procedural prerequisite and the mediation-in-advance institution were observed to be similar in terms of definition and both should be in the category of alternative dispute resolution (ADR) systems, before case filing and for cases of specific types.

6.1.1.2 Realistic Factor

Different mediation subjects may affect the nature of the mediation agreements concluded through the mediation procedural prerequisite.[9] The mediation procedural prerequisite is closely connected to the judicature, but essentially is in the category of ADR. Civil disputes before the case is filed are outwith the jurisdiction of the courts. In light of the principle of judicial objectivity, such judicial personnel as judges and judge assistants cannot intervene actively in such disputes. As the case filing registration system was implemented and the quota system of judges was reformed, the situation of more cases but fewer personnel became more prominent and the courts could hardly handle the burden of so many cases. However, with society constantly developing, people's mediation organizations, administrative mediation organizations, industrial mediation organizations, and commercial mediation organizations are becoming increasingly specialized and regularized, and all play an irreplaceable role in handling the disputes in their respective fields. Especially the mediators or organizations who work in courts, they are selected and trained by people's courts and accept the assignment of the court to participate in special mediation and be included on the list of names of special mediators or special organizations. They have gained a lot of special experiences and possess a rather high professional level. And the civil disputes suitable for the mediation procedural prerequisite are generally relatively simple disputes with relatively small target amounts, and thus the special mediators or special mediation organizations are very competent at handling such affairs.

6.1.1.3 Cost Factor

On the one hand, due to the sharp increase in cases accepted by the courts and the phenomenon of the reduced number of judges and personnel under the influence of the "quota system" reform, delay in litigation greatly increased and thus the justice desired by the parties was often "delayed justice." On the other hand, since many people's understanding of modern mediation still remained shallow, viewing mediation as "mixing water into mud," making the entitled people suffer losses and making the obligatory people benefit,[10] people were unwilling to participate positively in mediation. Due to the limited understanding of the voluntary principle of mediation, different types of mediation organizations and judicial organs were also limited to the "restriction" of the literal meaning of "voluntary" and, thus, mediators often wasted their efforts in advising the parties to agree with mediation rather than in performing the substantial medication process, leading to the strange phenomenon of "advising one hour, but mediating five minutes." In the meantime, as the relevant studies indicate, the success rate of mediation performed in a mandatory mode was no lower than the success rate of mediation performed according to the voluntary choice of the parties,[11] but without consideration of protecting the interests of the parties or based on the preferential choice of the parties, the mandatory institution in the field of civil affairs may be only a kind of basic tactic to maintain the operation of one institution without other, better incentive mechanisms.[12] Therefore, prior to the mandatory activation of the mediation procedure, it is essential to encourage the parties, by establishing and perfecting the consensus induction mechanism, to choose voluntarily to resolve disputes through mediation, so as to reduce the manpower cost of courts as well as reduce the time and economic costs of the parties and also make disputes properly resolved and have consensus positively performed.

6.1.1.4 Assurance of Their Right

As a basic human right, the parties cannot be deprived of their claim for judgment, but this can be rationally restricted for proper and necessary reasons. Based on the principle of procedural matching, the procedure should be designed to adapt to such factors as the nature of the case handled, the size of the disputes, or the importance and complexity of the dispute matters.[13] Especially where there are limited judicial resources, the beneficial result of procedure should not be ignored.[14] By establishing and perfecting the mediation procedural prerequisite, it is possible to reduce costs as well as provide the parties with a benefit not inferior to that obtainable only through litigation. Even with respect to the specific types of disputes, in most circumstances, it is also possible to provide the parties with a benefits superior to that obtainable only through litigation. It is worth emphasizing that such "justice" naturally included in such benefits is not "secondary justice," but like litigation, the rights of the parties are protected, and disputes are resolved under the moderation of a neutral third party. Furthermore, when the mediation fails, the mediation procedural prerequisite will not prevent the parties from properly exercising their litigation right and will not exclude the assurance for the claims of the parties, but, on the contrary, through the linking mechanism between the mediator or mediation organization and the court, filing the case can be completed, as is convenient for the parties to exercise their litigation rights.

6.1.2 Differentiation and Analysis of the Mediation Procedural Prerequisite and Relevant Concepts

The mediation procedural prerequisite has all kinds of connections with such concepts as mediation-in-advance, mandatory mediation, or pre-litigation mediation. Studies on the mediation procedural prerequisite investigate such mediation modes as mediation-in-advance and mandatory mediation and, consequently, as a new concept, the mediation procedural prerequisite is often confused with the other concepts, leading to chaos in terms of legislation, theory, and practice. But since there is actually an essential difference between the foregoing concepts, it is necessary to differentiate them and analyze them carefully so as to expressly manifest the legal principle and guide practice.

6.1.2.1 Mediation Procedural Prerequisite and Mediation-in-Advance

As discussed above, the mediation procedural prerequisite carried on and developed mediation-in-advance and both play a role before the disputes enter litigation, but in terms of mediation subjects and activation mode, the two observe significant differences. As for the mediation subjects, there is actually a debate regarding the subjects of mediation-in-advance in theory and practice,[15] but the mainstream viewpoint or practice view is that the subjects of mediation-in-advance include judges or judicial assistants as well as people's mediators, while the subjects of mediation procedural prerequisite are special mediators or special mediation organization. According to the provision of Article 1 of *The Provisions of the Supreme People's Court on Special Mediation of People's Court*, special mediators or special mediation organizations should be selected from the list of mediation organizations or individuals engaged in people's mediation, administrative mediation, commercial mediation, and industrial mediation. Obviously, the subjects of mediation procedural prerequisite are the social organizations or individuals, but do not include the judicial organs or judicial personnel. As for the mode, the performance of mediation-in-advance is based on the consensus of the parties, while the mode of mediation procedural prerequisite has two sides: one is to induce, by stating clearly the advantages and disadvantages and reducing costs, encouraging the parties to choose the mediation procedural prerequisite; the other works in a mandatory way for specific types of disputes in the event of meeting certain conditions, without the consensus of the parties.

6.1.2.2 The Mediation Procedural Prerequisite and Mandatory Mediation

In terms of activation, the mediation procedural prerequisite has changed the previous situation a, previously, mediation could not be activated if the parties were not willing, so some viewed mediation procedural prerequisite as a reflection of civil mandatory mediation.[16] Actually, due to differences over time, civil mandatory mediation is classified as pre-litigation mandatory mediation and mid-litigation mandatory mediation. Currently, Chinese law has not made any relevant provisions for the pre-litigation mandatory mediation, and the typical representative of the mid-litigation mandatory mediation is Article 14 of *The Provisions of the Supreme People's Court for Application of Summary Procedure in Trial of Civil Cases*. For the specific types of disputes applicable to the summary procedure, the people's court will mediate, first, prior to a court trial. On the contrary, the mediation procedural prerequisite is performed before case filing and it is in the category of pre-ligation mediation.

Besides, on the one hand, the activation of the mediation procedural prerequisite includes particularly three types: (1) voluntary choice of the parties; (2) choice of the parties under the guidance of the induction mechanism; and (3) mandatory activation, but the mandatory activation referred to in mandatory mediation is one of the activation modes in the mediation procedural prerequisite and is not the best choice for the mediation procedural prerequisite. On the other hand, the mediation subjects of the two are also different. As mentioned above, mandatory mediation includes pre-litigation and mid-litigation mandatory mediation. Accordingly, its mediation subjects include people's mediators or people's mediation organizations and other individuals or social organizations as well as judicial personnel or judicial organs, but the mediation subjects of mediation procedural prerequisite can only be special mediators or special mediation organizations.

6.1.2.3 Mediation Procedural Prerequisite and Non-Proceeding Mediation

Non-proceeding mediation is a relatively broad concept in China, including mainly people's mediation, administrative mediation, and arbitration mediation,[17] and to some extent, the mediation procedural prerequisite is also in the category of non-proceeding mediation in a narrow sense. Obviously, the two have various points in common in terms of subject and effect of mediation agreements, but, importantly, the mediation procedural prerequisite has a closer connection with judicial organs compared with non-proceeding mediation. First, a certain number of the disputes handled by the mediation procedural prerequisite is assigned by the courts, while almost all the disputes handled by non-proceeding mediation come from the voluntary choice of the parties. Second, in the mediation procedural prerequisite, the special mediators or organizations in charge of mediation are generally registered and listed by courts for management and training, while in non-proceeding mediation, the mediators are usually selected and engaged by different mediation organizations, and are under the management of the organization or judicial administrative organ. Finally, in the case of failing to conclude a mediation agreement through the mediation procedural prerequisite, the parties can continue to resolve the dispute through litigation after the case is filed by the court through the procedural link, but in the case of failing to resolve a dispute through non-proceeding mediation, the parties can generally submit a lawsuit to court by themselves.

6.1.3 Attributes of the Mediation Procedural Prerequisite

As a new dispute resolution procedure, the mediation procedural prerequisite is relatively independent from litigation procedure, but also is essentially different from the people's mediation in a traditional sense. Its aim is to establish the long-term mechanism of judicial guidance and control over social resources when entering the field of dispute resolution and it is currently an important reflection of the courts' initiative as a guiding role and realized the courts' effective regulation and control over other dispute resolution modes during the great development of folk mediation. By differentiating and analyzing the relevant concepts, we can discover mediation procedural prerequisite has a unique orientation and value because it has such special attributes as subjective specialty, double activation, limitations of scope, and judicial relevance.

6.1.3.1 Subjective Specialty

According to the provision of Article 27 of *The Suggestions for the Reform of Diversified Dispute Resolution Mechanism*, the mediation procedural prerequisite should take special mediation organizations or special mediators as the subjects. With reference to the provision of Article 1 of *The Provisions of the Supreme People's Court on Special Mediation of People's Court*, special mediation organizations or special mediators are formed by qualified people's mediation, administrative mediation, commercial mediation, industrial mediation, and some other mediation organizations or individuals, as trained by people's courts. In particular, people's mediation, administrative mediation, commercial mediation, industrial mediation, and other organizations with the mediation function established according to law can apply to courts for their names to be put on the list of special mediation organizations. People's courts can also actively invite the qualified mediation organizations to join the list of special mediation organization and invite the NPC deputies, CPPCC members, people's jurors, experts and scholars, lawyers, arbitrators, retired law workers, and other qualified individuals to put their name on the list of special mediators. On the surface, the source of special mediation organizations or special mediators is relatively complex, but actually a professional community is gradually being formed. First, before becoming the special mediation organizations or special mediators, the relevant organizations or individuals must also be selected and trained by people's courts. Upon becoming the special mediation organizations or special mediators, the name of the organizations or individuals will be included in the list for the uniform management of the court and the list will be provided for the parties to choose from. Third, no matter whether a special mediation organization or special mediator is found at the court, the place of its mediation is usually at the mediation office set up within the court. With the same selection and training procedure and the same working environment, special mediation organizations or special mediators gradually have different features from other dispute resolution subjects: different from the common folk mediation organizations or mediators, their professional capacity is stronger and their dispute resolution level is higher and they have more special knowledge in certain fields. Also different from judges or judicial assistants, their essential attribute is not in the category of judicial personnel, but is an organic part of the folk dispute resolution forces. Therefore, when we talk about the mediation subjects of mediation procedural prerequisite, we refer in particular to the special mediation organizations or special mediators on the court's list rather than other people.

6.1.3.2 Double Activation

It is usually considered that one of the most important basic principles of mediation is the voluntary principle, i.e., in the procedural sense, application of mediation to resolve disputes is subject to the prior agreement of the parties or conclusion of consensus, and in a substantial sense, whether a mediation agreement is finally concluded and what mediation agreement is concluded will all, on the premise of not violating the mandatory provisions of law and regulations, respect the choice and will of the parties. However, as the particular mediation procedure, mediation procedural prerequisite will still substantially follow the voluntary principle, but in the procedural sense, it has two activation modes: (1) voluntary activation; and (2) mandatory activation. Furthermore, the so-called voluntary activation no longer relies purely on the prior agreement of the parties or their consensus, but can rationally guide the choice of the parties with the leverage of dispute resolution costs or by specifying the positives and negatives, by establishing the consensus induction mechanism. It is significantly different from the activation mechanism of litigation. In the civil procedure, when one party brings a lawsuit to court, no matter whether the other party agrees or not, it will be "forced" to be involved in the procedure of dispute resolution. Even if it tries in vain to resist by non-appearance, the court still has the "default judgment" as a trump card. All in all, mediation procedural prerequisite takes the voluntary activation as the primary mode and mandatory activation as the supplementary mode. Different from the activation mechanism for mediation moderated by other folk mediation organizations and civil procedure, it takes into consideration the procedural option of the parties as well as ensuring the efficiency of mediation, showing a unique modality.

6.1.3.3 Limitations of Scope

Just as the supply capacity of judicial institution is limited by various factors such as the judicial system and its mission, the nature and structure of disputes and the complexity of the dispute,[18] as one of the mediation institutions, the mediation procedural prerequisite is also limited by the foregoing factors and is limited in its actions, which, particularly in the micro field, refer to the issue of the applicable scope of the mediation procedural prerequisite. The study of this issue should be undertaken with reference to the supply capacity of judicial institutions. In recent years, with the development of the judicial reform, the supply capacity of judicial institution has steadily been promoted and in terms of lawsuit submission and the acceptance principle, the courts have basically realized that each appeal is guaranteed access to the court, and they have established the identification and distribution mechanism, ensuring that disputes to be tried are resolved by courts and disputes not suitable for judgment are resolved by other channels. In the meantime, since people's demand for justice through the judicature is urgent and the lack of judicial institutions is glaring, as the courts can hand over the disputes not suitable for judgment to other channels for resolution, it has become a sincere consideration of the court to distribute also the disputes suitable for judgment but more suitable for resolution in other modes. Therefore, the scope of application of the mediation procedural prerequisite should mainly cover those cases to be resolved more suitably through mediation than through litigation. Due to the actual dual nature of the mediation procedural prerequisite and its informality, compared with the litigation process, its scope of application must be defined more prudently. In particular, it should comply with the following conditions: (1) the two parties are specific and particular; (2) disputes are substantial and less intensive; (3) the litigation target value and specialty are relatively low; and (4) the parties are seeking an informal approach to resolve the dispute.

6.1.3.4 Judicial Relevance

Before talking about the judicial relevance of the mediation procedural prerequisite, it is first of all necessary to define its non-judicial nature. Compared with other folk mediation, there is a closer relation between the mediation procedural prerequisite and judicial procedure. In view of the subjects, no matter whether it is an initiative request or an invitation by the court, special mediation organizations or special mediators will all eventually go through the selection and training of the court and, upon being enlisted, their routine work will also be under the management and supervision of the court. This is very different from other folk mediation organizations and individuals mainly following self-management and self-supervision. In view of the sources of disputes, in the cases handled by the mediation procedural prerequisite, usually after the parties refer a dispute to the court, because the dispute is more suitable for resolution through mediation, the court will assign the case. Compared with the disputes of other folk mediation organizations or individuals, which are mainly sourced from the voluntary choice of the parties, its reliance on the court is even higher. In view of the activation mode, except for voluntary activation, the mediation procedural prerequisite can still be activated in a mandatory mode in some circumstances, because of its relatively high special technique as well as being the result of mixing with the judicial authority to some extent. In view of the linkage procedure, when mediation fails, the special mediation organization or special mediator can return, through the internal approach, the disputes to the tribunal of case filing and get back on track for litigation, without the necessity for the parties to resubmit the lawsuit. When mediation succeeds, according to the needs of the parties, a more convenient channel is available for judicial confirmation or requesting a mediation statement, but it will not do so without the close connection of the mediation procedural prerequisite with the judicature. All in all, in all the aspects of shaping the mediation procedural prerequisite, the judicature plays a role and there is a close relationship between the mediation procedural prerequisite and the judicature.

6.2 Operation of the Mediation Procedural Prerequisite

6.2.1 Subjects of the Mediation Procedural Prerequisite

The mediation procedural prerequisite carries on and develops the mediation as the first resort. The Supreme People's Court has officially proposed the establishment of the mediation procedural prerequisite and stipulated it is provided through judicial interpretations. But due to the inertia of judicial operations, all the pilot courts still continued, to some extent, to follow some of the practices in mediation-in-advance, e.g., forming the three-subject model of the present mediation procedural prerequisite by improving the main theoretical viewpoints of mediation-in-advance: judicial subject theory,[19] folk subject theory,[20] and mixed subject theory.[21]

The first type can be called the judicial personnel mediation model. By optimizing the organizational structure and changing the internal work division, courts adopting the judicial personnel mediation model integrated some of the judges of the civil tribunal, the judges of the case filing tribunal, and judicial assistants into the litigation service center or litigation-mediation matchmaking center to specially take charge of handling the disputes brought by parties to the court, but not yet filed and suitable for resolution through mediation. The case-handling pressure of these courts is generally not especially high and they still have spare capacity to share some of the judges and judicial assistants to help in mediation. Accordingly, these courts have not established the list of names of special mediation organizations or special mediators and are in a position of causing relative delay in the process of diversified dispute resolution mechanism reform.[22] At the same time, it must be pointed out that the foregoing circumstance opens discussion on the mediation procedural prerequisite, because it complies with such time limits for mediating prior to the case filing of the court, but in terms of mediation subjects, it should be included in the category of court mediation.

The second type can be called the folk mediator mediation model. Generally, the courts adopting this model are in the eastern part or southern coastal region of China with a developed economy, with a huge number of cases accepted annually but with limited staff. With Shenzhen Futian District Court as an example, in 2016, it received 66,150 cases but only had a quota of 108 judges, with an average annual treatment of 487.6 cases of disputes per person.[23] As there are only about 250 working days generally in a year, it means that each person had to handle nearly two disputes each day, and this is impossible. To be precise, the courts in these regions also have unique advantages. With civic society expanding and social dispute resolution organizations developing, people's understanding of dispute resolution is further deepened and the folk dispute resolution organizations also have the capacity to provide dispute resolution resources for the whole of society. Therefore, accordingly, it is a matter of these courts, without a lot of effort, introducing folk dispute resolution forces in order to hand over for mediation the disputes brought by the parties to the courts, to the special mediation organization and special mediator. In particular, they can set up a litigation service center or litigation-mediation matchmaking center under the tribunal of case filing, which will establish a list of names of special mediation organizations and special mediators for the parties to choose from. Upon selection by the parties, the personnel of the center will contact the selected special mediation organization or special mediator to define the time and place of mediation. But the actual condition differs from such an institutional set-up, because many of the parties want to approach the court and choose a specific special mediation organization or special mediator and also like to know the background and special knowledge of the special mediation organization or special mediator. Therefore, there is mostly a risk of replacing "the choice of the parties" with the "court designation," and there is also the circumstance that some of the mediators in charge of mediation are not included in the list of names, while most of the listed special mediation organizations or special mediators only handle symbolically two or five cases annually.

The third type can be called the mixed model. Courts adopting this model currently shared the most, mainly selecting a number of people's mediators from different folk mediation organizations to work jointly with the judicial personnel in the mediation office that is set up at the courts. They are responsible enough to mediate in the civil disputes transferred from the tribunal of case filing or the litigation service center. These courts have adopted this mode because of lack of staff, on the one hand, and distrust of the professional level of people's mediators, on the other, thus selecting the compromise of the judicial personnel cooperating with people's mediators in jointly handling civil disputes. The typical representative is Dongguan No. 2 People's Court, which was the first nationally to undertake the pilot reform of the diversified dispute resolution mechanism. Through a field survey, we discovered that the court set up the litigation-mediation center within the tribunal of case filing, where the mediators included the people's mediators assigned to the court by the Bureau of Justice, as well as judge assistants on the court staff, showing a style of mixed subjects. Also, as the reform of diversified dispute resolution mechanism is continually being developed, these courts have also established the list of names of special mediation organizations and special mediators, but the personnel playing the main role of mediation are still the people's mediators originally working at the courts and some of the judicial personnel. However, unfortunately, these mainstay mediators are not included in the list of names.

6.2.2 Activation of the Mediation Procedural Prerequisite

In the early period of exploring the establishment of the diversified dispute resolution mechanism, all the pilot courts basically followed the voluntary principle of the parties to activate the mediation procedural prerequisite, but the fact that all mediation cases have to be activated upon consensus of the parties increased, without doubt, the difficulty for mediation activation and pushed up the cost of courts and the parties to resolve disputes. Thus, in terms of resolving the difficulty for mediation activation, all the pilot courts undertook further exploration, showing three different development stages but the simultaneous co-existence in the current judicial practice.

The first stage is to still stick with the traditional voluntary principle of the parties. Except for the types of disputes that should be mediated first, as provided by law, the courts adopting this principle will activate the mediation procedural prerequisite only when the two parties make a prior agreement or agree to choose the dispute resolution through mediation, and will file the case, if the parties fail to reach a prior agreement or a consensus. The court will resolve the dispute through immediate judgment proceedings, the summary procedure, special procedure, or ordinary procedure, according to the conditions of the case. This practice is adopted because the relevant courts considered that free will is the basic principle of mediation that cannot be violated and the mediation agreement concluded in the mode of voluntary mediation can be more easily performed by the parties.

The second stage refers to sticking to the voluntary principle of the parties as well as introducing the consensus induction mechanism. This practice gives up the strict voluntary principle of the parties, but increases the probability and efficiency of the parties to choose mediation for dispute resolution. *The Regulations of Xiamen Special Economic Zone for the Promotion of the Diversified Dispute Resolution Mechanism*, *The Regulations of Shandong Province for the Promotion of Diversified Dispute Resolution*, *The Suggestions of the Supreme People's Court for People's Courts to Deepen Further the Reform of Diversified Dispute Resolution Mechanism*, *The Regulations of Sichuan Province for the Promotion of Diversified Dispute Resolution (Draft)*, and *The Regulations of Heilongjiang Province for the Diversified Resolution of Social Contradictions and Disputes* all have set forth the requirements for mediation organizations or mediators to help the parties to conclude, on a voluntary basis, a mediation agreement and resolve disputes by convincing and persuading. Currently, the relatively mature practice is that the relevant courts offer a list of positives and negatives for the parties when providing the "mediation notice." The contents of the positive list include such advantages as a short mediation period and low cost and such features as failure in mediation will not affect litigation. The negative list mainly includes additional litigation fees and other disciplinary practices that may be applied when the litigation result is more unfavorable than the mediation result, if the parties refuse mediation without giving any proper reason. Through a mutual comparison, this allows the parties to gain a more intuitive understanding of the modes and advantages of resolving disputes. During the survey, Presiding Judge of the Tribunal of Case Filing under Dongguan No. 2 People's Court, Jiang Heping also said, frankly: with this mode adopted, the probability of the parties choosing mediation for dispute resolution has greatly increased, and the mediation success rate has not fallen duly either, but showed a trend of steady increase. On August 13, 2020, Shanghai Municipal Higher People's Court and Shanghai Municipal Bureau of Justice jointly issued *The (Trial) Suggestions for Exploring Mediation-in-advance and Advancing the Litigation-source Governance*, which stated that the ten types of disputes, including marriage, family, and inheritance disputes, should be mediated first, except where the parties have expressly refused. According to *The Suggestions*, Shanghai courts should set up at the litigation service center the special "non-litigation mediation window," increase information on the interpretation and guidance of dispute resolution modes and guide the parties to the "non-litigation window" or "alternative dispute resolution center" (people's mediation center) for mediation first.

The third stage refers to the activation of mediation by deploying mandatory means. Based on the realistic needs and the arrival of the third wave of "Access to Justice,"[24] scholars of both theory and practice intensified their studies on mandatory mediation. This type is no longer linked to such terms as "forced mediation" and "pressing mediation with judgment" and its legitimacy has gradually been accepted by different sectors. As for those disputes especially suitable for resolution through mediation in judicial practice, but in which the parties refuse to mediate without giving any proper reason, the courts also started to try the mandatory activation of mediation, especially in the fields of family disputes and neighborhood disputes, but currently the courts taking this practice are merely few and far between. Without any legislative provisions, the relevant courts can only include, in internal documents, some types of disputes in the scope of mandatory mediation. When the relevant types of case enter the courts, upon primary judgment of the judge at the tribunal of case filing, if it is not especially unsuitable for mediation, the tribunal of case filing will transfer them to the litigation service center or litigation-mediation matchmaking center and require the center first to assign the personnel for mediation. If the mediation succeeds, the aim of "closing the case as settled" is already achieved, without the need to file the case. If the mediation fails, the tribunal of the case file will file the case before handing it over to the tribunal of civil judgment for further treatment.

6.2.3 Assurance of Being Trustworthy of the Mediation Procedural Prerequisite

The healthy operation of procedures will not work without the assurance of being trustworthy of the relevant institutions, and the mediation procedural prerequisite is no exception. When facing circumstances, such as if the mediator has a personal connection of interests with one party and should not be the mediator, or that party intentionally destroys evidence and transfers properties, or if the two parties gang up with evil intentions and undertake false mediation, then assurance of being trustworthy of the relevant institutions is required so that mediation procedural prerequisite will not be abused by people with an ulterior motive. However, regarding whether the challenge system, the preservation system, and the punitive system should be established for mediation procedural prerequisite, *The Suggestions for the Reform of Diversified Dispute Resolution Mechanism* has not stipulated any relevant provisions, but due to the realistic needs, many of the courts have started to explore approaches suitable for their situation.

In terms of the challenge system, the practices of all the courts are about the same. When it comes to application, it can be a written application or an oral application. Regarding causes for application, basically with reference to the provisions of Article 44 of *The Civil Procedure Law* and Articles 43 and 44 of *The Interpretations of the Civil Procedure Law*, they set forth the reasons why a mediator can be challenged. For instance, such reasons as having a close relative or an interest relationship with one party or the agent, thus possibly affecting the justice of mediation are all reasons for the parties to apply for a challenge. In terms of application results, when one party applies for a challenge, the mediator suspends the mediation of the dispute, subject to the further examination by the judge. When the objection is upheld, the mediator is replaced. When the objection is not upheld, the original mediator proceeds with moderating the mediation. On the whole, compared with the challenge system in litigation, the challenge application and examination in mediation procedural prerequisite are both more convenient and efficient, due to the relatively sufficient supply of mediators as well as complying with the informality of mediation.

In terms of the preservation institution, there is no relevant mechanism for evidence preservation as well as property preservation in the mediation procedural prerequisite. In practice, it is frequently observed that when one party brings a dispute to the court and follows the court's arrangement to resolve the dispute first through mediation procedural prerequisite, it causes the other party to be alert and consequently "replace time with mediation" to accelerate the transfer of properties or destroy evidence. Facing such acts, the judicial practice has also gradually explored two solutions: one is that the party bringing the dispute to court first has the relevant properties and evidence notarized so that the properties and evidence are fixed through the notary organ; the other is to ask the party bringing the dispute to court to provide the guarantee and request the court for pre-litigation preservation and notify the other party to participate in mediation after the court completes the preservation.

In terms of a penalty mechanism, the mediation procedural prerequisite also appears to be relatively weak, because the personnel in charge of mediation in the mediation procedural prerequisite are all special mediation organizations or special mediators and have no power to impose penalty measures on the parties, such as advising, fining, or detaining. Furthermore, since mediation looks more at resolving disputes and repairing the social relationship and does not strictly follow, like judgment, the logic of "evidence–facts" and finds out the facts usually based on the parties' expression of the facts and relevant evidence submitted voluntarily,[25] this results in a natural limitation on clearly finding out the objective facts of the case and is more easily used in a bad way by a mediator who is intentionally seeking improper interests and damaging the interests of the third party or public interests. Currently, judicial practice mostly relies on the wisdom and experience of the mediator and judge to identify false mediation. In this regard, the mediator will, in the whole process of mediation, pay attention to investigating the basic circumstances of the dispute and making a comprehensive judgment, while the judge will only play a role when the parties request the court to issue the mediation statement and examine the mediation agreement. But even if these disputes are judged as false mediation, the judge's role is usually to terminate the mediation only, without imposing any other penalties. Hence, in such circumstance, the number of random people increases, and false mediation also shows a trend of high frequency.

6.2.4 Scope of the Mediation Procedural Prerequisite

From mediation-in-advance to the mediation procedural prerequisite, the legislative provisions and judicial practices regarding the scope of application are most abundant and most diverse, and are also the most disputed. Almost all the important judicial interpretations regarding the mediation institution will involve the provisions regarding the scope of application of mediation, some of which are rational and some are also irrational. There may be conflicts between judicial interpretations, which is worth examining and carefully analyzing. Furthermore, against such a background of legislation, the definition of the scope of application of the mediation procedural prerequisite in practices obviously also reflects the features of the locality and its expansion and needs to pay attention to the issue of the unity of application.

In terms of legislation, China mainly uses the combination of reverse exclusion and positive listing. For instance, Article 2 of the Provisions of *The Supreme People's Court on Issues of Civil Mediation of the People's Court* adopted the method of reverse exclusion to provide that:

> In the cases applicable to special procedure, supervision and urging procedure, procedure of public summons for exhortation, and procedure of bankruptcy and liquidation, confirmation cases of marriage relationship and status relationship and other civil cases for which mediation cannot be undertaken as per nature of cases, the people's court will not mediate.

Article 27 of *The Suggestions for the Reform of Diversified Dispute Resolution Mechanism* adopted the method of positive listing, considering that such disputes as family disputes, neighborhood disputes, small amount debts, consumer rights protection, traffic accidents, medical disputes, and property management are the disputes suitable for mediation-in-advance. There are also some circumstances where types of disputes applicable for mediation as provided by the judicial interpretations actually may not be suitable for resolution through mediation. For instance, as provided by Para. 2, Article 4 of *The Suggestions of the Supreme People's Court for Implementing Further the Work Principle of "Mediation-first and Mediation-judgment Combination,"* the following cases are not necessarily suitable for resolution through mediation:

> Cases related to the people's life and group interest and requiring the government and relevant departments to collaborate; group cases that may influence social harmony and stability, group litigation cases and bankruptcy cases; folk debt, marriage, family and heritage and other civil dispute cases; cases with complex details where it is hard to form evidence advantage; cases of serious confrontation of moods between the parties; cases which the relevant law and regulations have not been provided or have not clearly been provided and for which it is somewhat difficult to apply the law; cases where it is hard to enforce judgment; sensitive cases drawing the general concerns of society; the retrial cases and petition cases with intense moods and intensified contradictions of the parties.

After all, these types of disputes are related to social harmony, requiring the coordination of multiple departments, which the government and judicial authority as the representative of justice authority can hardly provide, how is it possible to be hopeful of the mediation which is still in development? Fortunately, in recent years, since people have gained a more profound understanding of the function of mediation, such phenomena no longer exist in the judicial interpretations that are newly promulgated.

In view of the practices, due to the legislative form of "reverse exclusion + positive listing" and the existence of miscellaneous provisions, the legislation has still left a relatively big space for the independence of judicial practice, and, by working on the premise of not violating the provisions of law and judicial interpretations, all the pilot courts have gradually explored some creative ways of working. For example, if a view of such actual circumstances as the local economy is developed, the sense of protecting rights is strong, intellectual property disputes are frequent and absolute, most of the intellectual property disputes are brought about by the intellectual property protection organizations, and the case are relatively simple, Shenzhen Futian District Court decided to include the simple intellectual property cases in the scope of application of the mediation procedural prerequisite. Because the local old city was being rebuilt and the shanty town was being upgrade, various disputes over relocation compensation arose, so Shenyang Huanggu

District included the disputes over housing relocation and land acquisition in the applicable scope of the mediation procedural prerequisite. In view of the actual conditions with numerous local Internet enterprises and frequent network disputes for small amounts, Hangzhou Xihu District Courts included also some of the network disputes in the applicable scope of the mediation procedural prerequisite and established a special team in this regard. As a whole, due to relatively many legislation vacancies and the encouragement for the qualified grass-roots people's courts to undertake the exploration of mediation procedural prerequisite, all pilot courts will define, according to their own conditions, the types of disputes applicable to the mediation procedural prerequisite. Further discussion is required on whether these practices are rational, but, without doubt, the trend of expanding the scope of mediation procedural prerequisite poses the threat of damaging the uniform application of the law.

6.2.5 Connections of the Mediation Procedural Prerequisite

In terms of internal connections, when the mediation fails through the mediation procedural prerequisite, the parties can submit a lawsuit to the court, as in theory and practice that causes almost no objection, but in how to make connections when the mediation succeeds, theory and practice differ. In the opinion of some scholars, reference can be made to the practices of Japan and the Taiwan Region of China, endowing the mediation agreement concluded through the mediation procedural prerequisite with the same effect as the judgment.[26] In the opinion of other scholars, except where the parties disagree, courts should undertake positively the judicial confirmation of the mediation agreement concluded through mediation-in-advance, as this is also the reflection of its judicial role on the basis of its non-judicial role.[27] But currently, judicial practices have differed from the theoretical proposals, and in view of the existing legal framework, three typical practices have been adopted. The first is that after the parties conclude a mediation agreement, the parties are informed they can, if necessary, jointly apply to the court for judicial confirmation. The second is the parties are informed they can, upon filing the case and paying certain fees, apply to the court to issue the mediation statement. The third is meant for the circumstance that, upon conclusion of a mediation agreement, the parties neither apply to the court for judicial confirmation, nor apply to the court to issue the mediation statement. In such a case, the court will generally wait until the two parties dispute over the content and performance of the mediation agreement and bring the case to the court, before making judgment, by examining the content and effect of the mediation agreement, on the substantial rights and obligation relations of the two parties, and will not accept the original dispute before the effect of the mediation agreement is overruled and will reject any matters exceeding the original agreement content.

In terms of external connections, the administrative organs, social organizations, enterprises, and institutions and other forces of other sectors cannot do a lot in the mediation procedural prerequisite. Actually, as early as in 2009, the Supreme People's Court issued *The Suggestions for Establishing and Perfecting the Resolution Mechanism of Contradictions and Dispute with Linkage of Litigation and Non-litigation*, requiring parties to take courts as the link to give proper play to the different dispute resolution forces and properly realize the connection and coordination of different dispute resolution modes. Later it issued again *The Suggestions for the Reform of Diversified Dispute Resolution Mechanism*, emphasizing this issue once more, and different provinces issued successively their own local regulations, e.g., *The Regulations of Xiamen Special Economic Zone for the Promotion of the Diversified Dispute Resolution Mechanism*, *The Regulations of Shandong Province for the Promotion of Diversified Dispute Resolution*, and *The Regulations of Heilongjiang Province for the Diversified Resolution of Social Contradictions and Disputes*, which also all mentioned this issue. Facing the big gap still observed between judicial practice and legislative provisions, we need to make the general arrangement at a higher level by intensifying these studies.

6.3 Existing Problems with the Mediation Procedural Prerequisite

6.3.1 Problems in Terms of Subjects of the Mediation Procedural Prerequisite

6.3.1.1 Confused Subject Model Resulting in the Unclear Effect of the Mediation Agreement

The judicial subject theory, folk subject theory, and mixed subject theory at the theoretical level caused, directly or indirectly, the subjects of mediation procedural prerequisite in practice to take three forms: (1) the judicial subject model; (2) the folk subject model; and (3) the mixed subject model. Such a state emerged due to the historical factors as well as different pilot courts following their own special circumstances, but, in any case, the problem of the subject model chaos in practices has already resulted in an important bad influence on the nature and legal effect of mediation agreements concluded through the mediation procedural prerequisite. According to the basic principle of the civil procedure, only after the case is filed can the disputes enter into litigation and can the judicial personnel handle the disputes, and if the mediation is undertaken by the judicial personnel, except for such exceptional circumstances as divorce cases, in which both parties have become reconciled after conciliation, cases in which an adoptive relationship has been maintained through conciliation, and cases in which the claims can be immediately satisfied as provided in Article 98 of *The Civil Procedure Law*, after the parties conclude a mediation agreement, the judicial personnel should prepare the civil mediation statement according to the content of the mediation agreement. However, the enforcement of the mediation statement is essentially different from the mediation agreement only with the civil contractual effect. According to the foregoing principle, it is seen that in the courts currently still taking the judicial personnel mediation model, it is illogical if the judicial personnel moderate the mediation before the case is filed and it is illegal if the judicial personnel moderate the mediation after the case is filed but only issue the mediation agreement, and it even destroys the pre-litigation mediation orientation of the mediation procedural prerequisite. In addition to the same problem as encountered by the courts adopting the judicial personnel mediation model, in view of the science, in the courts adopting the mixed mediation mode, it is possible to observe the chaos of different legal effects with the mediation consensus concluded by the parties through the same mediation procedural prerequisite, while all these resulted from the different mediation subjects moderating the mediation.

6.3.1.2 Empty Special Mediator or Special Mediation Organization

Actually, as the Supreme People's Court issued *The Suggestions for the Reform of Diversified Dispute Resolution Mechanism*, no matter which subject models are taken, the pilot courts have all established successively their list of names of special mediation organizations and special mediators, adequately absorbing the chamber of commerce mediation organization, trade union mediation organization, and such professionals as bankers, doctors, and lawyers as their special mediation organizations and special mediators. But behind the mediation changes that seemed to be progressing like a raging fire, a risk of empty special mediators or special mediation organizations is still concealed, because, actually, the listed special mediators and special mediation organizations annually only handled several cases of civil disputes symbolically, far from meeting the requirement of taking charge of the mediation procedural prerequisite. But the mediators working in the court mediation office as the mainstay in mediation procedural prerequisite are often not listed and consequently the disputes handled by them are mostly sourced from the direct assignment of the court or internal work division, rather than from the choice of the parties. Due to opaque and asymmetrical information, between the parties and the mediator working at the court mediation office, there is misunderstanding from the very beginning and the situation of trust cannot be established rapidly, as this also fails to comply with the requirement of "provide the list of names for the parties to choose from" as provided in the legislation. Actually, all these resulted from the relevant courts' unclear orientation of the mediator of the major mediation organizations working at court and the retired personnel, who contribute in spirit and love and are active in the cause of mediation. Since the mediators of the major mediation organizations working at court mediation and the retired personnel are not part of the staff at the courts and their salaries are not paid by the courts, many of the courts have a mentality of "mobilize all available resources," only assigning the task of mediation to them, but ignoring the management of these personnel. Actually, according to the relevant content of *The Provisions of the Supreme People's Court for Special Mediation of People's Courts*, these personnel should also be special mediators and should also be included on the list of names.

6.3.2 Issues with the Activation of the Mediation Procedural Prerequisite

6.3.2.1 The Will of the Parties for Voluntary Activation of Mediation Is Not Strong

The first step is always the most difficult, while the first step of mediation procedural prerequisite is the activation of mediation. Regarding the issue of the difficult activation of mediation, many pilot courts all have their own experiences and especially the pilot courts sticking to the traditional voluntary principle of the parties, then the activation of mediation is more difficult. Relying solely on the parties' prior agreement or conclusion of mediation consensus was the result of mechanically following the voluntary principle of mediation, as it not only lowered the possibility of the parties choosing mediation for dispute resolution, but also it caused the functional scope of mediation to decline, failing to give adequate play to the role of the mediation procedural prerequisite in dispute resolution. It is scarcely imaginable that the core significance of the voluntary principle of mediation is the voluntary will of the parties to conclude a certain mediation content or result, but not the voluntary activation of mediation. The reason for the parties being unwilling to choose mediation may result from the need to show a tough face and may also be based on consideration of China's relatively efficient and low-cost litigation procedure. It does not seem to be a responsible practice to worry the parties, without considering the principle of procedural matching and also without considering taking measures to guide the parties to choose the appropriate mode of dispute resolution.

6.3.2.2 The Consensus Induction Mechanism Faces Various Questions

Currently, a number of scholars have questioned the consensus induction mechanism, viewing its adoption as damaging judicial neutrality and making the parties question the neutrality of the judicial personnel, because adoption of the consensus induction mechanism to persuade the parties to choose mediation increases the probability and efficiency for the parties to choose that method. But when the court persuades the parties to use mediation, such tactics mainly are adopted as a combination of emotion, reason, and law, the carrot-and-stick method, divide and rule, and are actually due to the co-existence of such factors as regulatory system pressure, judges worried about their high-risk survival, the easy, non-troubling logic of grassroots courts, and opportunistic behavior of the parties. In such a consensus induction mechanism, judges follow the principle of being risk-averse, while the parties follow the principle of being loss-averse. On the surface, it seems that contradictions are resolved and the unity of legal effect and social effect is realized, but actually it may more easily bring future troubles, one after another, resulting in consequent new contradictions. Furthermore, with the result of persuading the parties to settle problems through mediation, judges will feel forced to be involved in the disputes, losing their neutral position.[28] Actually, such a worry is unnecessary, because those difficult and complex types of cases that are difficult to judge should not be included in the scope of the mediation procedural prerequisite.

6.3.2.3 The Mandatory Activation of Mediation Still Faces Legislative Obstacles

There are already many discussions on mandatory mediation. Based on the human right attribute of a just claim,[29] when having one's rights encroached on or disputing with others, the parties have the right to request the judicial organ for just judgment, but it can be reasonably restricted due to proper and necessary causes. This point has been reflected in the provisions of *The Civil Procedure Law* on the scope of acceptance and small-amount litigation, and the definition of a claim for judgment not only means the parties should acquire the just award, but also means the parties should obtain the relief in the correct time. Die to the litigation explosion, the mandatory activation of mediation procedural prerequisite provides the parties with another option of access to justice, and the justice is concluded through the mediation procedural prerequisite is not secondary justice, but like litigation, the rights of the parties are protected and disputes are resolved under the moderation of a neutral third party. Furthermore, the procedure should be designed to adapt to such factors as the nature of cases handled, the numbers of disputes, or the importance and complexity of the dispute matters.[30] Especially with limited judicial resources, the beneficial result of the procedure should not be ignored. As available studies indicate, the mediation success rate upon mandatory activation of mediation is no lower than the success rate of mediation actuated as per voluntary choice of the parties.[31] Since the theoretical misunderstanding is already resolved and there is also a need for judicial practice, it is imperative to overcome the legislative obstacles for mandatory mediation.

6.3.3 Problems in Terms of Assurance of the Mediation Procedural Prerequisite Being Trustworthy

6.3.3.1 A Challenge System Does Not Exist

In the mediation procedural prerequisite, the mode for the parties to apply for withdrawal basically refers to the provisions of *The Civil Procedure Law* on the challenge system, but in practice there are different methods used, regarding who decides on the time of application for withdrawal, if there are any circumstances for withdrawal except where the mediator withdraws at his own discretion.

In particular, there are generally two points in time when the parties can apply for withdrawal. One is after selecting the mediator and before formally starting the mediation procedure and the other is during the process of mediation. No matter when, either at the first or second time point, as long as the parties apply for withdrawal, some courts will grant consent and expect to enhance thus the parties' acceptance of the final mediation result. However, other courts will grant consent when the parties apply for withdrawal at the first time point, but when the parties apply for withdrawal at the second time point, the courts will generally reject it in order to keep the continuity of the mediation process and prevent one party from delaying the result by making use of mediation, where the mediator is not observed to be doing anything bad to affect justice, such as accepting bribes or playing favorites or committing irregularities. These two forms emerged because of the different understandings of the fairness and efficiency required by different courts. Further definition of this is required.

Regarding the issue of who grants consent on application for withdrawal and decides on withdrawal in the case of any circumstance for withdrawal, but the mediator fails to withdraw himself, currently, the courts in different places also have applied different rulings. Sometimes, it is decided by the chief mediator, sometimes it is decided by the director of the litigation-mediation center, sometimes by the presiding judge of the tribunal of case filing, sometimes by the presiding judge of the tribunal of civil affairs, and sometimes the foregoing circumstances are mixed and superposed, as the chaos of management resulting from the chaos of subjects in mediation procedural prerequisite shows. There are many discussions in practice on what position the mediation subjects should be in during the current new round of judicial reform. To further improve the challenge system in the mediation procedural prerequisite, it is necessary to properly control the relation between the two parties and to conclude, as soon as possible, uniform applicable rules.

6.3.3.2 Application of the Preservation Mechanism Is Inconvenient

Currently, the law and regulations have not stipulated relevant provisions regarding how to preserve the properties and evidence in the mediation procedural prerequisite, and the two practices explored in the judicial practice also have problems to some extent. The first mode of notarizing fixed assets and evidence deviated from the original purpose of notarization. The notary institution mainly looks at preventing the future possible disputes between the two parties, rather than resolving the existing disputes between the two parties,[32] and when one party wants to notarize the evidence and properties already under its control, it may be relatively smooth, but if the first party wants to notarize the evidence and properties under the control of the opposite party, the collaboration of the opposite party is required, and this makes it hard to achieve agreement between the two parties to the existing dispute. The second type is to preserve the properties and evidence using a pre-litigation preservation of court, which is currently the common as well as the most feasible method, but since the application for pre-litigation preservation involves the custody of court and the parties are also required to provide guarantees, the procedure is complex and the cost is relatively high, and according to the provision of Article 101 of *The Civil Procedure Law*, if the applicant fails to bring an action or apply for arbitration within 30 days after the people's court takes the measure of preservation, the pre-litigation preservation will be canceled, as has also imposed a strict restriction on the mediation time of such disputes.

6.3.3.3 The Penalty Is Excessively Light

In accordance with the provision of Article 111 of *The Civil Procedure Law*, with respect to the act of the parties hindering the litigation, the people's court has the right to impose a fine and detention according to the seriousness of the act and, if the act constitutes a crime, will investigate the criminal responsibility according to law. But with respect to how to handle the act of the parties hindering the mediation, the law has not stipulated any relevant provisions. Besides, Article 112 of *The Civil Procedure Law* has only provided that if the parties undertake false litigation or mediation, the people's court can also impose a fine and detention according to the seriousness of the act, or investigate the criminal responsibility, but the mediation in this provision refers to court mediation, and there is no legal basis for how to punish the parties when they undertake false mediation in the mediation procedural prerequisite in the category of non-proceeding mediation. After all, the mediation subjects of the mediation procedural prerequisite are special mediators or special mediation organizations rather than judges and they have no power to punish the parties. According to the principle of economic analysis, the cost of one illegal act is usually composed of three parts: tool cost, opportunity cost, and criminal consequence. For a rational actor, only by increasing the difficulty of obtaining the illegal tool, reducing the opportunity of illegal success, or enhancing the strength of punishing the illegal act will it be possible to make him understand that the loss outweighs the gain for an illegal act, thus effectively preventing the illegal act. For such an act as undertaking false mediation, the parties may also have many illegal opportunities without preparing an illegal tool. Therefore, in the case of reducing the act of the parties for false mediation, it is critical to restrict such an act by increasing the illegal cost of false mediation. Obviously, with respect to the act of undertaking false mediation through the mediation procedural prerequisite, the strength of the punishment is currently far from enough and only will "terminate the mediation once it is observed."

6.3.4 Problems with the Scope of the Mediation Procedural Prerequisite

6.3.4.1 No Mature Solution Is Available in Terms of Theoretical Exploration

As discussed above, in terms of legislation, China has adopted the legislative form of "reverse exclusion + positive listing" for the provisions on the scope of application of the mediation procedural prerequisite, but it is impossible for this method to cover all types of disputes. To solve the problem of undistributed legislative provisions, academic circles have successively proposed two theories: "the tripartite method" and "the individual case judgment method." Two scholars, Li Hao and Zhao Lei, put forward the tripartite method. Li Hao classified the scope of application of mediation-in-advance as disputes suitable for mediation-in-advance, disputes unsuitable for mediation-in-advance, and disputes possible for mediation-in-advance.[33] Based on this, Zhao Lei classified the scope of application of mediation-in-advance as cases that should be mediated in advance, cases that judges can mediate in advance according to the circumstances, and cases the parties choose through voluntary consultation.[34] But the first classification is logically not self-consistent, because "suitable" and "unsuitable" are already the complete classification of disputes and logically there should be no space for another classification. The latter revised the former to some extent and attempted to cover the mediation-in-advance with "mandatory," but as this author has said, this solution is not yet mature and further study and discussion are required as to which category some particular types of cases should belong to. The scholar holding the viewpoint of "individual case judgment method" is mainly Li Ende. In his opinion, for disputes brought to court, only by adopting the method of individual case judgment will it be possible not to reject any dispute as being "suitable for mediation,"[35] but this method is actually not feasible in judicial practice, which increases the judicial cost as well, and may damage the authority of the judicature. After all, it is extremely easy for the individual case judgment to cause the moderator of mediation to include personal experiences and it is hard to manage and supervise this process. Therefore, currently, the theoretical exploration is not helpful in resolving the problem of undistributed legislation. In practice, when a judge is puzzled about whether to resolve through mediation, there is not yet any appropriate referential standard.

6.3.4.2 The Scope Is Excessively Expanded in Judicial Practice

As a whole, due to the relatively many legislation vacancies and the encouragement for the qualified grass-roots people's courts to undertake the exploration of mediation procedural prerequisite, all pilot courts will define, according to their own conditions, the types of disputes applicable to the mediation procedural prerequisite. But during this process, in order to relax the pressure of "more cases but fewer personnel," some of the courts continue to include more types of disputes in the scope of application of the mediation procedural prerequisite. With the court sector of Shanghai as an example, in the first half of 2017, the domestic disputes, traffic accident disputes, folk loan disputes, and simple civil disputes resulting from service contracts applicable for the mediation procedural prerequisite in a traditional sense shared only 59.4 percent of the total cases received by Shanghai Court Litigation-mediation Matchmaking Center, while the remaining 40.6 percent of the disputes were in the category of other types.[36] This may be a reflection of increasingly complex social disputes, but from another angle, it also displays the fact that courts included more types of disputes in the scope of application of the mediation procedural prerequisite. Yet, mediation also has its limits of use, the play of its function depends on certain conditions, the basic status of the parties, the intensity and complexity of the disputes, and the target amount will all impact on the dispute resolution capacity of mediation. If its application scope is continually expanded without interference, till it exceeds the certain boundary, it will, on the contrary, prevent the parties from resolving disputes rapidly and efficiently. Especially when mediation can be actuated on a mandatory basis, the practice of continually expanding the scope of application of mediation procedural prerequisite without interference is inadvisable.

6.3.5 Problems with the Connection of the Mediation Procedural Prerequisite

6.3.5.1 When Mediation Fails, the Information Obtained Cannot Be Put to Good Use

According to the provisions of *The Civil Procedure Law*, where the parties fail to conclude a mediation agreement through the mediation procedural prerequisite, it will not prevent the parties from protecting their rights and interests in the mode of litigation, and the mediator can also, upon obtaining consent from both parties, record in writing the facts not disputed by the two parties in the process of mediation and the parties will confirm this in writing. But currently, there is an issue whether to submit to the judging judge the record of the facts not disputed, together with the mediation records, and which part of the record of facts not disputed and mediation notes in particular are to be submitted in the circumstance when the civil dispute mediation fails, after the litigation-mediation center returns the dispute to the tribunal of case filing through the internal procedure, and the judge of the tribunal of case filing distributes them to the relevant judge of the tribunal of civil affairs. Currently, in judicial practice, where mediation fails, some of the courts do not transfer any materials to the tribunal of civil affairs, but allow the parties to provide materials to the court according to their needs. Some courts only transfer to the tribunal of civil affairs the records of facts not disputed rather than the mediation notes. Some of the courts transfer to the tribunal of civil affairs neither the record of facts not disputed nor the mediation notes, but provide a copy of illustrations recording the basic information of the parties (especially the delivery information) and reflecting the moods of the parties without involving the substantial contents of the dispute. Through the survey, it is known that different courts have taken up different practices mainly because they have no clear idea about the effect of the record of facts not disputed and against the background of litigation-mediation separation, lies the fear of affecting the judge's discretion by submitting excessive information to the judge. However, it also substantially results in failure to make adequate use of the information obtained by the mediator in the process of mediation, as this is suspected of increasing the caseloads of the parties.

6.3.5.2 When Mediation Succeeds, Courts Tend to Intervene Positively

Some scholars mentioned that reference can be made to the practices in Japan and the Taiwan Region of China, endowing the mediation agreement concluded through mediation procedural prerequisite with the same effect as judgment. But since *The Civil Procedure Law of China* currently has not yet taken the settlement of action as an independent case-closing mode, it can hardly settle down within a short period of time. However, based on the characteristic of the mediation procedural prerequisite as enjoying a close connection with the judicature, in the opinion of some scholars, in such a practice, except where the parties expressly indicate their disapproval, the court should positively undertake the judicial confirmation for the mediation agreement concluded through mediation-in-advance, but this created great waves in judicial practice. Due to this impact, the courts previously following the passive examination in judicial practice also started to explore the model of positively undertaking the judicial confirmation of mediation agreements. After all, for the parties, judicial confirmation will not increase the cost too much, and for the courts, the initiative of judicial confirmation can also consolidate the mediation achievements and prevent the disputes from arising again. But such a practice is actually suspected of encroaching on the option of the parties and increasing the cost and causing the parties to misunderstand that the mediation agreement has the same legal effect upon completion as the judicial confirmation. Thus, in a long-term view, it is not favorable for the parties to actively and positively fulfill the mediation agreement.

6.4 Path of the Mediation Procedural Prerequisite

6.4.1 Perfect the Register with Special Mediators as the Subjects

We should emphasize cultivating the professional community of special mediators and, with special mediators or special mediation organizations as the important support, structure the subject model of the mediation procedural prerequisite. Actually, in order to relax the contradiction of "more cases but fewer personnel," the subjects of mediation procedural prerequisite are really experiencing the changing process of "judicial subject – mixed subject–-folk subject." Nowadays, many of the courts are still willing to send some judicial personnel to participate in mediation and adopt the practice of "judicial subject" or "mixed subject," as it is simply a question of not trusting the mediation capacity of special mediators and special mediation organizations. However, with such rapid social and economic development, different types of folk mediation organizations have also developed and are already able to deliver to the courts a number of special mediators with mediation experience and mediation capacity, and under the uniform management and uniform training of the courts, special mediators have gradually formed a professional community. Next, the people's courts should intensify the guidance for special mediators according to the legislative provisions, in such aspects as guidance, management, service, training and performance assessment, promote the integration of the mediators from different major mediation organizations with those selected and engaged by the courts and perfect the construction of a professional community.

As for the courts, they also have the following advantages to perfect the institution of a register and should insist on constructing the mediation procedural prerequisite in line with special mediators, by doing the following: (1) relax the problem of personnel shortage and liberate judicial personnel from the mediation procedural prerequisite so that they can take part in litigation as it needs more personnel; (2) make it convenient for courts to supervise and manage and correct in time the irregular conduct of special mediators; (3) improve the present situation where the currently listed special mediators and special mediation organizations are unable to undertake the mediation procedural prerequisite. In this regard, the work of courts still needs to be improved in the following aspects: first, define the nature of working court mediators also as special mediators, and improve their working conditions at courts; second, perfect the register, include the mediators who work at court in the list of names of special mediators for the parties to choose and only when the parties fail to conclude consensus will the court designate a mediator; finally, the courts that are still adopting the practice of "judicial subject" or "mixed subject" should separate the roles of judicial personnel and special mediator so that the special mediators take charge of mediation, the judicial assistants communicate and coordinate therein, and judges are responsible to supervise and guide the mediation. In this way, it is possible to sort out the division of rights and obligations between different subjects, realize the optimal allocation of human resources and resolve fundamentally the problem that it is hard to determine the nature of mediation agreements.

6.4.2 Implement the Activation Mode of a Dual Model

In order to resolve the awkward situation of "advising one hour, but mediating five minutes" in practice and resolve the problem of the present separation of theoretical exploration and practical needs, it is necessary to limit the mandatory mediation to a certain scope and structure the "dual model" to activate the mediation procedural prerequisite. In particular, combine the consensus induction mechanism with the mandatory activation and make sure that the two are not equal in terms of application sequence. As for the disputes suitable for resolution through the mediation procedural prerequisite, generally, it is necessary to give, as much as possible, adequate play to the role of the induction mechanism to persuade the parties. Only when the parties refuse without giving any proper reason will the mediation procedural prerequisite be activated in the mandatory mode. By adopting this mode, on the one hand, it can give consideration to the options of the parties, ensure that the disputes really suitable for mediation are resolved through the mediation procedural prerequisite and ensure that the disputes not suitable for resolution through mediation can enter the litigation procedure in time to increase the acceptance of the parties of the mediation procedural prerequisite. On the other hand, it can completely resolve the problem of difficult activation of mediation currently resulting from sticking to the voluntary principle of the parties in judicial practice, and allow mediators to put more effort into the process of resolving disputes through mediation rather than in persuading the parties to resolve problems through mediation.

Besides, facing the worry and questions by the relevant scholars about the consensus induction mechanism, while adopting the dual model of activation, we should also properly carry out the auxiliary work in the following two aspects: first define the standard for judging whether a dispute is suitable for mediation. Currently, legal provisions, theoretical exploration, and judicial practice all adopt listing types of disputes suitable for mediation. Consequently, the circumstance of "the same case, but different treatment" is rather serious and the individual problem of law application by defining the judgment standard must be urgently resolved. Second, improve further the consensus induction mechanism. With respect to the pilot courts currently adopting the consensus induction mechanism, their mode is still individual and not regular. While implementing the list and applying the leverage of litigation fees to regulate the conduct of the parties, it is also necessary to strengthen the construction of the expectations of the parties, correct the expectations of the parties by providing the judgment or mediation results of similar cases, give adequate play to the guiding function of judgment, and help the parties make rational choices.

6.4.3 Perfect the Connection with the Existing Litigation Assurance Mechanism

Based on the efficiency and informality of mediation compared with litigation, it is neither realistic nor necessary to seek the establishment of challenge, preservation, and penalty in the mediation procedural prerequisite, while it is effective to strengthen the connection with the existing litigation institution.

As for the issue of time for the parties to apply for the withdrawal of the mediator, like the mode and cause for the parties to apply for withdrawal, reference should also be made to the provisions of *The Civil Procedure Law* and *The Judicial Interpretations of the Civil Procedure Law*, allowing the parties to apply for withdrawal after selecting the mediator and before starting formally the mediation procedure, as well as allowing the parties to apply for withdrawal during the process of mediation. After all, in the case of any conflict between fairness and efficiency, the status of fairness is higher than that of efficiency, fairness should be prior to efficiency, and, as compared with the judgment procedure, the mediation procedural prerequisite is efficiency. Therefore, without making the mediation procedural prerequisite bloated, it is more important to try to ensure in particular fairness and help the parties to accept the mediation results. As for the issue about who will decide the withdrawal, when the mediator should withdraw, but fails to withdraw at his own discretion, in the opinion of the author, it is appropriate for the director of the litigation-mediation center to decide. As discussed above, since the mediation in the mediation procedural prerequisite is in the category of non-proceeding mediation, it does not comply with the basic legal principle for the presiding judge of the tribunal of case filing and the tribunal of civil affairs to intervene excessively, while it is of relatively high randomness for the chief mediator to decide, and it is not convenient for the court to give play to its role of supervision either. In the long-term view, it is a relatively steady and proper practice for all major courts to gradually set up a litigation-mediation center to promote the connection of mediation and judgment so that the director of the center decides on the withdrawal of mediators, as this complies with its duty as well as being an important approach for the court to give play to its function of supervision.

With respect to assuring the rights of the parties in practice through the notarial institution and pre-litigation preservation institution, these should first of all be affirmed, but there is still room for the two to be improved. Since the notarial purpose is to provide assurance to the parties and prevent future possible disputes from arising, when any dispute appears, except where there is the risk of evidence being destroyed or lost, or the parties demand the certification of evidence, generally, the parties should be no longer guided to notarization, but should be guided to prevent, in the mode of pre-litigation preservation, the opposite party from destroying evidence and transferring properties so as to avoid further expansion of their losses. Compared with the notarial institution, since pre-litigation preservation includes pre-litigation evidence preservation and pre-litigation property preservation, its system is better and can play a role in protecting the evidence and properties out of their control. Furthermore, according to the provision of Article 101 of *The Civil Procedure Law*, after receiving an application, the people's court must make an order within 48 hours, and if the order for the adoption of property preservation measures is made, the execution thereof shall begin immediately. Its efficiency is also higher and has more strength and the pre-litigation evidence preservation actually has a certain function of evidence disclosure,[37] as helps the mediator to further understand and judge the circumstances of the disputes according to the pre-litigation evidence preservation and can prevent false mediation. However, the present legal provisions have also imposed certain restrictions on pre-litigation preservation: the applicant should bring an action or request for arbitration within 30 days after the people's court has adopted the preservation measures so that the pre-litigation preservation can continue to be effective, otherwise, the people's court shall timely cancel the preservation, but if the parties undertake the mediation through the mediation procedural prerequisite, it has no function to make the pre-litigation preservation remain effective. Therefore, for the measures currently available, in mediation, for the dispute for which the pre-litigation preservation is already applied, the mediation time limit should be controlled, strictly within 30 days. Where the mediation fails, it should be timely transferred to the relevant tribunal of civil affairs to prevent the invalidation of the pre-litigation preservation. In the long-term view, it is better to include, by amending the legislation, the circumstance so that the parties resolve disputes through the mediation procedural prerequisite and it also allows the pre-litigation preservation to remain effective.

If the penalty mechanism of mediation procedural prerequisite is excessively unitary and weak, it is necessary, on the basis of "terminate the mediation once it is observed" for false mediation, to establish and perfect the penalty mechanism covering the whole process of mediation. Thus, the objects of penalty are not only the acts of false mediation, but also should include the circumstance where the parties refuse mediation without giving any proper reason. In particular, with respect to the act of false mediation, the party recognizance institution can be introduced in advance, asking the parties to sign a guarantee before the formal mediation procedure begins and informing the parties of the unfavorable consequences of making a false statement. In the process, if one party is observed in the act of false mediation, the other party should be notified in time to take relevant measures. If the two parties gang up evilly for false mediation, the mediation should be terminated. Furthermore, it, after the mediation is terminated, the parties again bring an action to court, the court can order the party involved in false mediation to pay more litigation fees so as to give adequate play to the leverage of litigation fees. If the parties refuse mediation without giving any proper reason, there is no room for application of "terminate the mediation." Currently, the relatively reliable practice is to tell the parties about the various advantages of mediation and give adequate play to the regulating role of litigation fees while actively guiding the parties.

6.4.4 Define the Scope of Application with the Element Method as Guidance

The scope of application of the mediation procedural prerequisite has a "domino" effect, because both the dispute resolution capacity of the subjects in mediation procedural prerequisite and the dual activation model of mediation procedural prerequisite set out a relatively high requirement for the definition of the scope of application of the mediation procedural prerequisite. If the scope of application is excessively wide, it will lead to the possibility that the disputes applicable to mediation procedural prerequisite are not suitable for mediation and it may not activated in a mandatory mode. If the scope of application is excessively narrow, it will lead to the failure to resolve some of the disputes through mediation, failing to give the parties "access to justice" as well as failing to relax the court's situation of more cases but fewer personnel. This deviates from the original intention when setting up the mediation procedural prerequisite.

Except for the types of disputes, which are applicable or non-applicable for mediation, as provided expressly by law and judicial interpretations, we maybe can fill in the legal blanks with stereotyped thoughts for the purpose of promoting the efficiency and effect of the application of the law. It can be observed that the disputes suitable for mediation generally have the following elements: (1) both of the parties usually have a relationship of acquaintance; (2) the relationship between the two parties will continue in the future; (3) the strength is relatively balanced between the two parties; (4) the target amount involved in disputes is relatively small; (5) the rights and obligation relation between the two parties are relatively definite. The first element makes it possible for the mediator or mediation organization to timely confirm and contact the two parties, providing the most fundamental precondition for undertaking mediation, because "default mediation" is impossible. The second element makes it possible for the two parties to a dispute to choose the dispute resolution through an informal channel, for the sake of maintaining the relationship of the two parties. The third element makes it possible for the mediator to gradually comprehend the basic information of the dispute in the confrontation process of the parties, without the necessity to call for evidence, generally according to the function and power when necessary, like judges, in compliance with the requirement of increasing the efficiency as well as following the institutional design that mediators have no power to investigate and collect evidence. The fourth element complies with the principle of procedural matching from the angle of the judicial organ and also complies with the choice of the rational economic man from the angle of the parties, because generally in cases with larger target amounts and more complex details, people are more willing to choose a more specialized and more formal dispute resolution mode, The fifth element considers the dispute resolution capacity of the mediator and the informal feature of mediation so that the mediator can focus on the crux of the disputes and rapidly resolve the disputes. If there is some doubt about whether one dispute is applicable to mediation procedural prerequisite, the person in charge of the case distribution can take the aforementioned five elements as guidance and can even also take the same as an important reference in measuring whether the legal provision is rational.

6.4.5 Insist on Relative Mediation-Trial Separation and Passive Examination Mode

Mediation and trial have different faces in at least 12 aspects,[38] but it is also only a theoretical ideal to say "mediation is mediation and trial is trial" and realize the absolute mediation-trial separation, with deviation from the development stage and development requirement of China's present judicial practice. Currently, China's judicial institution is already relatively perfect and through efforts made over a long period of time, the judicature has also gradually established its own authority and become the approach of dispute resolution most trusted by people. In the meantime, China's mediation cause has also observed great development, but its specialty, regularity, and authority have not yet been widely recognized. It not only has the conditions for independent development, but also, on the contrary, requires the rational guidance of the judicial organs. The concept of absolute separation of mediation and trial is established on the idea of authority, but fails to notice that this practice may possibly initiate the internal differentiation of judges and increase the judicial costs.[39] Therefore, it is necessary to structure the institution with appropriate separation of mediation and trial, while what is the so-called "appropriate" is reflected as: mediation procedure and trial procedure both have the space of relative independence, but the two are also connected to each other. The limit of such connection is that the information presented by the mediation procedure cannot affect the justice of the trial and the function of the trial cannot intervene with the mediation-in-advance procedure. Therefore, the information on the parties and the basic status of the disputes obtained in the mediation procedural prerequisite can, on the premise of not affecting the trial justice, be partially submitted to court, especially the circumstances regarding the delivery of information, the special position of the parties, the moods of the parties, and the intensity of the disputes, so as to make adequate use of the information collected in the process of mediation.

Besides, some pilot courts wanted to examine the mediation agreements in the mode of intervening positively. On the one hand, the thought of judicial centralism causes trouble, without forming a clear picture of the status and function of courts in the reform of diversified dispute resolution mechanism. On the other hand, the courts are eager to acknowledge the mediation achievements and prevent the efforts made for mediation from being wasted. Actually, the purpose of establishing the judicial confirmation procedure is to keep it in a state of "being ready but not used" as a supplementary measure for the present irregular quality and insufficient authority of the mediators, as this is the best choice.[40] Currently, courts must urgently carry out proper supervision and training, concentrate more on promoting the regularity of the mediation procedure and the specialty of mediators and make the contents of mediation agreements reflect the real will of the parties, without the need to replace "passive examination" with "initiative intervention," increasing any unnecessary burden on judicial personnel.

6.5 Future Prospects of the Mediation Procedural Prerequisite

Mediation has lasted a long time and has been running in the blood of the Chinese people and rooted in China's social habits, social mentality, and lifestyles and is honored as a beautiful flower in the oriental dispute resolution experiences. But with the impact of the Western discourse system after the reform and opening-up and due to the need to realize the specialization of China's judgment, the traditional mediation was deeply affected by judicial policies rising and falling, and showed, as a whole, a decline. Until the beginning of the twenty-first century, as the scope of functioning of civil judgment power gradually became clear, the judicature returned from the previous initiative penetration into every corner of society to a modest and passive nature, no longer bringing all types of cases under the umbrella of judicial judgment. In the meantime, the "society of acquaintance" continually broke up and differentiated, releasing the disputes that could originally be resolved by the units or groups, requiring new social organizations to replace the original units or groups in playing the role of dispute resolution. Thus, it opened the path to explore how to further learn from the Western mediation ideas to transform native mediation resources into the modern mediation on the basis of traditional mediation. This process is still developing even now.

The fundamental basis for measuring the legal governance level of a society or the status of the social order is not the frequency and intensity of social conflicts in society, but is the resolution capacity and effect of the dispute resolution mechanism for realistic social conflicts.[41] Against the background of the socialization of civil procedure,[42] dispute resolution power is continually spreading to social organizations, and more and more social organizations are also gradually possessing the special and efficient dispute resolution capacity. Facing the reform of the quota system for judges and the courts' situation of "more cases but fewer personnel," the establishment and perfection of the mediation procedural prerequisite provided new dispute resolution approaches for simple civil disputes, favorable to relaxing the phenomenon of litigation delay and to assuring the rights of the parties, rationally allocating the dispute resolution resources, and realizing the modernization of the state governance system and governance capacity. Currently, due to the rough legislation, diverse theories, various practices, and the unique form of development of "bottom-up + top-down" in China's judicial reform, the structure of the mediation procedural prerequisite lacks a uniform standard, but we cannot give up an undertaking on account of a small obstacle and we should have a clear picture of the important role of the mediation procedural prerequisite in resolving disputes and assuring the rights as well as understanding that the mediation procedural prerequisite was based on the national conditions of China and developed step by step from "mediation-first" to "mediation-in-advance," and then to "mediation procedural prerequisite," complying with the development trend and having a strong vitality. Currently, we should concentrate on the five most important dimensions of mediation procedural prerequisite: subject, activation, assurance, scope, and connection, and promote the development of the mediation procedural prerequisite in terms of legislation and judicature, strive to provide, on the supply side, appropriate resolution mechanisms for social contradictions of different intensity, continually optimize the state governance system, promote the state governance capacity, and strive to make every citizen feel the fairness and justice in every judicial case.

Notes

1 Zheng Kangsheng: Three Decades of Reform and Opening-up: the Chinese Society in Rapid Transformation–Significant Features of the Chinese Society from the Prospect of Sociology, *Social Science Research*, 2008 (4), p. 2.
2 Gu Peidong: *Social Conflicts and Litigation Mechanism* (Beijing: Law Press, 2016), pp. 7–14.
3 Wu Yingzi: "Mediation-first": Reform Pattern and Legal Interpretation – with the Reform of O City Court as an Example, *Chinese and Foreign Law*, 2013 (3), p. 538.
4 Nadjia Marie Alexander: *Global Trend in Mediation*, trans. Wang Fuhua, et al. (Beijing: China Legal Publishing House, 2011), Preface by translator: International Trends of Mediation Development and China's Opportunities.
5 Part 3 of *The Decision for Strengthening Further the Grass-roots Construction of People's Courts* printed and distributed by the Supreme People's Court.
6 Article 17 of T*he Provisions of the Supreme People's Court on the Civil Mediation Work of People's Courts.*
7 Article 122 of *The Civil Procedure Law of the People's Republic of China.*
8 *The Provisions of the Supreme People's Court on Special Mediation of People's Courts* and *The Suggestions for Deepening Further the Reform of Diversified Dispute Resolution Mechanism.*
9 Xu Shaobo: On the Effect of Mediation-first Agreement, *Jiangsu Social Sciences*, 2014 (6), pp. 83–84.
10 Long Fei: Get out of the Misunderstanding of "Mediation," *People's Court Daily*, July 12, 2013, Edition 6.
11 Nadjia Marie Alexander: *Global Trend in Mediation,* p. 24.
12 Tang Li: Studies on Inducement Mechanism of Litigation and Mediation Consensus, *Studies in Law and Business*, 2016 (4), pp. 121–130.
13 Liu Min: *Principle and Institution: Studies on Amendment of Civil Procedure Law* (Beijing: Law Press, 2009), p. 29.
14 Xiao Jianguo: *Value Theory of Civil Procedure* (Beijing: China Renmin University Press, 2000), pp. 212–213.
15 Discussions on subjects of mediation-in-advance include mainly the social subject theory, judicial subject theory, and mixed subject theory. Those holding the social subject theory consider that the subjects of mediation-in-advance should include different folk mediation organizations inclusive of people's mediation organization, while as the controller, the court mainly plays a role of planning as a whole and supervision. Those holding the judicial subject theory considered the subjects of mediation-in-advance should be limited to people's courts, but do not exclude the "assistance" of the relevant units and individuals. Those holding the mixed subject theory considered that it is necessary to set up a special mediation

department in courts, for the judicial personnel and people's mediators to jointly moderate mediation. Fan Yu: Comparative Study on Trusted Mediation – Comment on Mediation-in-advance, *Tsinghua University Law Journal*, 2013 (3), p. 74; Zhao Gang: Issues on "Mediation-in-advance," *Law Review*, 2013 (3), p. 35; Xie Shaojing: On the Structure of China's Civil Pre-litigation Mediation Procedure – with the Addition of "Mediation First" in the Amendments of Civil Procedure Law (Draft) as the Breakthrough Point, *Journal of North China Electric Power University (Social Sciences)*, 2012 (3), p. 57.

16 Fan Yu: Issues on Connection of Litigation and Alternative Dispute Resolution – with the Amendments of the Civil Procedure Law as the Breakthrough Point, *Journal of Law Application*, 2011 (9), pp. 30–34.

17 Yan Qingxia: Comparison of Chinese and Japanese Alternative Dispute Resolution Institutions, *Jinan Journal (Philosophy and Social Sciences)*, 2006 (4), p. 87.

18 Wu Yingzi: Judicial Limitation: between Judicial Activism and Judicial Restraint, *Chinese Journal of Law*, 2009 (5), pp. 111–130.

19 Fan Yu: Comparative Study on Trusted Mediation -- On Mediation-in-advance, *Tsinghua University Law Journal*, 2013 (3), p. 74.

20 Zhao Gang: Issues on "Mediation-in-advance," *Law Review*, 2013 (3), p. 35.

21 Xie Shaojing: On Structuring of China's Civil Pre-litigation Mediation Procedure – with the Addition of "Mediation First" in the Amendments of Civil Procedure Law (Draft) as the Breakthrough, p. 57.

22 Han Bao: Empirical Study on "Judicial Process" of Grass-roots Courts: Dilemma of Court Mediation – with the Northwest Region of China as an Example, *On Civil Procedure*, 2012 (5), pp. 138–143.

23 Official WeChat ID of Shenzhen Futian District Court, available at: https://mp.weixin.qq.com/s/ggR6hV96h8jOTgVkPaO86g (accessed December 26, 2017).

24 The third wave of "Access to Justice" has mainly two basic ideas: one is to provide, through the summary procedure, convenient conditions and increase the opportunities for the public to make use of the judicature; the other is to no longer equate justice with the judicature, re-understand and define justice, claim to allow citizens, through the socialization of judicature, the opportunity to access to particular justice complying with the actual conditions. Mauro Cappelletti: *Welfare States and Access to Justice*, trans. Liu Junxiang (Beijing: Law Press, 2000), pp. 125–160.

25 Lang Lihui: Influence of Judicial Reform on Affirmation of Civil Case Facts, *Hebei Law Science*, 2017 (12), pp. 190–200.

26 Yang Xiaoli: Research on Issues of China's Court Mediation Institution – With Reference to Japanese Dispute Resolution Mechanism through Consensus of Legal Parties, *Journal of Law Application*, 2010 (10), pp. 36–38.

27 Xu Shaobo: On the Effect of Mediation-in-advance Agreement, *Jiangsu Social Sciences*, 2014 (6), pp. 83–84.

28 Wang Yongtao and Chen Peng: Inducible Mediation: A Interpretation Framework of Court Mediation, *Law and Social Development*, 2017 (5), pp. 45–46.

29 Wu Yingzi: On the Human Right Attribute of Just Claim – From the Perspective of Historical Evolution, *Social Sciences in China*, 2015 (6), pp. 112–130.

30 Liu Min: *Principles and Institution: A Study on Amendments of Civil Procedure Law* (Beijing: Law Press, 2009), p. 29.

31 Nadjia Marie Alexander: *Global Trend in Mediation*, p. 24.

32 Liu Kunlun: Idea and Value of People's Mediation Institution, *Law and Economy*, 2015 (6), pp. 97–108.
33 Li Hao: A Study on Mediation-in-advance Institution, *Jianghai Academic Journal*, 2013 (3), pp. 141–144.
34 Zhao Lei: Type of Research on Mediation-in-advance Cases, *Journal of Law Application*, 2016 (10), pp. 10–14.
35 Li Ende: Restatement of Mediation-in-advance Institution: Time Limit and Applicable Expansion, *Legal Forum*, 2015 (2), p. 49.
36 Author's note: the data is sourced from the meeting materials for The Supreme People's Court, "Seminar on Pilot Work of Exploration for Reform of Mediation Procedural Prerequisite," in July 2017, pp. 3–4.
37 Xiong Yuemin: Analysis on the Evidence Collection Institution in Civil Procedure of Continental Law System – with German Civil Procedure as the Center, *Journal of Gansu Political Science and Law Institute*, 2004 (4), pp. 1–6.
38 Li Hao: Mediation Is Mediation and Trial Is Trial: Mediation-Trial Separation in Civil Adjudication, *China Legal Science*, 2013 (3), pp. 5–18.
39 Hu Daocai: Appropriate Separation of Mediation and Trial: Another Path of "Mediation is Mediation and Trial is Trial" – with the Pilot Reform of Nanjing Courts at Two Levels as the Research Objects, *Contemporary Law Review*, 2014 (2), pp. 76–86.
40 Pan Jianfeng: Thinking of "Mediation-Litigation Matchmaking" Mechanism against the Background of Amendments of the Civil Procedure Law, *Contemporary Law Review*, 2013 (3), pp. 107–111.
41 Gu Peidong: *Social Conflicts and Litigation Mechanism* (Beijing: Law Press, 2016), p. 19.
42 Wang Fuhua: Socialization of Civil Procedure, *China Legal Science*, 2018 (1), pp. 28–52.

References

Alexander, Nadjia Marie: *Global Trend in Mediation*, trans. Wang Fuhua, et al., Beijing, China Legal Publishing House 2011, Preface by translator: International Trends of Mediation Development and China's Opportunities.

Cappelletti, Mauro: *Welfare States and Access to Justice*, trans. Liu Junxiang, Beijing, Law Press, 2000.

Fan Yu: Comparative Study on Trusted Mediation – Comment on Mediation-in-advance, *Tsinghua University Law Journal*, 2013 (3): 74.

Fan Yu: Issues on Connection of Litigation and Alternative Dispute Resolution – with the Amendments of the Civil Procedure Law as the Breakthrough Point, *Journal of Law Application*, 2011 (9): 30–34.

Gu Peidong: *Social Conflicts and Litigation Mechanism*, Beijing: Law Press, 2016.

Han Bao: Empirical Study on "Judicial Process" of Grass-roots Courts: Dilemma of Court Mediation – with the Northwest Region of China as an Example, *On Civil Procedure*, 2012 (5): 138–143.

Hu Daocai: Appropriate Separation of Mediation and Trial: Another Path of "Mediation Is Mediation and Trial Is Trial" – with the Pilot Reform of Nanjing Courts at Two Levels as the Research Objects, *Contemporary Law Review*, 2014 (2): 76–86.

Lang Lihui: Influence of Judicial Reform on Affirmation of Civil Case Facts, *Hebei Law Science*, 2017 (12): 190–200.

Li Ende: Restatement of Mediation-in-advance Institution: Time Limit and Applicable Expansion, *Legal Forum*, 2015 (2): 49.

Li Hao: A Study on Mediation-in-advance Institution, *Jianghai Academic Journal*, 2013 (3): 141–144.

Li Hao: Mediation Is Mediation and Trial Is Trial: Mediation-Trial Separation in Civil Adjudication, *China Legal Science*, 2013 (3): 5–18.

Liu Kunlun: Idea and Value of People's Mediation Institution, *Law and Economy*, 2015 (6): 97–108.

Liu Min: *Principle and Institution: Studies on Amendment of Civil Procedure Law*, Beijing: Law Press, 2009.

Long Fei: Get out of the Misunderstanding of "Mediation," *People's Court Daily*, July 12, 2013, Edition 6.

Pan Jianfeng: Thinking of "Mediation-Litigation Matchmaking" Mechanism under the Background of Almendments of the Civil Procedure Law, *Contemporary Law Review*, 2013 (3): 107–111.

Tang Li: Studies on Inducement Mechanism of Litigation and Mediation Consensus, *Studies in Law and Business*, 2016 (4): 121–130.

The Decision for Strengthening Further the Grass-roots Construction of People's Courts, printed and distributed by the Supreme People's Court, issued in 2004.

The Provisions of the Supreme People's Court on Special Mediation of People's Courts and *the Suggestions for Deepening Further the Reform of Diversified Dispute Resolution Mechanism,* issued in 2016.

Wang Fuhua: Socialization of Civil Procedure, *China Legal Science*, 2018 (1): 28–52.

Wang Yongtao, Chen Peng: Inducible Mediation: A Interpretation Framework of Court Mediation, *Law and Social Development*, 2017 (5): 45–46.

Wu Yingzi: "Mediation-first": Reform Pattern and Legal Interpretation – with the Reform of O City Court as an Example, *Chinese and Foreign Law*, 2013 (3): 538.

Wu Yingzi: Judicial Limitation: between Judicial Activism and Judicial Restraint, *Chinese Journal of Law*, 2009 (5): 111–130.

Wu Yingzi: On the Human Right Attribute of Just Claim – From the Perspective of Historical Evolution, *Social Sciences in China*, 2015 (6): 112–130.

Xiao Jianguo: *Value Theory of Civil Procedure*, Beijing: China Renmin University Press 2000.

Xie Shaojing: On Structuring of China's Civil Pre-litigation Mediation Procedure – with the Addition of "Mediation First in the Amendments of Civil Procedure Law (Draft) as the Breakthrough Point," *Journal of North China Electric Power University (Social Sciences)*, 2012 (3): 57.

Xiong Yuemin: Analysis on the Evidence Collection Institution in Civil Procedure of Continental Law System – with German Civil Procedure as the Center, *Journal of Gansu Political Science and Law Institute*, 2004 (4): 1–6.

Xu Shaobo: On the Effect of Mediation-first Agreement, Jiangsu *Social Sciences*, 2014a (6): 83–84.

Xu Shaobo: On the Effect of Mediation-in-advance Agreement, *Jiangsu Social Sciences*, 2014b (6): 83–84.

Yan Qingxia: Comparison of Chinese and Japanese Alternative Dispute Resolution Institutions, *Jinan Journal (Philosophy and Social Sci*ences), 2006 (4): 87.

Yang Xiaoli: Research on Issues of China's Court Mediation Institution – With Reference to Japanese Dispute Resolution Mechanism through Consensus of Legal Parties, *Journal of Law Application*, 2010 (10): 36–38.

Zhao Gang: Issues on "Mediation-in-advance," *Law Review*, 2013 (3): 35.

Zhao Lei: Type of Research on Mediation-in-advance Cases, *Journal of Law Application*, 2016 (10): 10–14.

Zheng Kangsheng: Three Decades of Reform and Opening-up: the Chinese Society in Rapid Transformation--Significant Features of the Chinese Society from the Prospect of Sociology, *Social Science Research*, 2008 (4): 2.

7 Basic Conception for the Formulation of the "Mediation Law" in China

7.1 Questions

Since the launch of the reform and opening-up, China has experienced an unprecedented fierce social transformation and spent almost 30 years to complete the social modern transformation that took the Western countries three hundred years. In such a short and fierce process, China's different contradictions and disputes emerged in large numbers and showed an explosive trend of rushing to the courts, making China shift from a "non-litigation society" to a "society of litigation" like the Western countries with developed legal governance.[1] In order to overcome the limitations of the state judicial resources, relax the contradiction of "more cases but fewer personnel," and give the public more convenient "access to justice," efficiently and economically, as the main alternative solution to social contradictions and disputes, mediation has become a global trend. In the previous chapters of this book, we have already expounded adequately why mediation has deep cultural roots in Chinese society dispute resolution and analyzed the new problems faced by the traditional Chinese mediation in the new era and the new ideas to be reshaped for contemporary Chinese mediation. In the basic national conditions with new changes in society, how should the new ideas and new thoughts of mediation be integrated into the modern legal governance system? In the previous chapters, we have reviewed the past, present, and future of such Chinese mediation practices as people's mediation, court mediation, administrative mediation, commercial mediation, industrial mediation, and lawyer mediation, and summarized their achievements and deficiencies. Based on this, this chapter has a foothold in the practical experiences of mediation in China, explores the issue of mediation legislative regulation, and promotes the integration of mediation and legal governance.

The Decision on Major Issues of Promoting Comprehensively the Legal State Governance, adopted at the Fourth Plenary Session of the 18th CPC Central Committee, expressly proposed: "Construction of the socialist legal governance system with Chinese characteristics must insist on legislation first, give play to the leading and promoting role of legislation and has as its base

DOI: 10.4324/9781003385882-7

such a key as legislation quality." Yet, in the "New Sixteen-word Policy" for legal state governance in the new era, "scientific legislation" comes first. In the overall general plan for the comprehensive legal state governance, the complete and improved legal regulation system is the foundation stone for the construction of a socialist legal governance system. The following question is whether it is necessary to legislate specially for mediation. If it is necessary to legislate specially for mediation, how to do so? In this regard, with mediation legislation as the subject matter, this chapter is based on China's practical experiences in relevant legislation to emphasize the legislation resources and provide some referential conceptions for the formulation of the "mediation law."

7.2 The Need for the Formulation of the "Mediation Law"

Formulation of a law makes the claim of a certain class (stratum or stratum alliance) on the state will as a normative legal document and eventually as the code of conduct to be followed by all the members of society.[2] In terms of macro strategies, as an important element in the construction of legal governance in China, the formulation of the "mediation law" at the right time is of extremely important theoretical value and significance in promoting the modernization of the social governance system and the governance capacity, coping with the present demand for resolution of major social contradictions and disputes, and complying with the global trend of inclusive mediation. Therefore, years ago, academic circles called for the formulation of the "mediation law."[3] In view of the Chinese mediation practice, this is now a realistic necessity.

7.2.1 Overcome the Deficiency of The People's Mediation Law

To formulate a uniform "mediation law," first of all, it is necessary to answer how to orientate the prevailing *People's Mediation Law* and why it is still required to formulate a "mediation law" while *The People's Mediation Law* has been formulated. In November, 2006, at the National Political and Law Work Conference, Comrade Luo Gan, then acting as a Member of the Standing Committee of the Political Bureau under the CPC Central Committee, promoted for the first time the concept of the "Grand Mediation work system":

> [To] emphasize giving play to the role of mediation in resolving social contradictions and disputes and set forth efforts in structuring the Grand Mediation work system with mutual connection and cooperation of three types of mediation measures based on the people's mediation and intensifying the administrative mediation and judicial mediation under the leadership of the CPC committee.[4]

Afterwards, in China's official documents, the mediation system has always been expressed as three major types: people's mediation, administrative mediation, and judicial mediation. *The People's Mediation Law*, as adopted in 2010, continued with such a "one-into-three" mediation framework system, attempting to bring all types of non-judicial and non-administrative social mediation into the scope of regulation of *The People's Mediation Law*. As *The People's Mediation Law* was promulgated in 2010, China's mediation legislation chose the approach of "distributed advances." People's mediation has already penetrated gradually into other types of mediation, resulting in the general concept of people's mediation.

However, China's mediation types are extremely numerous, including such types as administrative mediation and judicial mediation, moderated by the official institutions as well as social mediation, moderated by non-governmental organizations, e.g., such types as individual mediation, people's mediation, industrial mediation, commercial mediation, lawyer mediation, arbitration mediation, and notary mediation. *The People's Mediation Law* has failed to establish the diversified social mediation system with respect to the features of different disputes, but has broken the original institutional orientation of traditional people's mediation as regional and autonomous, attempting to integrate all types of folk social mediation into the unified people's mediation. Such a unified integration model resulted in the expression of its subsequent relevant policy documents capturing, in the "name of people," the types of different new mediation organizations emerging in practice as "people's mediation" or including them in the "collection bag" of people's mediation. Such a general concept concealed the institutional characteristics of commercial mediation, industrial mediation, professional mediation, and other diverse social mediation modes, resulting in unclear legal orientation of such a non-official mediation, causing the legislation of mediation to lag behind the practice of new mediation, and severely constraining the coordinated development of diverse mediation forms, and this was unfavorable to international exchange and cooperation of dispute resolution. Therefore, it is necessary for China to bypass *The People's Mediation Law* and formulate a uniform "mediation law."

7.2.2 Raise the Legal Status of ADR

Since the reform and opening-up, China has gradually formed the litigation-centralized dispute resolution system and mediation has been marginalized as it is deemed to be the opposite of legal governance. Against the realistic background of right discourse flooding, as advertised by the "struggle for rights," "go to court to ask for an explanation," and "one Yuan case," courts became the main line of defense for the resolution of social contradictions and disputes. Since 1978, the cases of different types accepted by the Chinese courts have increased sharply from 613,000 to 22,600,000 in some year (exact date to be verified), with a growth of nearly 37 times, while the number of judges increased from more than 60,000 in 1981 to more than 120,000 in some year (exact date to be verified), and thus the situation of "more cases but fewer personnel" in people's courts' was valid. The scarcity of judicial resources and limitations of confrontational litigation also determined that litigation should not be the only or main mode to "run the whole show" and "guarantee to cure all ills." Currently, since China is in a period of social transformation, a period of prominent contradictions, and a period of interest adjustment, social contradictions and disputes are full of reality and unreality and many disputes cannot be resolved in the litigation mode of comparing and distinguishing the right and the wrong. Compared to a judicial trial, mediation has the comparative advantages in such aspects as: being voluntary, conciliation, consultancy, openness, flexibility and confidentiality.[5] Mediation plays an indispensable role in maintaining social harmony and stability. Therefore, we should break the dispute resolution idea of litigation-centralism and advocate or guide the people to resolve disputes through mediation and conciliation.

It is worth noting that Article 122 of *The Civil Procedure Law of China* has established the mediation-in-advance institution. In Article 27 of *The Suggestions for Deepening Further the Reform of Diversified Dispute Resolution Mechanism*, the Supreme People's Court also proposed to explore the establishment of the mediation procedural prerequisite. The mediation procedural prerequisite established by *The Civil Procedure Law* and the future mediation procedural prerequisite should be oriented for all the non-proceeding social mediation, i.e., for the disputes in need of the mediation prerequisite, the parties can apply to people's mediation organizations as well as to other types of mediation organizations, and all types of mediation organizations certified by the state can undertake the prerequisite mediation in some of the disputes. Substantially, all types of non-proceeding social mediation essentially abide by the voluntary and autonomous principle of the parties showing no essential difference in terms of nature of mediation agreements either. Therefore, these non-proceeding mediation agreements should be granted with judicial confirmation, rather than limited only to people's mediation agreements. However, except where it is already provided by *The People's Mediation Law*, in practice, a large number of new non-proceeding social mediation cases are in the situation of having no law to abide by or regulations to follow, and this has greatly weakened the operation effect of the mediation-in-advance institution. It is important to meet the demand of the people for the diversified dispute resolution by raising the legal status of non-proceeding social mediation, giving adequate play to its advantages compared with litigation, and reducing the costs in time and money of the parties for dispute resolution by forming the "mediation law" so that it becomes the first line of defense in resolving social contradictions and disputes. Formulation of the "mediation law" and definition of the legal status and function of different mediation types is useful to support the parties to resolve disputes through mediation, endow mediation with the legitimacy and legality of resolving disputes, and increase its efficiency.

7.2.3 Promote the Regularization of Modern Mediation

Traditional mediation is mostly in the category of "spontaneous order," but the mediation in the modern society of legal governance will definitely accept the regulation of law, and most mediation types are formed under the "shadow of the law." Especially in the modern commercial society, the demand of commercial subjects for mediation service is already different from the previous conciliation contradiction in a pure sense, and it has a higher requirement for the procedural assurance of mediation and its quality. However, currently in China, except where the people's mediation organizations and people's mediator team are regulated specially by *The People's Mediation Law*, in terms of new mediation such as commercial mediation, industrial mediation, and lawyer mediation, there is no regular mediation organization certification system and mediator qualification certification symbolic rules, and the development of mediation professionalization has not yet formed the scientific top-level design and overall arrangement. No play is given to the variety of advantages of mediation types, different types of mediation act in their own way and form their own system, with no uniform code of conduct and access standard, and the social status, special authority and professional regulation of mediators have not yet formed a rational structure.[6] Since the relevant mechanism to apply a mediation procedure has not been formed either, consequently, the quality of mediation can hardly be assured in practice.

As some scholars proposed, due to the prospect of modern transformation, China's mediation institution takes the approach of responsive mediation. The responsive mediation corresponds to the responsive legislation and shapes policy and plays an active role in relaxing the strictness of law and promoting the generation of new laws.[7] If mediation itself fails to operate in a regularized way, the modernized function of mediation is out of the question. The function of the "mediation law" is to make clear the qualification conditions for different types of mediation organizations, define the duties and scope of authority of local governments at all levels for supporting, assuring, supervising, and managing different types of mediation organizations, to establish the basic principle and procedural norms of mediation, promote the legitimacy, legality, and rationality of mediation, reduce the defects and probability of mistakes in mediation and provide the necessary relief mechanism for the parties.[8] Therefore, formulation of the "mediation law" corresponds to the operation chaos of the present mediation system. It coordinates the conflicts and contradictions between the prevailing legal articles, regulates the order of different mediation types in the process of resolving social contradictions and disputes as well as comprehensively controlling, in an overall sense, the advantageous and disadvantageous situations of different types of mediation, making best use of the advantages and bypassing the disadvantages, and structures the modernized mediation system. Only in this way will it be possible to promote the mediation quality and advance the professionalization of mediation.

7.2.4 Conform to the Global Mediation Development Trend

In the tide of the global civil judicial reform, the alternative dispute resolution (ADR) mechanism draws general concerns, of which mediation is the typical representative. In view of the legislative and judicial practices of different countries and regions all over the world, mediation is the ADR mechanism with the fastest development. Some scholars even proposed that the perfect legislation would provide the solid foundation of legal governance for the development of mediation in different countries in the world, and the legalization of mediation also responded to the realistic demand with a remarkable achievement.[9] Obviously, formulation of the "mediation law" is the natural choice to comply in time with the development trend of mediation. As is well known, China is energetically advancing the development and construction of "One Belt and One Road" and in the dispute resolution of the countries related to "One Belt and One Road," the litigation mechanism cannot play a role in foreign disputes, being limited by the local protectionism of judicial sovereignty of different countries. Especially in those countries or regions with extremely fast modernization of legal governance, due to massively using the substantive law and procedural law of other countries, transplantation of law was often accompanied by the problem of being unaccustomed to the different climate and these legal rules cannot avoid conflicting with the original social rules. Therefore, those playing a major role in dispute resolution are often such ADR mechanisms as mediation and arbitration accepted by the countries over a long period of time.

> The dispute treatment institutions are not only to resolve disputes, but also they deliver to society the information of how a dispute is understood and respected and they promote and reflect the dispute culture. In the tendency that the discussion on the legal reform concentrates on the mutual integration of the two major law systems, mediation symbolized the birth of an informal new form of justice dominated by consumers, as maintains the generality rather than the typicality of legal procedure.[10]

For China, mediation is a more mature dispute resolution mode than arbitration. Formulation of the "mediation law" will maintain the universality of legal procedure and conform to the inclusion of mediation in the long term and is the natural choice to conform to the global mediation development trend in the short term. On June 27, 2018, at its 51st meeting, the United Nations Commission on International Trade Law (UNCITRAL) adopted the *Convention on International Settlement Agreements Resulting from Mediation* (also known as the *Singapore Convention*), as the first multilateral treaty to resolve commercial disputes using mediation and was deemed a great milestone in the field of the international dispute mediation. It has also made it obviously urgent for China to formulate the "mediation law." To help the parties to choose and trust the conciliation agreements concluded through mediation by Chinese mediation organizations, it is necessary to promote the regularity of Chinese mediation organizations and the mediation procedure. Especially in the process of constructing the "One Belt and One Road" strategy, the generation of various commercial contradictions and their resolution solutions need to be recognized by all the parties. China, as a large responsible country, must take on the role of a lead runner, and formulate the universal dispute resolution mechanism. With the concept of a community with the shared future for mankind, the dream of the Chinese people is closely related to the dream of the people of all nations and the inclusive and mutual benefit development must be carried out and implemented. In the Western developed countries, more and more attention is turned to developing the specialization of the mediation institution and rules and the professionalization of mediators.[11] To conform to the trend of the times, while actively building the international commercial dispute resolution center, it is necessary for China to modernize its mediation institution, actively formulate the uniform "mediation law" inclusive of commercial mediation, and establish and perfect the scientific and regular mediation rule system.[12]

7.3 Guiding Principles for Formulating the "Mediation Law"

The rationality of mediation includes such aspects as procedure, economy, and morality and the idea of mediation is to be transformed in terms of guiding principles. At present, with the diversified development of mediation, we should lay stress on the rational application of different types of mediation and avoid the infinite generalization of one mediation mode. The diverse mediation system aims to meet the demands of different groups for mediation at different levels.

Under the Western value orientation of seeking the rights and interests and advocating confrontation, a trial has always held the core position, while under the social idea in China of pursuing compromise and advocating a harmonious society, mediation has always held an important position. Especially at present with unbalanced and inadequate social development, the optimal status of the diversified mediation system is to realize coordination and balance in the application of different types of mediation. Therefore, to formulate the "mediation law," it is necessary to sort out the relationship between different mediation modes and establish the new guiding idea, as it directly determines the structure of the mediation system.

7.3.1 Core Socialist Values

The core socialist values are the soul of the socialist legal governance construction. *The Suggestions for Cultivating and Practicing the Core Socialist Values* printed and distributed by the General Office under the CPC Central Committee, proposed to implement the core socialist values in all aspects of legislation, enforcement, judicature, law popularization, and legal governance.

China's General Provisions of the Civil Law included the core socialist values in the legislation. The idea of China's "mediation law" has a corresponding nature with the core socialist values. The core socialist values advocate civilization, democracy, and harmony at the national level, advocate freedom, equality, justice, and legal governance at the social level, and advocate good faith and friendship at the civil level. These value targets, value orientations, and value pursuits are all consistent with the idea of mediation. Mediation is consistent with such traditional cultural values of China as "no litigation" and "harmony is most precious." Under the nurture of the traditional Confucianism of "The gentleman understands what is moral. And the mean man understands what is profitable," the vast majority of common people were not used to the competitive litigation confrontation and often looked for more relaxed resolution approaches for the disputes that occurred in the society of acquaintance. The mediation in the traditional society without exception implemented the spirit of "keep a good neighborhood to settle disputes" and "make clear benefit for the subsequent rationality of customs," and the idea of harmony upheld by mediation could arouse the acceptance hidden in the heart of the people.[13] Mediation pursued the interpersonal civilization and harmony in terms of closure for settlement; displayed the subject status of the parties, respected the autonomy of the parties and reflected the freedom and democracy in social communication in terms of the dispute resolution process; emphasized that the parties should be honest and friendly and abide by the law and contracts, and reflected equality, justice, and legal governance in terms of the dispute resolution results. Therefore, among the numerous dispute resolution mechanisms, without any doubt, mediation is the dispute resolution mechanism that can best manifest the core socialist values, as demonstrated from the point of view that the formulation of the "mediation law" must take the core socialist values as the guide.

Formulation of the "mediation law" with the core socialist values as the guide complies with the legislation policy guidelines of the CPC and the central government in recent years. In December, 2016, the General Office of the CPC Central Committee and the General Office of the State Council printed and distributed *The Guidelines for Integrating Further the Core Socialist Values into the Construction of Legal Governance*, requiring all the regions and all the departments to sincerely carry out and implement the core socialist values in the actual conditions. As the important guidance for the construction of socialist legal governance, integration of the core socialist values fits into the construction of legal governance, it is the natural requirement to insist on legal and moral governance of the state and this is the important approach to advance the construction of core socialist values. In October, 2017, in the report to the 19th National Congress of the CPC, General Secretary Xi Jinping restated China must "integrate the core socialist values into all the aspects of social development" and build the socialist legal governance culture of China. *The Planning for Integrating Core Socialist Values into Legislation and Amendment of Legal Governance Construction*, printed and distributed by the CPC Central Committee in May 2018 emphasized that it must insist on issue-orientation to advance the inclusion of core socialist values in law and regulations. The formulation of the "mediation law" is a benign practice of encouraging the application of mediation in the resolution of social contradictions and disputes, meeting the demand of the parties for dispute resolution at different levels, by combining such elements as emotion, reason, and law, and advancing the integration of core socialist values into legislation.[14]

7.3.2 The New Development Idea

The new development idea was originally the concept proposed at the Fifth Plenary Session of the 18th CPC Central Committee. *The Suggestions of the CPC Central Committee for Formulating the 13th Five-year Plan of National Economic and Social Development* expressly proposed: "to realize the '13th Five-year' development target, break through the development difficulties and plant deeply the development advantages, it is necessary to establish firmly the development idea of innovation, coordination, green, open and sharing."[15] In the report to the 19th National Congress of the CPC, General Secretary Xi Jinping restated: "it is necessary to implement firmly the development idea of innovation, coordination, green, open and sharing." In order to rationally structure the social contradiction and dispute mediation system and give adequate play to the advantageous position of different types of mediation in resolution of different disputes, China should insist on the new development idea and guide the formulation of the "mediation law" accordingly.

"The relation between the new development idea and the legal governance of China is actually the relation between the political discourse system and the legal governance discourse system."[16] The "mediation law" is formulated in such a context, of guiding the legal governance with the new development idea of the political discourse system, for the reason that the two are consistent in terms of the final target. Specifically, the new development idea is the policy guidance proposed by the Communist Party of China to advance social and economic development. As the ruling party, in the process of advancing the state governance and administration, the Communist Party of China will definitely carry out and implement the new development idea in the development of the market economy. The market economy is substantially in the category of legal governance economy, and the "mediation law" is formulated with the purpose of properly regulating the order of contradiction and dispute mediation in the development of the market economy, so that the relevant conduct has the law to follow. Not all the policies are transformed into law, but the best method for realizing the policy value is to make use of legal governance to integrate the content and principle of policies into legislation and law practice. To some extent, mediation naturally corresponds to the new development idea. With the green idea as an example, the green idea can be understood as the idea of sustainable development to some extent. The report of *Our Common Future*, by the World Commission of Environment and Development, in 1987, defined sustainable development as the development that can meet the needs of the contemporary people without constituting any harm to the capacity of the later generations to meet their needs.[17] In the field of the resolution of social contradictions and disputes, different types of dispute resolution mechanisms have their respective features. Litigation is the typical example of justice and legal governance, but to some extent will cause the parties to "be completely isolated from each other all their lives." Comparatively speaking, mediation is relatively "mild" and lays more stress on repairing and maintaining the mentality and social relation of the two parties, and is a mere coincidence with the idea of sustainable development. Activation and the process of mediation and conclusion and fulfillment of the mediation agreement all advocate following the independent will of the parties, mediating in disputes in a relatively peaceful environment, as is really the typical example of the green idea in dispute resolution.

> As the course of legal governance development in civilized society indicates, the generation and evolution of each legal governance revolution condensed specific social and legal governance development ideas, reflecting the profound changes of the social and legal governance development ideas and showing the orientation of the significant and unique, social and legal governance development idea.[18]

Formulation of the "mediation law" can be deemed a profound reform in the field of mediation, but it is not meant to overturn and rebuild the Chinese mediation system but is meant to reasonably dispose of some of the existing traditional norms. Only in this way can it more properly eliminate the chaos in mediation practice.

7.3.3 Non-proceeding Idea

In Section 7.3.2, the author has already expounded the new idea and new thought of modern mediation. To a certain extent, the process of mediation modernization is the process for the mediation law system to advance with the times. In order to do this, it is necessary to take the new idea and new thought of mediation as the guide. As the dispute resolution institution, the institutional design of the "mediation law" should be different from the institutional design of the civil procedure law. In this regard, as a non-proceeding law, the "mediation law" should insist on the following basic ideas.

First, it is necessary to insist on making the idea of a community of interests. With the claims as the core, the litigation idea structures the logic of self-consistency and seamless abstract "axiom system," while the modern mediation institution takes the interest equilibrium as the value origin. The litigation idea pursues the one-dimensional formal justice, while the value destination pursued by the modern mediation institution is a kind of comprehensive "co-existential justice."[19] The social basis for "co-existential justice" is that people always co-exist with others rather than live in solitude on an isolated island like Robinson Crusoe, so mutual compromise is required to form the equilibrium of interests. The basic structure of civil procedure is "confrontation and judgment." Since the two parties have a confrontation of interests and try their best by attacking and defending to win the favorable litigation results, for a long time, litigation has been labeled as costing a lot of time and money, and litigation delay is also inconsistent with the efficiency pursued by the transactions of the market economy. In modern mediation, mediators mostly take the common interests between the two parties to a dispute as the axis and undertake the dispute mediation with the thought of mutual benefit and win-win, consensus and co-construction. Compared with the confrontation attribute of litigation, the formulation of the "mediation law" with the new idea and new thought of mediation as guidance is meant to strive to realize the purpose of pursuing dispute resolution at the minimum cost between the parties, pursue the common interests between the parties to disputes and strive to explore the mediation approach in the area of win-win, as conforms to the transaction principle currently encouraged by the market economy.

Second, it is necessary to establish the outlook of dynamic interests. Among the numerous dispute resolution modes, the litigation mechanism undertaken on the basis of litigation target represents a kind of unitary static interest idea and due to its own flexible, open and inclusive attributes, mediation becomes the outlook of dynamic interests advocating diversity. Self-evidently, the litigation mechanism representing the outlook of unitary static interests fails all the more to adapt to the diversified demand of the parties for interest appeals in the period of transformation, while mediation is the dispute resolution mode with consideration to both present and long-term interests, both material interests and non-material interests, and both the interests within litigation and the interests outside litigation, and its flexibility, openness, and inclusiveness are its advantages. With the main social contradiction changing, the parties set forth even higher requirements for the mode, target, process, and result of dispute resolution, and as compared with the value idea of static interests, consideration for the non-disputed, indirect and long-term interests is more favored by the parties. Therefore, the idea and thought of dynamic interests should be absorbed by the "mediation law."

Third, it is necessary to establish the comprehensive thought. Litigation pursues the "only correct answer" with the positive law as the basis, while the modern mediation institution takes the compatibility and unification of emotion, reason, and law as the value criterion. Due to the influence of litigation target theory, the litigation mechanism shows, in dispute resolution, the "sliced" thinking. The rigid judgment is made to pull out forcibly the right and obligation between the parties from the social relation between the two parties and behind the mandatory judgment. It often fails to properly meet the internal real will between different parties. Comparatively, with the consensus between the parties as the premise, mediation is a kind of comprehensive dispute resolution thought, not only paying attention to the rights and obligation relation between the parties, but also giving more consideration to the continuity of the emotional relation and business contacts of the natural person or legal purpose organizations and even the third party, and in the multidimensional vision, observing comprehensively the cause, issue, and resolution of disputes. Since the civil procedure takes the "sliced" thinking as the guidance, judges can only make a ruling on the legal relation of the dispute, otherwise it will violate the legal principle of litigation. Yet, with "consensual principle" as guidance, the modern mediation applies the comprehensive thinking to combine the legal relation of several related disputes. To put it bluntly, in resolving disputes, mediation is brimming over with the humanities not available with litigation, as this is its unique charm.

Finally, it is necessary to guide the parties to establish forward-looking-thought. In litigation, with the aid of evidence materials, judges explore the case facts of the existing contradictions and disputes, as is a process of recalling the historic facts. No matter whether it is the authority doctrine model or the adversary system model, its purpose is to discover legal facts through evidences and then make judgment on the legal rights and obligations according to the case facts discovered, as based on the prominent backward-looking thinking. Yet, mediation is different. The culture of mediation advocates the idea of "harmony" and the disputes between the parties should not cause any irreconcilable rift to the relation between the two parties and consensus for application of mediation indicates that the two parties are resolutely not pursuing the dispute resolution result of "being completely isolated from each other all their lives." Being driven by the trend of globalized development, the contacts between people, between organizations, and between states become increasingly frequent and the world becomes increasingly an entirety of close contacts. In the commercial contact, the process of interaction and exchange is accompanied by the dispute and confrontation of interests and cannot avoid frictions and disputes, but the commercial activities have their objective law that must be followed and the maximization of interests is absolutely not concerned with the short term, while the long-term interests and sustainable interests are the extreme target. In the field of mediation, disregarding people's mediation, administrative mediation and industrial mediation or commercial mediation, the resolution of disputes between natural persons is not limited to the scope of existing disputes, and especially the sustainability and continuity of commercial development and its essential attribute of pursuing interests determines that the resolution of commercial disputes is often not so concerned about the temporary gains and losses in the short term, but will often consider the acceptance or rejection of present interests and long-term interests. Actually, maximization of interests usually does not occur under the confrontation mechanism, but in the mutual benefit and win-win cooperation and it is a kind of sustainable interests.

> The forward-looking thought of commercial mediation requires that the dispute resolution should not stop on resolution of present disputes and recovery of current interests, but should be oriented for the future to take the mode of "making the cake bigger" rather than "cutting and distributing the cake" to seek the new interest growth point of both parties to the dispute and facilitate the new cooperation solution so that the disputes are prevented in the long-term cooperation of mutual benefit and win-win.[20]

People often are helpless and pursue justice with the aid of litigation, but mediation is chosen for resolution of disputes more or less not only for the purpose of pursuing dispute resolution, and the optimization of dispute resolution effects mediation pursues includes the total consideration of dynamic interests, comprehensive interests, long-term interests and common interests, as it is a kind of dispute resolution idea conforming to the demand of the times. No matter the core socialist values and new development idea, or the new idea and new thought of contemporary mediation, they are all the scientific guiding thoughts conforming to the world mediation development trend and verified in practice. The "mediation law" must be formulated with them as the ideological guidance so as to eventually realize the scientific legislation.

7.4 The Basic Principles of "Mediation Law"

According to the definition in *Black's Law Dictionary*, a legal principle refers to the fundamental principle or truth of law, proving the fundamental or original comprehensive norms for other rules, and is the rule reflecting the decisive values of legal acts.[21] To formulate a "mediation law" in a comprehensive sense, a legal principle is imperative. China's prevailing mediation types are abundant and various and different types of mediation have their own special principles to be followed, as will not be discussed in details herein, while the general principles of mediation are the key points herein. The basic principles of mediation include but are not limited to the voluntary principle, the non-disclosure principle, the legality principle, and the principle of honesty and credit,[22] which are particularly expounded mainly hereinafter.

7.4.1 The Voluntary Principle

The voluntary principle of mediation refers to the fact that consent must be obtained from the two parties for mediation in the disputes of the parties, without forcing them. The voluntary principle is the prime principle for undertaking the mediation and any practice of undertaking mediation in disputes by force against the independent will of the parties will conflict with the act and purpose of the mediation. Only by insisting on the voluntary principle will the activities of mediation have the significance and can the act and results of mediation be accepted by the parties to eventually eliminate the misunderstanding of the parties and resolve the dispute. The definition of mediation's voluntary principle should be understood in two dimensions as procedural voluntary and substantial voluntary, mainly including: first, choice of the mediation mode to resolve the dispute must be on the voluntary basis of the parties' will; second, in the process of mediation, the two parties are willing to cooperate in the mediation of the mediator, without being forced by others; third, the conclusion and fulfillment of the mediation agreement must be based on the parties' voluntary will. In the judicial practice, the voluntary attribute of mediation is more or less observed with the phenomenon of procedural "softening." In the opinion of Lord Woolf, the appropriately mandatory mediation is rational and especially when the case pressure of the court sector is huge, mediation can become an important assistance in case distribution. In order to cope with the judicial delay, Italy stipulated the expansion of the scope of application of mediation in Bill No. 5492. Article 15a of *The Code of Civil Procedure (EGZPO)* promulgated by German Federal Government in 2000 was also the particular provision for mandatory mediation.[23]

Currently, people have a certain misunderstanding of the voluntary principle of mediation. For instance, people may misunderstand the relation between the voluntary principle of mediation and mediation-in-advance. Actually they are two different concepts. Mediation-in-advance is only meant for the activation of the mediation procedure and at the substantial level of dispute resolution, it should naturally follow the disposal of mediation's voluntary principle. As a kind of guiding norm for procedure application, mediation-in-advance is only applied in court mediation. *The Miscellaneous Provisions of Article 14 of the Provisions for Application of Summary Procedure in Trial of Civil Cases* (FS [2003] No. 15): "except for the disputes that cannot be mediated or are unnecessary for mediation according to the nature of cases and actual conditions of the parties" has such a meaning. For another example, mediation's voluntary principle may be different from the active and initiative mediation of the people's mediation committee in disputes.[24] In our opinion, upon the occurrence of a dispute, the two parties should actively approach the people's mediation committee to moderate the mediation, and this is the people's mediation in a regular sense. When the member of the people's mediation committee actively approaches the parties for mediation, if the parties express no objection or initially oppose but afterwards choose the mediation upon the proposal of the people's mediator, it is still in the category of mediation's voluntary principle. The voluntary principle does not always require that the parties cannot have an opposing opinion or expression of will. The expression of independent will should give adequate consideration to the parties. changing their minds As mentioned above, Germany, Japan, and the Taiwan Region of China have all established the pre-litigation mandatory mediation procedure for specific types of disputes. China has currently not yet established the mandatory mediation institution in any substantial way,[25] but the voices of the sector of judicial practice for the establishment of such an institution are strong. However, many scholars in theoretical circles still hold a conservative view in this regard. The biggest worry of the academic circles about the litigation mediation prerequisite is that forcing the parties to choose mediation first raises suspicions of encroaching on the claim of the parties. This is actually misunderstanding the mediation procedural prerequisite, taking the mediation-in-advance for specific types of disputes as the prerequisite condition for the parties to take action, as is mandatory only for the parties to first make use of the mediation procedure. Regarding whether the parties are willing to conclude the mediation and the particular contents of the mediation agreement, it is still required to follow the voluntary and legal principle completely for the parties to decide. Therefore, as for such types of common disputes as marriage and family, neighborhood quarrels, small-amount debt, consumers' right protection, motor vehicle accident, medical and property suitable for mediation, as verified in the long-term judicial practice, it is legitimate and rational to set up the mediation procedural prerequisite, guide the parties to resolve the disputes through the mediation procedure before litigation and regard the mediation for specific types of disputes as the necessary procedure when entering litigation. This has not deprived the parties of the right to ask for judgment, but applies an appropriate procedural limitation for the parties to make use of the litigation procedure, gives adequate play to the use of alternative dispute resolution resources, reduces the caseloads of the judges, makes the judicial judgment function of the courts smoother, and realizes the rational and optimal allocation of judicial resources.[26]

It should be made clear that the voluntary principle in a substantial sense is the acceptance of mediation results, as they must be strictly interpreted.[27] As the consensus of the parties on the dispute resolution through mediation, the mediation agreement includes the disposal of the substantial rights and interests between the two parties. If the mediation agreement is concluded in violation of the voluntary principle, it is substantially a direct infringement on the substantive rights of the two parties, and will directly lead to the failure to fulfill the mediation agreement. Usually, a mediation agreement has the nature of a civil contract. Such basic principles of contract law as freedom, consensus, no cheating or threatening or no major default should also be included in the mediation agreement. Behind the mediation's voluntary principle, it also reflects the freedom of the parties for the disposal of substantive rights. Since civil disputes are in the category of private right disputes, the conclusion of a mediation agreement is subject to the binding of the autonomous principle of private rights. It is not related to the types of mediation applicable for disputes. As for people's mediation, social mediation, or administrative mediation, the mediation's voluntary principle is of indisputable legitimacy. Otherwise, the act of mediation is in violation of the original intention of its operation, and will even further result in increasing the conflict between the two parties.

7.4.2 The Non-disclosure Principle

With reference to Article 134 of *The Civil Procedure Law*, public hearing is a basic principle of China's civil procedure. Comparatively, mediation in China follows the non-disclosure principle. The non-disclosure principle of mediation is deemed an important measure to maintain the will and freedom of the parties of mediation. In the field of mediation, the meaning of the non-disclosure principle should include three aspects of content: first, the process of mediation is not open to the public and the mediation procedure only allows the parties, their agents and witnesses and other persons related to the case and must take part in mediation to participate, persons not related to the case are not allowed to participate or attend as a visitor, and the news media are not allowed to report externally.[28] Second, in the subsequent arbitration procedure or litigation procedure, the two parties should not use as evidence the notes prepared in the process of mediation, and any opinion or proposal expressed by the mediation agreement, the mediator, or the parties. Third, the mediator is obliged to keep the mediation confidential and should not participate in the treatment of the disputes between the two parties as a witness or other judicial assistants.

The non-disclosure principle also can be breached in some exceptional circumstances. The relevant information of mediation the two parties agree to publish or as provided by law expressly is not subject to the binding of the non-disclosure principle of mediation. For instance, according to the recording mechanism of non-disputed facts provided in Article 23 of *The Suggestions of the Supreme People's Court for People's Courts to Deepen Further the Reform of Diversified Dispute Resolution Mechanism* (FF [2016] No. 14),

> when the mediation procedure is terminated, where the parties fail to conclude a mediation agreement, upon obtaining the consent from all the parties, the mediator can record in writing the facts not disputed by the two parties in the process of mediation and have the parties confirm it in writing. In the litigation procedure, except where the national interests, public interests and legal rights of others are involved, the parties are not required to produce evidence for the non-disputed facts as already confirmed in the process of mediation ... Confidentiality of the mediation procedure is one of the important reasons for mediation being favored by the parties and ensuring confidentiality is extremely critical for the successful promotion of mediation.[29]

Without doubt, recording the non-disputed facts breaks the binding force of the non-disclosure principle of mediation. As the dispute resolution mechanism was innovated independently by China, it applied the flexibility of the non-disclosure principle of mediation to the judicial reform of China, and reminded the legislators to collate and stipulate the non-disclosure principle and its exceptional circumstances in any future mediation legislation.

As a fundamental criterion of the ADR mechanism, the significance of the non-disclosure principle is not only to maintain the stability of the mediation procedure, but also to ensure the justice of the judicial procedure.[30] Different from litigation, the progress and success or failure of mediation are directly determined by the independent will of the parties, so how to properly protect the independent will of the parties is a core issue of mediation, and public mediation will damage the free expression of the parties' will to some extent. Starting with compromising the contradiction between the stability of the mediation procedure and the stability of the litigation procedure, some scholar proposed to keep confidential the mediation information by levels.[31] According to him, the non-disputed facts in the recording mechanism of non-disputed facts are in the category of "primary confidential information," but the category of "higher confidential information" is currently not yet expressly defined. We agree with the viewpoint of breaking the non-disclosure principle of mediation. Confidentiality is the opposite of open, and the open principle belongs to the category of a civil trial. In order to realize the vision of "making every citizen experience the fairness and justice of judicature in every case," the open principle of a trial must be implemented in the civil trial. Relatively speaking, mediation in a general sense is the free will of the two parties, without the need to be open generally to public supervision such as the judicature, and even the court mediation is merely the mediation of disputes undertaken by the judge as an intermediate mediator rather than the judicial act of the judge to exercise the adjudicatory power. In China's judicial practices, for such disputes involving personal privacy as marriage and family disputes, even if they are brought to court, the parties will also be advised to first approach the resident committee (or villager committee) at the place of household registration or habitual residence of the two parties for mediation. It is also the same in commercial mediation. As the most basic procedural rights, non-openness is the fundamental reason for mediation to be widely and successfully applied in the resolution of commercial disputes.[32]

7.4.3 The Legality Principle

The legality principle refers to the fact that mediation activities should not be contrary to the mandatory provisions of the law, regulations, and national policies, and should not be contrary to public order and good morals. With the strategy of legal governance of the state advancing comprehensively, the idea of legal governance is without doubt gradually winning support among the people. As one of the basic principles of mediation, people's understanding of the legality principle has also gradually developed. The legality principle of mediation has two connotations: (1) the procedural operation of mediation must be legal, and (2), the contents of the agreement concluded through mediation should be legal.[33] Actually, the procedural and substantive connotations of mediation are extremely rich, e.g., the application scope of mediation, the appointment of mediators, the application norms of mediation, the contents of mediation agreements, and so on must be rational and legal. The application norms of mediation are discussed hereinafter.

In addition to the statutory norms in a regular sense, the application norms of mediation include also the customs in a general sense[34] and local rules and regulations. Here, the local rules and regulations must be emphasized. As is well known, China people's mediation is mostly applied in the countryside. In the vast rural areas, the function of people's mediation is undertaken by the villager committees. The report to the 19th National Congress of the CPC proposed: "implement the rural development strategy. … Perfect the rural governance system with the combination of autonomy, legal governance and moral governance." As an important part of the rural governance system, rural mediation with the characteristics of rural autonomy must be given due attention in the new round of rural development. Some scholars proposed that the common law does not allow "directly suing the government," and it is necessary to follow the "principle of rural governance first," and the enforcement right of rural organizations for mediation first is also recognized by the state. They advocate a tendency of "prohibiting the direct action to the government."[35] Some scholar also proposed that since the vast rural areas are generally relatively closed, the status of the rural communities with the profound basic characteristics is gradually being marginalized in the national overall structure, but these local rules and regulations are, to some extent, deemed the combination of the natural demand of villagers' life and the rules of the state for the governance of rural society. They are not only the crystallization of village wisdom, but also the important content for the local government to rebuild rural order and still play an irreplaceable role in the rural governance.[36] Numerous scholars all emphasized the important significance of the local rules and regulations in the rural governance, but we must be aware of the conflict and coordination issues between the local rules and regulations and the national law. The mediation norms in the local rules and regulations shared only one part of the overall mediation norms, and their scope is, after all, limited. The "illegal" points of the local rules and regulations may be considered the exceptional circumstances in the binary branch structure. After all, regarding the national law or local rules and regulations, in terms of mediation in social disputes, the two share the common value target. Furthermore, we should not undertake the immutable and solidified interpretation of the legality principle of mediation. Just as some scholars have said, the dispute resolution modes provided in the local rules and regulations mainly include villagers' consultation on their own, village committee mediation, administrative organ mediation, and so on. "Mediation" is the uppermost dispute resolution mode and as the autonomous norms, the local rules and regulations do not have the coercive force of the state behind them in resolving disputes and mostly rely on the pressure of public opinion within villages or the coercive force of communities and rely on the force of the common law. The dispute mediation undertaken on the basis of local rules and regulations can even achieve more effective dispute resolution results than the national law in the present rural governance.[37]

The legality principle is the basic criterion that must be followed in all the mediation activities. Essentially, as a written contract or contractual provision concluded between the two parties, the mediation agreement concluded through mediation should follow the provision of Article 7 of *The Contract Law*. Legal norms are not the only basis of mediation and in the rural dispute mediation, emotional, custom, moral norms, and so on often become the negotiation counter for the mediator to moderate the mediation. The legality principle claimed by the author should be understood thus: as an act in the sense of private law, mediation is not naturally applicable to the irreconcilable contradiction between law and reason. As long as the mediation undertaken by the parties does not violate the prohibitory provisions of the law and does not harm the legal rights of the state, collectives or third parties, it can be deemed to be legal.

7.4.4 The Principle of Honesty and Credit

By consulting the references, one can see that introducing the concept of such moral categories as "good faith" into the legal norms was first undertaken in Ancient Roman law. In modern life, the principle of honesty and credit has such unique functions as restricting the contractual freedom, maintaining the public order and good morals, restricting the abuse of power and facilitating the formation of good habits to pay debts honestly. Its essence is morality and is the legal formalization of moral norms.[38] Establishment of the principle of honesty and credit in the "mediation law" is related to the moral rationality of mediation. This has been particularly discussed in Chapter 2 of this book, and will not be discussed further. In a dialectical sense, establishment of the principle of good faith between the parties is not only favorable to mediation, but also favorable to the conclusion and fulfillment of the mediation agreement. It avoids further waste of the parties' time and money, promotes the establishment of the social credit system, and restricts the arbitrariness and excessive discretionary power of their mediation by regulating the conduct of mediators, as is especially important for relaxing the crisis of credit observed with mediation.[39] This is also the original intention of the author to claim to regard the principle of honesty and credit as the basic principle of the "mediation law."

With the Notice of the State Council for Printing and Distributing *The Planning Outline for the Construction of Social Credit System* (2014–2020) (GF [2014]) No. 21) published, in the form of the state principles and policies, honesty and credit came into the public view as an important part of the construction outline of the social credit system, and the principle of honesty and credit is placed at a new high level in the contemporary social development. Essentially speaking, as the contractual consensus between the two parties, the mediation agreement is the particular fulfillment content planned by the two parties for dispute resolution. As the social credit system is gradually established, the act of participating in mediation and fulfilling the mediation agreement certainly should be included in the scope of application of the social credit system. It has laid down the strong policy keynote to include the principle of honesty and credit as the basic principle of the "mediation law." Article 7 of *The General Provisions of the Civil Law* provided: "the parties to civil legal relations shall conduct civil activities under the principle of good faith, adhere to honesty, and fulfill their promises." Article 13 of *The Civil Procedure Law* provided: "civil procedure should follow the principle of honesty and credit." In these two most important statutory laws, the principle of honesty and credit is the additional article, and especially the latter established the principle of honesty and credit at the legislative level, because such circumstances emerged in an endless stream and cannot be stopped, despite repeated bans in civil procedure, such as abusing of litigious rights, and infringing the legal rights of the state, collectives, and others. On the surface, the parties undertake the activities of civil procedure subject to the binding of the legal framework, but actually a number of litigious acts are observed against good faith. As an activity of civil affairs with weaker binding of law, mediation should without doubt properly follow the principle of honesty and credit, facing the social reality of "high arbitrariness of mediation and low fulfillment rate of mediation agreements."

7.5 Content Framework of the "Mediation Law"

As a comprehensive legislation in the field of mediation, the "mediation law" is a complex systematic project. To formulate the "mediation law," it is necessary to insist on the issue-orientation, highlight the key points and give adequate consideration to set up the legislative framework on the basis of the prevailing relevant mediation rules, with respect to such problems as the irregular connection between different types of mediation and between mediation and other dispute resolution mechanisms.

> As for to what fine extent the legislative framework draws the outline of the content of the act, there is no fixed model, but one point should be noted that excessive in-depth details may lead to the opaque basic framework and cause the logic relevance to be worse.[40]

In a vertical view of the countries that follow the statutory laws of the continental law system, France, Germany, Italy, and Japan all undertook the legislation, without exception, in the form of executive summary and separate narration. With France as an example, its proud "*Civil Code*" has been formulated for more than two hundred years. It has provided the example and reference system for the civil legislation of many countries in the world, with a major influence worldwide.[41] China's prevailing relatively mature statutory law styles, such as *The Criminal Law* and *The Civil Code*, are all formulated in the form of general provisions and special provisions. Currently, as the only law that regulates the particular types of mediation, *The People's Mediation Law* has in total 6 chapters and 35 articles, particularly including the general provisions, people's mediation committee, people's mediator, mediation procedure, mediation agreement, and supplementary provisions. Without the previous experiences to follow, it is better to prepare with reference to the existing relatively mature legislation style. The framework of the "mediation law" should take *The Constitution* as the guidance and *The People's Mediation Law*, the documents of the two general offices of the CPC Central Committee and the State Council for mediation reform,[42] the reform documents of the central commission of comprehensive governance,[43] the relevant reform documents of the court sector,[44] the rules of different provinces for the promotion of diversified dispute resolution mechanism,[45] measures of the governments at all levels for purchase of mediation services, rules of the relevant organizations,[46] and the foreign legislation models[47] as the major normative references. The contents of the "mediation law" must include: the principle of mediation, the scope of application of mediation, mediation organizations, mediators, mediation procedure, mediation rules, mediation agreement, relief procedure, and mediation fees. It is necessary to note that in the process of application, the mediation modes in various types must give consideration to the differentiation of China's economic and social development and should not simply copy *The People's Mediation Law* or other laws and regulations, but should, on the premise of establishing the overall framework, grasp the principle and flexibility of legislation application, follow the differential demand of local practices, and structure a kind of "binary regulation framework."[48]

7.5.1 Four Major Types of Mediation

The dispute mediation system is concerned with the framework content of the "mediation law." Actually, before *The People's Mediation Law* was published, academic circles quietly undertook the debate on what type of mediation law should be formulated. According to some viewpoints, it is necessary to structure the "mediation law" inclusive of people's mediation, court mediation, and all other types.[49] According to other viewpoints, the "mediation law" should include all types of mediation rather than litigious mediation and the application of the "mediation law" must lay stress on the coordination and integration between different types of mediation. Where *The Civil Procedure Law*, *The Administrative Procedure Law* and *The Criminal Procedure Law* have stipulated the particular provisions on relevant mediation, the "mediation law" is only taken as the macro guidance.[50] According to other viewpoints, the people's mediation law regulates the existing people's mediation organizations and their dispute resolution activities and other folk social mediation or dispute resolution mechanisms are applied with the macro regulation with the comprehensive mediation law or attached, by categories, to different substantive laws or procedural laws.[51] Also according to some viewpoints, the types of mediation applicable to the "mediation law" should not include litigious mediation, arbitration mediation, and administrative mediation.[52] According to others, the mediation under the binding of the "mediation law" should not involve the mediation in terms of administration and labor service and it is not suitable to combine the mediation in arbitration and litigation procedure and it is necessary to maintain the mediation pattern shaped by the prevailing *Civil Procedure Law*, *The Arbitration Law* and relevant laws.[53] In the opinion of the author, the existing types of dispute mediation have a multitude of names, but no type of mediation is suitable for regulation in the "mediation law." For instance, as a kind of industrial association, the notary association can be applicable with reference to the provisions of industrial mediation. Since the online mediation itself is undertaken with the aid of a network platform and the form and content of its mediation have no substantial difference from that of the spot mediation, it should be regulated in the provisions on the place of mediation. In order to make the framework set-up more compliant with the standard of logical rigor and inner and outer distribution, the types of mediation regulated by the "mediation law" should have certain differences. Comprehensively considered, in our opinion, the system framework of the "mediation law" should be set up in four major types of mediation: (1) people's mediation; (2) administrative mediation; (3), industrial mediation; and (4) commercial mediation, as well as give consideration to the new mediation modes to emerge continually and define the legal status of different mediation.[54]

First, amend and perfect the norms of people's mediation. People's mediation organizations are established on the basis of grass-roots autonomy and have the special attribute of the organizational form of a grass-roots regime. Since China is a socialist country of the people's democratic dictatorship, the nature of people's mediation should be oriented as mass character, autonomy, and public welfare. In addition to the function of resolving folk disputes, people's mediation also has such a function as social governance, cultural heritage, moral education, and assistance in judicature. Currently, the only statutory law available in China on mediation is *The People's Mediation Law* as adopted at the 16th meeting of the 11th NPC Standing Committee on August 28, 2010, and thus obviously, people's mediation is important in the Grand Mediation system in China and in the maturity of its legislation. But, the importance of people's mediation we have emphasized is actually a kind of misunderstanding and due to its labeling, people's mediation has carried various things it should not have carried.[55] Therefore, to formulate the "mediation law," a rational understanding must be held of people's mediation so that people's mediation returns to its pure features. The main framework and provisions of people's mediation in the "mediation law" should make reference to the provisions of the prevailing *People's Mediation Law*.

Second, integrate the norms of administrative mediation. The past and even present administrative mediation has been closely connected with "rule by man" to a great extent, and the special functional set-up of China's administrative organs has determined that administrative mediation has the nature of administrative guidance. The people have denounced various points in administrative mediation, but such advantages of administrative mediation as efficiency, low cost, openness, and authority cannot be matched by other mediation modes. Administrative mediation was generated on the premise of democratic consultation and the voluntary will of the parties and in the special period of the functional transformation of Chinese government and change of the administration model, administrative mediation not only has the function of dispute resolution, but also can assist in formulating the policies, so it is necessary without doubt for administrative mediation to be compiled independently. As administrative mediation includes the norms of positive law, it is currently urgent to integrate it into the form of legislation and form a system.

Third, rationally tap the potential of industrial mediation. Industrial mediation should be a mediation mode with a commercial nature as well as the nature of government's purchase of social mediation services. As China's socialist market economy continually has developed, the role of industrial mediation in resolving the industrial disputes became increasingly prominent, and especially in terms of the recognition between the members of industry, industrial mediation is often deemed a shortcut for dispute resolution under the guidance of collective consciousness. The special issues between different industrial disputes are extremely difficult for the mediators in a general sense to mediate upon, and the existence of the self-repair and self-correction mechanism in the industry is also an advantage of industrial mediation to resolve disputes. When formulating the norms of industrial mediation, we should especially lay stress on the treatment of relations between the autonomy of industrial associations and the intervention of state power, and especially should expressly define the concept, nature, and scope of application of industrial mediation so as to establish the uniqueness of industrial mediation different from other mediation.

Fourth, actively develop the advantages of commercial mediation. With China's basic national policy of opening-up and "One Belt and One Road" being advanced, commercial mediation possesses a vast stage. Arbitration is still the internationally more recognized and major dispute resolution mode, but commercial mediation will naturally mature as China's socialist market economy develops. Currently, the Chinese commercial mediation institutions are developing like bamboo shoots after a spring rain shower and the commercial mediation should insist on operating with the market-based mechanism and provide specialized and high-end chargeable services. Actually, the Supreme People's Court set up separately the international commercial court, because the level of foreign legal services fails to match the speed of China's economic and social opening-up and development, and China is in urgent need of a fair, just, and rational international commercial dispute resolution mechanism to accompany China's market economic development, while the commercial mediation is more efficient, convenient, and low-cost than commercial trial and it became one of the rational modes for dispute resolution.[56] It must be noted that "lawyer mediation" should be better defined as the act of commercial mediation, particularly with reference to the norms of commercial mediation for application. As the General Office of the CPC Central Committee and the General Office of the State Council printed and distributed *The Suggestions for Deepening the Reform of Lawyer Institution* and *The Suggestions of the Supreme People's Court and Ministry of Justice of Undertaking the Pilot Work of Lawyer Mediation*, all the places nationwide actively undertook the pilot work of the lawyer mediation reform, but with many problems being observed in the pilot work of lawyer mediation, its nature of commercial mediation became without doubt prominent. Upon carrying out the field interviews with some lawyer mediators and analyzing, with reference to the development experiences of the USA and other countries in terms of lawyer mediation, we consider that the advancing direction of lawyer mediation should be a market-based operation, while such welfare modes as the form of government's purchase of services currently at the pilot stage will continue, and will eventually be integrated into the commercial mediation system.

7.5.2 The Procedural Connection Mechanism

The diversity of disputes mediation demands substantially emphasizes the need to formulate a "mediation law" with a comprehensive vision. In the particular disputes mediation, we should pay attention to the coordination and interaction between different types of mediation and between mediation and other dispute resolution modes to realize the procedural connection mechanism of performing the respective function, carrying out the multi-party link, and forming joint forces. The "mediation law" should attach importance to the following procedural connection mechanisms.

First, in order to change the pattern of undertaking an individual fight and acting their own way in the mediation mode, it is necessary to structure the effective connection mechanism between different mediation institutions, i.e., the connection between people's mediation, administrative mediation, industrial mediation, and commercial mediation. With the connection of people's mediation and administrative mediation as an example, due to various factors, in many circumstances, the present administrative mediation plays its role with the aid of the platform of people's mediation, while people's mediation also, in the reverse manner. relies on the coordination of administrative mediation. Therefore, part of civil disputes can be brought into the scope of administrative mediation. When mediating in civil disputes, the administrative organ should properly treat the relations between the mediation of civil disputes as per their function and power. If civil disputes exceed the scope of its function power, the scope of civil disputes for administrative mediation should be rationally confined. The parties to civil disputes are not prohibited from applying for resolution of disputes through administrative mediation, as it is not meant to ignore the use of people's mediation in resolution of civil disputes. But it is meant not to consolidate the rights of the parties to choose different types of mediation to resolve disputes, assuring the procedural option of the parties. Actually, it is closely connected with the special national conditions of China. For instance, in the mediation of group contradictions and disputes, the advantage of people's mediation is that it can timely control and report the early warning information, properly carry out the work of preliminary persuasion and stability maintenance, and take a pre-emptive opportunity for dispute resolution. The advantage and disadvantage of administrative mediation are both very evident. The advantage is that it can control the stability by relying on the strong administrative power and function, and its disadvantage is that the mediation organizations of administrative have been under pressure for years. In order to make best use of the advantages and bypass the disadvantages, it is necessary to give play to the maximum value of administrative mediation and people's mediation for the sake of realizing their complementary advantages. Besides, in the process of formulating the "mediation law," stipulate the prohibitive limitations on the scope of application of mediation in the general provisions, while for the mediation scope of positive application, appropriate guidance is undertaken only where applicable in administrative mediation or industrial mediation. Since commercial mediation completely insists on market-based development, the particular application scope has not yet been guided. The scope of application for different types of mediation is extremely important for the internal connection of mediation procedure. Since voluntary mediation is regarded as the prime principle for mediating, the internal connection of mediation procedure should adequately assure the independence and voluntary will of the parties to choose the mode of mediation. The norms of the scope of application of mediation can guide, as much as possible, the parties in choosing the appropriate mode to undertake the disputes mediation.

Second, actively explore the recording of non-disputed facts and the recognition of non-objected mediation solutions. In order to avoid any subsequent worries of the parties and assure smooth mediation, with respect to the acceptance of case facts by the parties to conclude a mediation or conciliation agreement, the law generally prohibits the opposite party or judge from taking the recording as the evidence unfavorable to one party in the subsequent litigation. But in the alternative dispute resolution, in order to avoid any unnecessary waste of the achievement of dispute resolution, in a dispute for which no mediation agreement is eventually concluded, upon obtaining the unanimous consent from the parties, the mediation organization can record, in writing, the non-disputed facts and have the two parties confirm it in writing. In litigation, the parties are not required to produce any evidence for the non-disputed facts as confirmed in the process of mediation, and this has substantially reduced the focus of disputes and enhanced the efficiency of dispute resolution. However, where the parties have no major objection to the major disputed facts, but have only disputes on individual matters, upon obtaining the consent from the parties, the mediator can propose a mediation solution and deliver the same in writing to the two parties. Where the parties fail to object within the specified period of time, the mediation agreement on a voluntary basis should be considered concluded. Where an objection is raised, the mediation agreement should be considered as not established. Such a recording mechanism of non-disputed facts and the recognition mechanism of non-disputed mediation solution have already started to be used in practice and were reflected in the judicial reform documents of the Supreme People's Court.

Third, expand the scope of application of the judicial confirmation procedure for a mediation agreement. A mediation agreement is deemed a manifestation of the intention of the two parties to achieve consensus and has a contractual power. However, the "contract" is not as simple as it seems to be from conclusion to fulfillment. The mediation agreement is not a joke, but currently, since the desire of some of the parties to fulfill the statutory obligations is lacking and China's good faith system is not yet established, the voluntary and non-mandatory nature of mediation is often accompanied by the uncertainty in fulfilling the mediation agreement. As is well known, *The Civil Procedure Law* established the judicial confirmation mechanism of mediation agreements, and limited the scope of application of judicial confirmation procedure to people's mediation agreement. Actually, in the process of legislation, there used to be different opinions about the scope of application of judicial confirmation procedure for mediation agreements. With reference to the provisions of Article 33 of *The People's Mediation Law*, some people proposed that judicial confirmation could be applied only for people's mediation agreement. Others also proposed that in practice, it does not mean that people's mediation dominates exclusively and judicial confirmation could also be applied for such mediation of administrative organs as public order mediation, traffic accident compensation mediation, medical dispute mediation, social group mediation, and commercial mediation. Due to the relatively complex circumstances of administrative mediation and commercial mediation, the then legislators temporarily could not reach a common agreement on whether to provide the judicial confirmation for the mediation agreement concluded through such a mediation, and took a prudent attitude toward the judicial confirmation procedure considering the features of Chinese folk disputes and the actual conditions of people's mediation.[57] But against the present background of various types of mediation in operation, numerous mediation agreements failed to be eventually fulfilled, all due to the problem of effect. The judicial confirmation procedure for mediation agreements is after all to "lock" the mediation agreement, consolidate the achievement of mediation activities, promote the effective connection between judicature and non-proceeding mediation, and promote the improvement of the diversified dispute resolution mechanism, as conforms to formulating the "mediation law." Therefore, the "mediation law" with the new idea and new thought of mediation as the guidance should expand the scope of judicial confirmation in combination with realistic demands so that it covers such mediation agreements as administrative mediation, industrial mediation, and commercial mediation.

Fourth, lay stress on the rational connection between mediation and such dispute resolution mechanisms as litigation and arbitration. As known in the industry, facing the chaos of social contradictions and disputes, relying merely on the mediation mode already fails to meet the realistic demands of dispute resolution, and the diversified resolution of disputes becomes the subject matter of the present dispute resolution. With the reality of connection between mediation and litigation, all places nationwide already have had various practical experiences: from the exploration of practices in different places, Zhejiang Province has gradually established the mechanism of connection of people's mediation and administrative mediation with litigation procedure, with the representative practices including the work coordination mechanism with the joint meeting as support,[58] the case distribution mechanism with court's case filing hall as pivot,[59] the dispute resolution mechanism with the comprehensive governance center as the platform,[60] the authority formation mechanism of people's mediation with judicial confirmation as assurance, and the professional training mechanism of people's mediators with people's courts leaders.[61] The court sector of Langfang, Hebei, has formed in recent years ten main mechanisms inclusive of pre-litigation mediation, special mediator, voluntary mediation, tour mediation, non-proceeding mediation agreement judicial confirmation, promoting the undertaking of litigious mediation and connection with people's mediation. In terms of the connection between administrative mediation and litigious mediation, Hebei Xinglong Court undertook a large number of exploration studies, and applied, on a pilot basis, the administrative coordination liaison officer institution, built the administrative coordination platform by establishing the "one-network, three-visit and four-coordination"[62] mechanism to promote the benign interaction between the judicature and administration.[63] The rich pilot experiences in different places have provided extremely valuable references to design the connection between mediation and external relevant dispute resolution mechanism, which should be absorbed in the formulation of the "mediation law."

7.5.3 Facilitate the Assurance Measures

Deficient motive for development and weak supporting strength are the problems to be urgently resolved in China's mediation system. In this regard, the state must make a series of assurance measures of facilitation and motivate the activeness and initiative of different dispute participants, as is also the function of the "mediation law."

First, provide the parties with dispute mediation path guidance. The dispute mediation mechanism should be "varied" as well as "rational and orderly" and avoid confusion in application, a tree with twisting roots and gnarled branches. Facing the "varied" mediation mechanisms, the awareness of the

Chinese public that they can choose a mediation mode is not profound, and in the circumstance with a clear picture of the overall situation of disputes, they may choose litigation or may choose a mediation type without considering the particular conditions. We cannot expect the parties to automatically choose, in the circumstance of incomplete information, the best dispute mediation path, but must structure, with a practical attitude, the appropriate dispute mediation guidance mechanism. In terms of the features of statutory law and case law and judging the development trend, some scholars introduced the cases into the mediation procedure in compliance with the development requirement of civil judgment mode reform.[64] With the aid of the regulation and guidance of British case law, some scholars proposed that in exploring the reform of diversified mediation mechanism, China should rationally adopt the voluntary principle of mediation.[65] Therefore, in addition to following the basic general law of relying mainly on territorial and personal jurisdiction and jurisdiction of dispute nature subsidiary, the choice of the mediation mechanism should also set up a relatively comprehensive and one-stop mediation service platform, define the obligation of all participants to inform the dispute mediation mode, and strengthen the propaganda and education, to enhance the understanding and acceptance of the public about the mediation mechanism, and form an atmosphere of mediation culture.

Second, intensify the support, supervision, and examination of the Party committee and government for the mediation work. With reference to the division of subject duty, implement the leadership responsibility system for the heads of the Party and government to guide and coordinate the resolution of major contradictions and disputes.[66] Intensify the human, financial, and material assurance and try as much as possible to meet the demand for mediation. All departments at all levels should intensify the information comprehension, timely report the contradictions and disputes discovered and accepted by the unit and the circumstance of the mediation work, exchange mediation experiences, strengthen the Grand Mediation system of contradictions and disputes, establish the database of information, grasp dynamically and in time the overall status of disputes and the progress of individual cases, realize the horizontal and vertical information sharing of dispute resolution to drive the regularization with information, and promote the work efficiency of the Grand Mediation. Intensify the collection, analysis, and circulation of relevant mediation information. Urge all departments and units to sincerely implement the departmental and unit responsibility system and take the proper mediation as an important part in the examination of the comprehensive governance of public order. Organize the relevant departments and units to carry out the special inspection of the connection of Grand Mediation and resolve the problems observed in work. Praise and reward the units (organizations) and individuals for doing well in mediation of disputes according to the national provisions. In the places and units where the leader's failure to pay attention, where improper mediation and major contradictions and disputes endanger the social order and social stability, track down those responsible and circulate criticism, impose warnings and even apply the one vote veto according to the circumstances.[67]

Third, introduce the market-based mechanism to promote the service quality of dispute mediation. China's prevailing mediation mechanisms are mainly of welfare and currently for such mediation as people's mediation, administrative mediation, and even industrial mediation, or lawyer mediation, the proportion of the government's purchase of services is not low. In terms of commercial mediation and industrial mediation, market-based mechanism is a shortcut to bring the relevant mediation services to maturity, which can attract high-end talents with special knowledge to join the mediation team as well as realizing the survival of the fittest through market-based competition mechanism, promoting the dispute mediation quality and meeting the demands of the parties for dispute mediation at different levels. While insisting on the free charge of traditional people's mediation and administrative mediation, the "mediation law" should encourage other mediation mechanisms such as commercial mediation and industrial mediation to take the market-based approach and realize the two-way development model of welfare mediation mechanism and market-based mediation mechanism. In the meantime, the local governments should issue such preferential and supporting policies as procedure simplification and tax reduction and exemption according to local conditions and encourage the social forces to participate in dispute resolution by actively purchasing the dispute resolution services from the social mediation organizations.[68]

Fourth, strengthen the professionalization of the mediator team. Since the beginning of the twenty-first century, the mediation institution has been highly favored and the specialized and professionalized development trend is prominent. The professionalization of the mediator team is the natural requirement of the complexity of social disputes as well as the important identification of the maturity and development of mediation skills. But, currently, different types of mediation all face different professional dilemmas: people's mediation lacks the complete career development system and has no full-time people's mediator group and the funding assurance is deficient; industrial mediation has a low utilization rate, the dispute resolution capacity of industrial mediators is lacking and there is no definite regular career assurance; the legislation of commercial mediation lags behind, the set-up of commercial mediation institutions is short of regularity and folk credibility is missing.[69] In view of the development experiences in other countries, the change in the attitude of the Italian public toward mediation originated from the attention of the legislators to the mediation procedure, while the attention of legislators was rooted in the application of mediation when resolving corporate disputes and the professional training undertaken for mediators.[70] From the legislative purpose to the particular provisions, Japan's *Law on the Promotion of Alternative Dispute Resolution Procedure* stipulated the qualification certification of the practitioners of alternative dispute resolution as an important part. Therefore, the Chinese government and the relevant departments should strengthen the specialization and professionalization of the mediator team, intensify the qualification certification and management of dispute resolution practitioners, and promote their career assurance.

7.6 Conclusion

During the period of the Republic of China, in the legislation proposal for *The Civil Mediation Law*, the President of Legislative Yuan, Hu Hanmin proposed the necessity for the mediation legislation:

> China always attaches importance to comity and is ashamed of going to court for lawsuits. In case of any minor disputes, approach the elders of noble character and high prestige to judge the right and wrong and settle the disputes in a few words, as passes from mouth to mouth with approbation. Nowadays, such a tradition has been gradually lost and people are fond of taking action for judging the win and loss and settling the difficult disputes. In terms of the past, it is better to learn from the ancient practice and in terms of the present, it is to adopt the European and American regulations and make necessary accommodation for judges to moderate the matter, as is called mediation. This is to define its effect and form the decree document for implementation nationwide.[71]

This was the beginning of the state legalizing the folk mediation. This law was promulgated in 1930 and was again abolished in a hurry in 1935, but mediation was thus formally planted in the national litigation institution and became a part of China's practice of civil law with most Chinese characteristics.

The past has gone for a thousand years. Traditional China has already experienced "great changes unprecedented for a thousand years," but different from the litigation-centralism dispute resolution ideas of the Western countries, China's Confucian cultural tradition with harmony as most precious continued in an endless succession and has lasted up to now, and corresponded to the contemporary mediation idea. Facing the changes in main contradictions in society in the new era, mediation still has the mission to "stop and settle disputes and reduce caseloads." Based on this, China should keep a foothold in its own historical tradition and realistic national conditions to structure the "mediation law" with Chinese characteristics and contribute China's wisdom and China's experiences to the co-governance of human fate. In the future, in the field of mediation, China should form a mediation law system with the harmony, co-existence, and co-flourishing of people's mediation, administrative mediation, industrial mediation, commercial mediation, and judicial mediation. We expect that China will be able, in the future, to continually promote the function and application of mediation in dispute resolution, remold the glory of the mediation institution and provide all people with a kind of relatively convenient and relatively low-cost access to justice. Mediation should contribute forces, jointly with litigation, arbitration and other dispute resolution mechanisms, to the diversified dispute resolution law system. This is the real significance of formulating the "mediation law."

Notes

1 The concept of the "society of litigation" was first proposed by Professor Zhang Wenxian in China. It is generally viewed that if a society has annually about 10 percent of the population involved in litigation, this society can be considered a "society of litigation." Zhang Wenxian: Chinese Judicature between Modernity and Post-Modernity – Chinese Courts in Society of Litigation, *Modern Law Science*, 2014 (1).

2 Shen Zongling (Chief Ed.): *Jurisprudence* (Beijing: Higher Education Press, 1994), p. 273.

3 Fan Yu: Issues on Formulation of the Mediation Law (I), *Justice of China*, 2005 (10); Tang Weijian: Thinking about Formulation of Social Mediation Law, *Studies in Law and Business*, 2007 (1).

4 Luo Gan: Political and Law Organs Bear the Major Historical Mission and Political Responsibility, *Qiushi*, 2007 (3), p. 7.

5 Li Hao: Comparative Advantages of Mediation and Reform of Court Mediation Institution, *Journal of Nanjing Normal University (Social Sciences)*, 2002 (4).

6 Liao Yongan and Liu Qing: On the Dilemma and Way-out of China's Mediation Professionalization, *Journal of Xiangtan University (Philosophy and Social Sciences)*, 2016 (6), p. 49.

7 Tang Weijian: Chinese Mediation Institution in the Perspective of Modern Transformation, *Chaoyang Law Review*, 2010 (2), pp. 165–166.

8 Fan Yu: Issues on Formulation of the Mediation Law (I), *Justice of China*, 2005(10).

9 Qi Shujie (Chief Ed.): *New Development of Foreign ADR System* (Xiamen: Xiamen University Press, 2017), pp. 22–24.

10 Nadjia Marie Alexander: *Global Trends in Mediation*, trans. Wang Fuhua, et al. (Beijing: China Legal Publishing House, 2011), p. 33.

11 Qi Shujie (Chief Ed.): *New Development of Foreign ADR System*, pp. 22–30.

12 Xu Guangming: Diversified Resolution of Commercial Disputes under the Background of One Belt and One Road, *People's Court Daily*, September 15, 2017, Edition 5.

13 Sun Yunfeng (Ed.): *How to Carry out Mediation Work Properly: Practical Skills and Cases of Mediation* (Beijing: China Legal Publishing House, 2013), pp. 12–13.

14 Li Jin: Path Option for Integration of Core Socialist Values into Scientific Legislation, *Journal of Xinjiang Normal University (Philosophy and Social Sciences)*, 2019 (1), pp. 29–30.

15 *The Suggestions of the CPC Central Committee for Formulating the 13th Five-year Planning of National Economic and Social Development*, *The People's Daily*, November 4, 2015, Edition 1.

16 Zhou Youyong: Logic and Approach – How New Development Idea Leads the Construction of Legal Governance in China, *Law and Social Development*, 2018 (3), p. 35.

17 Liu Jinguo and Jiang Jinshan (Chief Eds.): *New Jurisprudence* (Beijing: China University of Political Science and Law Press, 2006), p. 3.

18 Gong Pixiang: New Development Idea: Strategic Leading of China's Legal Governance Modernization, *Law and Modernization*, 2017 (1), p. 23.

19 The words "Co-existential Justice" refer to the concept proposed by the famous Italian comparative jurist Mauro Cappelletti when discussing ADR. In the opinion of Cappelletti, Alternative Dispute Resolution is a kind of co-existential justice and litigation pursues a kind of "contentious justice." See Mauro Cappelletti, Access To Justice as a Theoretical Approach to Law and a Practical Programme for Reform, *South African Law Journal* (1992) (109): 22, Mauro Cappelletti, Alternative Dispute Resolution Processes Within the Framework of the Worldwide Access-to-Justice Movement, *The Modern Law Review* 1995 (56): 287.

20 Liao Yongan: New Idea and New Thinking of Contemporary Mediation, *People's Court Daily*, June 16, 2017, Edition 2.

21 Guo Daohu: *Essentials of Jurisprudence* (Changsha: Hunan People's Publishing House, 2005), p. 235.

22 Some scholars proposed the "principle that mediation is not the necessary procedure of litigation." Chang Yi (Chief Ed.): *Chinese Mediation System* (Beijing: Law Press, 2013), pp. 59–61.

23 Li De'en and Liu Shiguo: Structuring of Mediation Principle Based on the Substantial Regression of Mediation, *Journal of South-Central Minzu University (Humanities and Social Sciences)*, 2010 (2), p. 135.

24 Chang Yi (Chief Ed.): *Chinese Mediation System* (Beijing: Law Press, 2013), p. 55.

25 Wang Ge: Studies on Mandatory Mediation Model, *Review of Political Science and Law*, 2014 (6), p. 104.

26 Li Shaoping (Chief Ed.): *Understanding and Application of The Suggestions of the Supreme People's Court for the Reform of Diversified Dispute Resolution Mediation and Provisions on Special Mediation* (Beijing: People's Court Press, 2017), p. 249.

27 Li De'en: *Systematic Studies on Civil Mediation Theory: Based on the Autonomous Principle of the Parties* (Beijing: China Legal Publishing House, 2012), p. 96.

28 Qiu Xingmei and Wang Qiulan: *Mediation Law* (Xiamen: Xiamen University Press, 2008), p. 81.

29 Zhan Yun: Issues in Mediation Legislation in Judicial Reform of Hong Kong, *Southeast Justice Review*, 2011, p. 31.

30 Guo Yujun and Mei Qiuling: Research on Confidentiality of Arbitration, *Law Review*, 2004 (2), p. 26; Wang Zuxing: Exploration of Non-disclosure Institution Related to ADR, *Modern Law Science*, 2005 (3), p. 56.

31 Zhou Jianhua: Non-Disclosure Principle of Judicial Mediation, *Law of the Times*, 2008 (5), p. 76.

32 Yin Li: Interpretation and Analysis of Non-disclosure Norms for Commercial Case Mediation, *Oriental Law*, 2008 (6), p. 72.

33 Chang Yi (Chief Ed.): *Chinese Mediation System*, p. 56.

34 Article 10 of *General Provisions of the Civil Law of the People's Republic of China* provided: "civil disputes shall be resolved in accordance with the law, or if the law is silent, customs may apply, but not contrary to the public order and good morals." Obviously, in the civil law system, customs have become the judgment basis in a proper sense under the legal hierarchy.

35 Gao Qicai: *China's Common Law Theory* (Changsha: Hunan Publishing House, 1995), pp. 77–79.

36 Zhang Mingxin: From Local Rules and Regulations to Articles of Villagers' Autonomy – Evolution of Local Rules and Regulations, *Jiangsu Social Sciences*, 2006 (4), p. 174.

37 Chen Hanfei and Gao Qicai: Empirical Study on the Active Roles of Local Rules and Regulations in Rural Governance, *Tsinghua University Law Journal*, 2018 (1), p. 75.

38 Zhang Guoyan and Lin Zhe: Principle of Honesty and Credit and Legal Governance Target of Modern Society, *Political Science and Law*, 2000 (5), p. 23–25. Professor Liang Huixing also holds a similar viewpoint, see Liang Huixing: Principle of Honesty and Credit and the Existence of Loopholes, *Chinese Journal of Law*, 1994 (2), pp. 23–24.

39 Ma Aiping and Liu Fangfang: *Principle of Honesty and Credit and Perfection of ADR, Journal of Shanxi University (Philosophy and Social Sciences)*, 2006 (4), pp. 129–130.

40 Cao Dieyun: *Legislation Techniques* (Beijing: China Democratic Legal System Press, 1993), p. 157.

41 *French Civil Code*, trans. Luo Jiezheng (Beijing: China Legal Publishing House, 1999), pp. 1–2.

42 For example, *The Suggestions for Perfecting the Diversified Resolution Mechanism of Contradictions and Disputes*.

43 For example, *The Guidelines for Promoting Profoundly the Grand Mediation Work of Contradictions and Disputes*.

44 For example, the Supreme People's Court's *Provisions on the Issues for Civil Mediation Work of People's Courts*, the *Suggestions of the Supreme People's Court for Implementing Further the Work Principle of "Mediation-first and Mediation-judgment Combination,"* the *Provisions on the Judicial Confirmation Procedure of People's Mediation Agreement*, *General Program for Expanding the Pilot Work of Reform of Contradiction and Dispute Resolution Mechanism with the Linkage of Litigation and Non-litigation*, *The Suggestions for People's Courts to Deepen Further the Reform of Diversified Dispute Resolution Mechanism*, *The Suggestions for Establishing and Perfecting the Resolution Mechanism of Contradictions and Disputes with the Linkage of Litigation and Non-litigation*, *The Guidelines of Jilin Provincial Higher People's Court for Advancing the Construction of Diversified Dispute Resolution Mechanism*, and *The Provisions of Guangdong Provincial Higher People's Court for Intensifying Further the Litigation-mediation Matchmaking Work*.

45 For example, *The Regulations of Xiamen Special Economic Zone for the Promotion of the Diversified Dispute Resolution Mechanism Xiamen*, *The Regulations of Shandong Province for the Promotion of Diversified Dispute Resolution*, *The Regulations of Heilongjiang Province for the Diversified Resolution of Social Contradictions and Disputes*, *The Regulations of Fujian Province for Diversified Dispute Resolution*, and *The Regulations of Anhui Province for the Promotion of Diversified Dispute Resolution*.

46 *The Mediation Rules of the United Nations Commission of International Trade Law*, *The Model Law on International Commercial Conciliation of the United Nations Commission of International Trade Law*, *The Mediation Rules of China International Economic and Trade Arbitration Commission South China Branch Mediation Center*, *The Mediation Rules of China Council for the Promotion of*

International Trade/International Chamber of Commerce Mediation Center, and *Beijing Arbitration Commission Mediation Center Mediation Rules*.

47 Japanese *Civil Mediation Law*, South Korean *Civil Mediation Law*, American *Uniform Mediation Act*, and Australian *Civil Dispute Resolution Act*.

48 Some scholars proposed that the "binary regulation framework" is a kind of harmonic resolution solution and the regulation of mediation should enter a simplified legislation framework for the organic balance of quality and flexibility; in terms of legislation, affirm the value of the co-existence of uniform central legislation and local regional practice and in terms of regulation content, separate explicitly. Xiong Hao: On the Transformation of Chinese Mediation Law Regulation Model, *Studies in Law and Business*, 2018 (3), p. 119.

49 Song Chaowu, et al.: *Studies on Mediation Legislation* (Beijing: China University of Political Science and Law Press, 2008), p. 246.

50 Yang Rongxin: Structuring of Harmonious Society Calls for Mediation Law, *Legal Daily*, March 3, 2005.

51 Fan Yu: Issues on Formulation of the Mediation Law (II), *Justice of China*, 2005 (11), p. 69.

52 Qu Kunshan: *My Opinion about the Legislation of Uniform "Mediation Law,"* website of China International Chamber of Commerce Mediation Center (accessed March 19, 2014), cited in Wang Qiulan, et al.: *Studies on Legislation, Theory and Practice of Chinese Mediation* (Beijing: China University of Political Science and Law Press, 2014), p. 53.

53 Wang Qiulan, et al:. *Studies on Legislation, Theory and Practice of Chinese Mediation* (Beijing: China University of Political Science and Law Press, 2014), p. 53.

54 The process of compiling mainly forms three representative mediation system classifications: (1) classify such seven parts as general provisions, people's mediation, administrative mediation, commercial mediation, lawyer mediation, and supplementary provisions; (2) classify such five parts as general provisions, people's mediation, administrative mediation, social mediation, and supplementary provisions, of which social mediation includes lawyer mediation, industrial mediation, and commercial mediation; (3) classify such six parts as general provisions, people's mediation, administrative mediation, industrial mediation, commercial mediation, and supplementary provisions.

55 Wu Jun: Deficiency of "*People's Mediation Law*" and Necessity for Uniform Mediation Law, *Judicial Reform Review*, 2016 (15), p. 196.

56 *The Provisions of the Supreme People's Court on Issues of Setting up the International Commercial Court* (FS [2018] No. 11).

57 Commission of Legislative Affairs under the NPC Standing Committee: *Interpretations of the Civil Procedure Law of the People's Republic of China*: Latest Amended Version (Beijing: Law Press, 2012), pp. 457–458.

58 The work coordination mechanism with joint meeting as support refers to the establishment of the communication and consultation institution in such forms as judicial joint meeting for such organizations as the court, public security, judicial administration and relevant administrative departments and trade unions, youth leagues and women's federations, formulate the planning of mediation work, regularly hold meetings, circulate to each other the mediation information and status of social contradictions and disputes, jointly study the solutions for major and

difficult disputes, analyze the existing problems and difficulties, and define the duties and work division of the relevant departments.

59 The case distribution mechanism with the court's case filing hall as pivot refers to the fact that the court establishes the reception hall of case filing integrated with such functions as accepting lawsuits, entertaining inquiries, guiding the limitation, receiving, settling, and returning litigation fees, for the sake of distributing the cases, according to such factors as the nature of disputes, appeals purpose and moods of the parties, to such modes as mediation and immediate judgment for treatment, where it is suitable to handle in advance through such approaches as people's mediation, actively guide the parties to choose the people's mediation.

60 The dispute resolution mechanism with the comprehensive governance center as the platform refers to the fact that the comprehensive governance center led by the party committee or the comprehensive governance commission with the court, judicial administration, public security, urban construction, labor, civil affairs, and so on as the member units, establishes the joint meeting institution of Grand Mediation for social contradictions and disputes and intensifies the coordination and cooperation between the relevant departments.

61 Project Team of Zhejiang Provincial Higher People's Court: Survey and Thinking of the Connection Mechanism of People's Mediation, Administrative Mediation and Litigation Procedure, *Research on Rule of Law*, 2008 (3), pp. 4–6.

62 "One-network" means to structure the network of administrative coordination liaison officers so that the administrative coordination interweaves vertically and horizontally and forms a scale, and the courts coordinate with the office of legal affairs of the government, township government, bureau of public security, administration of land resources, and other administrative enforcement organs to define the coordination liaison offices and make clear the relevant duties and contact modes. "Three-visit" means to implement the coordination and communication mechanism of "visit in advance, after-case visit, and regular visit" for the administrative enforcement organs. "Four-coordination" refers to the coordination of case filing and examination, coordination in trial, post-judgment coordination, and coordination in non-proceeding enforcement case examination, so as to carry out the administrative coordination from beginning to end.

63 Liang Ping: Theoretical Structuring and Empirical Exploration of "Grand Mediation" Connection Mechanism, *Science of Law*, 2011 (5), pp. 156–158.

64 Wang Liankun: Give Play to the Guiding and Demonstrating Role of Judicial Precedents in Mediation, *People's Justice*, 2002 (10), p. 48.

65 Zhang Yonghong: Regulation and Guidance of British Case Law for Mediation, *Journal of Law Application*, 2016 (Z1), p. 189.

66 *The Provisions for the Party and Governmental Principals to Fulfill the Duty of the First Responsible Persons to Promote the Construction of Legal Governance* published by the General Office of CPC Central Committee and General Office of the State Council made clear and definite that the Party and governmental principals must fulfill the duty of the first responsible persons to promote the construction of legal governance. This is an important part in undertaking the construction of legal governance to formulate the "mediation law" and advance the orderly mediation, as it is important to the construction of the country with legal governance, government with legal governance, and society with legal governance.

67 Article 19 and Article 20 of *The Guidelines for Promoting Profoundly the Grand Mediation Work of Contradictions and Disputes.*

68 Liao Yongan and Jiang Fengming: New Conception for Development of Social Mediation in the New Era, *Chinese Social Sciences Today*, January 18, 2018. Edition 1.

69 Liao Yongan and Liu Qing: On the Dilemma and Way-out of China's Mediation Professionalization, *Journal of Xiangtan University (Philosophy and Social Sciences)*, 2016 (6), pp. 48–49.

70 Giuseppe D. Palo and Veronica Alvisi: Professional Evolution of Italian Mediation, trans. Jiang Liping, *People's Court Daily*, June 17, 2011, Edition 6.

71 The Civil Mediation Law formulated in the period of the Republic of China was mainly meant for court mediation, but upon textual research, some scholars pointed out the establishment of "mediation" as a formal name originated in this law. Previously, the practice of civil mediation was popular among the people for a long time, but there had been no uniform name. Wang Chunzi: Development and Evolution of China's Civil Mediation Institution in the Modern Times -- Focusing on the Civil Mediation Law (1930), *Shengjing Law Review*, 2016 (2).

References

Alexander, Nadjia Marie: *Global Trends in Mediation* trans. Wang Fuhua, et al., Beijing: China Legal Publishing House, 2011.

Cao Dieyun: *Legislation Techniques*, Beijing: China Democratic Legal System Press, 1993.

Cappelletti, Mauro: Access to Justice as a Theoretical Approach to Law and a Practical Programme for Reform, *South African Law Journal* 1992 (109): 22.

Chang Yi (Chief Ed.): *Chinese Mediation System*, Beijing: Law Press, 2013.

Chen Hanfei and Gao Qicai: Empirical Study on the Active Roles of Local Rules and Regulations in Rural Governance, *Tsinghua University Law Journal*, 2018 (1): 75.

Commission of Legislative Affairs under the NPC Standing Committee: *Interpretations of the Civil Procedure Law of the People's Republic of China: Latest Amended Version*, Beijing: Law Press, 2012.

Fan Yu: Issues on Formulation of the Mediation Law (I), *Justice of China*, 2005(10): 71–74.

Fan Yu: Issues on Formulation of the Mediation Law (II), *Justice of China*, 2005 (11): 66–69.

Gao Qicai: *China's Common Law Theory*, Changsha: Hunan Publishing House, 1995.

Gong Pixiang: New Development Idea: Strategic Leading of China's Legal Governance Modernization, *Law and Modernization*, 2017 (1): 23.

Guo Daohu: *Essentials of Jurisprudence*, Changsha: Hunan People's Publishing House, 2005.

Guo Yujun and Mei Qiuling: Research on Confidentiality of Arbitration, *Law Review*, 2004 (2): 26.

Li De'en and Liu Shiguo: Structuring of Mediation Principle Based on the Substantial Regression of Mediation, *Journal of South-Central Minzu University (Humanities and Social Sciences)*, 2010 (2): 135.

Li De'en: *Systematic Studies on Civil Mediation Theory: Based on the Autonomous Principle of the Parties*, Beijing: China Legal Publishing House, 2012.

Li Hao: Comparative Advantages of Mediation and Reform of Court Mediation Institution, *Journal of Nanjing Normal University (Social Sciences)*, 2002 (4): 19–27.

Li Jin: Path Option for Integration of Core Socialist Values into Scientific Legislation, *Journal of Xinjiang Normal University (Philosophy and Social Sciences)*, 2019 (1): 29–30.

Li Shaoping (Chief Ed.): *Understanding and Application of The Suggestions of the Supreme People's Court for the Reform of Diversified Dispute Resolution Mediation and Provisions on Special Mediation*, Beijing: People's Court Press, 2017.

Liang Huixing: Principle of Honesty and Credit and Existence of Loopholes, *Chinese Journal of Law*, 1994 (2): 23–24.

Liang Ping: Theoretical Structuring and Empirical Exploration of "Grand Mediation" Connection Mechanism, *Science of Law*, 2011 (5): 156–158.

Liao Yongan and Jiang Fengming: New Conception for Development of Social Mediation in the New Era, *Chinese Social Sciences Today*, January 18, 2018 Edition 1.

Liao Yongan and Liu Qing: On the Dilemma and Way-out of China's Mediation Professionalization, *Journal of Xiangtan University (Philosophy and Social Sciences)*, 2016 (6): 48–49.

Liao Yongan: New Idea and New Thinking of Contemporary Mediation, *People's Court Daily*, June 16, 2017, Edition 2.

Liu Jinguo and Jiang Jinshan (Chief Eds.): *New Jurisprudence*, Beijing: China University of Political Science and Law Press, 2006.

Luo Gan: Political and Law Organs Bear the Major Historical Mission and Political Responsibility, *Qiushi*, 2007 (3): 7.

Luo Jiezheng (Trans.): *French Civil Code*, Beijing: China Legal Publishing House, 1999.

Ma Aiping and Liu Fangfang: Principle of Honesty and Credit and Perfection of ADR, *Journal of Shanxi University (Philosophy and Social Sciences)*, 2006 (4): 129–130.

Palo, Giuseppe D. and Veronica Alvisi: Professional Evolution of Italian Mediation, trans. Jiang Liping, *People's Court Daily*, June 17, 2011, Edition 6.

Project Team of Zhejiang Provincial Higher People's Court: Survey and Thinking of the Connection Mechanism of People's Mediation, Administrative Mediation and Litigation Procedure, *Research on Rule of Law*, 2008 (3): 4–6.

Qi Shujie (Chief Ed.): *New Development of Foreign ADR System*, Xiamen: Xiamen University Press, 2017, pp. 22–24.

Qiu Xingmei and Wang Qiulan: *Mediation Law*, Xiamen: Xiamen University Press, 2008, p. 81.

Qu Kunshan: My Opinion about the Legislation of Uniform "Mediation Law," cited in Wang Qiulan, et al: *Studies on Legislation, Theory and Practice of Chinese Mediation*, Beijing: China University of Political Science and Law Press, 2014, p. 53.

Shen Zongling (Chief Ed.): *Jurisprudence*, Beijing: Higher Education Press, 1994.

Song Chaowu, et al.: *Studies on Mediation Legislation*, Beijing: China University of Political Science and Law Press, 2008.

Sun Yunfeng (Ed.): *How to Carry out Mediation Work Properly: Practical Skills and Cases of Mediation*, Beijing: China Legal Publishing House, 2013.

Tang Weijian: Chinese Mediation Institution in the Perspective of Modern Transformation, *Chaoyang Law Review*, 2010 (2): 165–166.

Tang Weijian: Thinking about Formulation of Social Mediation Law, *Studies in Law and Business*, 2007 (1): 59–64.

The Suggestions of the CPC Central Committee for Formulating the 13th Five-year Planning of National Economic and Social Development, *The People's Daily*, November 4, 2015 Edition 1.

Wang Chunzi: Development and Evolution of China's Civil Mediation Institution in the Modern Times -- Focusing on the Civil Mediation Law (1930), *Shengjing Law Review*, 2016 (2): 169–185.

Wang Ge: Studies on Mandatory Mediation Model, *Review of Political Science and Law*, 2014 (6): 104.

Wang Liankun: *Give Play to the Guiding and Demonstrating Role of Judicial Precedents in Mediation, People's Justice*, 2002 (10): 48.

Wang Qiulan, et al.: *Studies on Legislation, Theory and Practice of Chinese Mediation*, Beijing: China University of Political Science and Law Press, 2014.

Wang Zuxing: Exploration of Non-disclosure Institution Related to ADR, *Modern Law Science*, 2005 (3): 56.

Wu Jun: Deficiency of "People's Mediation Law" and Necessity for Uniform Mediation Law, *Judicial Reform Review*, 2016 (15): 196.

Xiong Hao: On Transformation of Chinese Mediation Law Regulation Model, *Studies in Law and Business*, 2018 (3): 119.

Xu Guangming: Diversified Resolution of Commercial Disputes under the Background of One Belt and One Road, *People's Court Daily*, September 15, 2017, Edition 5.

Yang Rongxin: Structuring of Harmonious Society Calls for Mediation Law, *Legal Daily*, March 3, 200.

Yin Li: Interpretation and Analysis of Non-disclosure Norms for Commercial Case Mediation, *Oriental Law*, 2008 (6): 72.

Zhan Yun: Issues on Mediation Legislation in Judicial Reform of Hong Kong, *Southeast Justice Review*, 2011, p. 31.

Zhang Guoyan and Lin Zhe: Principle of Honesty and Credit and Legal Governance Target of Modern Society, *Political Science and Law*, 2000 (5): 23–25.

Zhang Mingxin: From Local Rules and Regulations to Articles of Villagers' Autonomy – Evolution of Local Rules and Regulations, *Jiangsu Social Sciences*, 2006 (4): 174.

Zhang Wenxian: Chinese Judicature between Modernity and Post-Modernity – Chinese Courts in Society of Litigation, *Modern Law Science*, 2014(1): 3–8.

Zhang Yonghong: Regulation and Guidance of British Case Law for Mediation, *Journal of Law Application*, 2016 (Z1): 189.

Zhou Jianhua: Non-Disclosure Principle of Judicial Mediation, *Law of the Times*, 2008 (5): 76.

Zhou Youyong: Logic and Approach – How New Development Idea Leads the Construction of Legal Governance in China, *Law and Social Development*, 2018 (3): 35.

8 The Structure of the Mediation Discourse System with Chinese Characteristics

8.1 Why Law in the New Era Needs to Attach Importance to the Structure of the Chinese Discourse System

Since the capitalist countries grew in modern times, the Oriental countries have suffered from the oppression of imperialism for a long time and the Oriental civilization has always been distorted by the West. While undertaking the military invasion and political and economic changes, Western capitalism also continued with the cultural change, consolidating the hegemonic Western culture and intensifying its legal authority to become the judge of what were "backward" nations and interpret Oriental culture. The fate of Oriental culture was just as Karl Marx said in *The Eighteenth Brumaire of Louis Bonaparte*: "they cannot express, themselves, and they must be expressed by others." In the 1970s, the scholar Edward Said proposed the concept of "Orientalism," creating a great upheaval in Western academic circles. He attempted to deploy the discourse power theory of Foucault to challenge the hegemony of Western discourse and reshape Oriental and Western relations. He criticized "Orientalism" not only as a discipline of teaching, writing, and studying the Orient, but also as a Western thinking mode and a discourse and as "a mode used by the West to control, restructure and rule the Orient." Western culture "was just to treat and even create the Orient through such a discipline in a political, sociological, military, ideological, scientific and imaginative mode."[1]

Against such an overall background, law could not emerge from the domination of "Orientalism" discourse either, and formed the discourse system of "legal Orientalism." The West exported law with an attitude of progressive and superior legal subjects, while China was deemed to be backward, rigid, and not living under the law.[2] Since the legal reform movement in the late Qing Dynasty, to defeat the inferior mentality of "lagging behind leaves one vulnerable to attack," China transplanted the legal systems on a large scale from the West. These transplanted legal systems made important contributions to the progress of China to accelerate the legal governance construction in a specific historical period, but the Western legal governance discourse transplanted to China also created a bad reaction as it did not fit with the Chinese culture.

DOI: 10.4324/9781003385882-8

Many scholars were excessively infatuated with the Western legal governance model, deeming the "Chinese characteristics" as the proof of backwardness, looking upon the Western institutions as the criterion, "homogenizing the Chinese problems with the foreign problems, taking the theory and institution for resolving foreign problems as the theoretical basis and design standard to propose the solution for resolving Chinese problems."[3] Consequently, the ideal prospect of the Western legal governance was taken dogmatically as the ideal template for China's legal governance, resulting in a phenomenon of "Chinese law without Chinese features." The result failed to achieve the success of "Westernization" as well as losing its own "tradition" and falling into an awkward situation of "rootless wandering."

As recently as more than one decade ago, Professor Deng Zhenglai pointed out sharply that Chinese law failed to lead the development of legal institutions in China for the fundamental reason that Chinese law suffered from the structural crisis of "totality." He emphasized: "We must end this old era of law created by the 'Western modernization paradigm' and thus start a new era of law to consciously study the 'ideal prospect of Chinese law'."[4] With more than one decade passing swiftly, Professor Deng Zhenglai passed away at a young age, and his unfulfilled wish remained and the "paradigm" crisis of China's law was not solved either, and we have eventually observed the best opportunity of starting the new era in China's law.

Since the Fourth Plenary Session of the 18th CPC Central Committee, the comprehensive promotion of governing the state according to law has taken an unprecedented step and thus China's legal governance construction has observed its "golden period." On May 17, 2016, in the important speech made at the National Seminar on Philosophy and Social Science, General Secretary Xi Jinping proposed to accelerate the structuring of the discipline system, the academic system, and the discourse system of philosophy and social sciences with Chinese characteristics. The speech was of major significance as a milestone in the development history of contemporary China's humanities and social sciences and was the manifesto of opening the period of the Sinicization of the humanities and social sciences, setting forth the new requirements and new direction for structuring the discipline system, the academic system, and the discourse system of law with Chinese characteristics. Immediately, we are in urgent need to carry out one new academic transformation, replacing those theoretical systems transplanted and copied from the West with the philosophy and social sciences with Chinese characteristics and changing the model of academic Westernization over the years.[5]

Given this best historical opportunity, the Chinese legal scholars should seize this good opportunity for a brilliant future to really keep a foothold in China's legal governance practice, consciously undertake the mission of structuring the discourse system of law with Chinese characteristics and contribute to the comprehensive establishment of a "new era of China's law." On May 3, 2017, when speaking at the China University of Political Science and Law,

General Secretary Xi Jinping emphasized that China's legal governance practice should not copy the Western theories completely:

> Our state governance has the specialty and complexity that cannot be compared to other countries as well as having our own experiences and advantages accumulated over a long period of time, so we should have self-confidence in constructing the discipline system of law.

This requires that our research on law should get rid of the Chinese "status of apprentice,"[6] and treat Western discourse with a clearer and open mentality: "get rid of nonsense, recognize fairy tales and do away with myth,"[7] to establish China's own ideal prospect of law with a more initiative attitude. China's law should turn from the "imitative legal governance approach" laying particular stress on transplanted ideas and making reference to the Western law institutions to become the "independent legal governance approach" with its basis in self-development and independent innovation."[8] It should stick to the approach of self-confidence: institutional self-confidence, theoretical self-confidence, and cultural self-confidence in China's legal governance construction, be based on the national conditions of China to undertake the research of law with a definite issue-oriented ideology, and provide the theoretical support to structure the discourse system of socialist law with Chinese characteristics.

"China's academic discourse must speak 'Chinese'."[9] To structure China's legal discourse system, we must get rid of the "foreign accent" and use the national language and national spirit of China. The representative of the German historical law school, Savigny pointed out that law is comparable to national language, an organic connection is observed between law and national character, and "the national common sense is the specific residence of law."[10] In the whole legal discourse system, mediation is one of the few native legal institutions and the genuine national language, using such terminologies of daily life with Chinese characteristics as "*Pingpingli* (reason things out)" and "*Zuogongzuo* (persuade)" expressed, in a popular and easily comprehensible way; this is the unique definition of the Chinese mediation institution.[11] Only when we are rooted in such a "living language" can the academic discourse system of socialist law with Chinese characteristics be generated, develop, and flourish.

At present, the world mediation institution mainly has two development paths. One is the primitive institution developed on the basis of partially improving the traditional mediation institution. The other is the post-institution created and developed on the basis of the Western modern legal governance. The former existed mainly in the Oriental countries under the influence of the Confucian tradition, represented by China. The latter originated in the late 1970s, with the main symbol of the ADR (alternate dispute resolution) movement arising in the West. China's primitive mediation institution began earlier than the West in a genetic sense and played an important role in the social governance, but since the late 1980s–1990s, the mainstream discourse of litigation-centralism looked down on the mediation value and depreciated the mediation culture, thus leading to the present legal discourse system of "strong litigation and weak mediation."

Due to the influence of "legal Orientalism" discourse, we can easily discover that the studies in line with mediation were also disregarded by the "Western modernity paradigm." On the one hand, when discussing mediation in China, many scholars implied the premise as: the culture of Western adversarial proceedings represented the advanced legal governance culture, while the mediation in China is the backward legal governance culture which should be abandoned.[12] On the other hand, due to the upsurge in the ADR movement in the West, Chinese scholars' understanding of the value of mediation strongly relied on the Western academic discourse, and the value of mediation was transplanted from the Western ADR academic discourse system, while the Chinese mediation studies were still lacking the systematic, self-consistent, and native mediation discourse system to modernize the Chinese legal governance. This resulted in the discarding of the academic discourse right of mediation in China. The huge cultural advantage of mediation in China suffered due to the strong pressure of Western legal governance discourse, and thus it became an important starting point for the new understanding of the modernity of Chinese law and restructuring China's legal discourse system. Only by directly facing such a discourse difference and continually digging deep into the historic practice of mediation in China will it be possible to structure the Chinese discourse system of mediation.

Socialism with Chinese characteristics entered the new era and major contradictions in Chinese society were observed with new changes, and this is the national condition of contemporary China. In order to respond to the new changes and major contradictions in society and meet the increasingly extensive requirements of people for a better life, at the Meeting of the Central Political and Legal Work in 2019, General Secretary Xi Jinping proposed an important thesis to "insist on highlighting the alternative dispute resolution." The Fourth Plenary Session of the 19th CPC Central Committee again set forth new requirements for perfecting the effective mechanism of correctly treating the people's internal contradictions in the new situation, emphasizing development of the "Fengqiao Experience" in the new era and perfecting the system to combine people's mediation, administrative mediation, and judicial mediation. Against this contemporary background, mediation again has a revival opportunity to show its brilliance. China's legal circles need to seize the opportunity, "make up for missed lessons at once," actively respond to the realistic demand, and compose a discipline system and an academic system of mediation suitable for the national conditions of China, thus structuring a mediation discourse system with Chinese characteristics.[13] Based on this, by summarizing the practical experiences of Chinese mediation, this book attempts to judge, comprehend, and define the Chinese mediation institution and primarily point out the direction for mediation discourse system with Chinese characteristics.

8.2 Cultural Self-Confidence of Mediation in China: A Combination of the Advantages of Confucian Cultural Tradition and Core Values

Culture is what our life relies on. Culture seems to be intangible, but is the soul of a country and a nation. "The cultural rationality should first of all be understood by itself … and there is no universal law or truth for measuring and requiring the cultures of different forms."[14] Therefore, since the cultural specialty of different nations determines the specifics of their legal institutions, we should not deem the native traditional culture as dross and esteem the Western legal culture as the essence, but should be aware that the Chinese and Western civilizations have their respective literary excellence and their respective advantages. General Secretary Xi Jinping pointed out:

> To stick to the road of self-confidence, theoretical self-confidence and institutional self-confidence of the socialism with Chinese characteristics, it is after all to stick to the cultural self-confidence. Cultural self-confidence is the more basic, more profound and more lasting force.[15]

When treating the socialist mediation institution with Chinese characteristics, we should especially establish such a cultural self-confidence, inherit and combine the ancient Confucian cultural tradition and modern core socialist values, and form the cultural advantages of the mediation institution with Chinese characteristics.

8.2.1 Historical Basis of Mediation: The "Non-Litigation" Cultural Tradition of Moderation and Harmony

Law is not only abstract clauses, but is more the product of culture in society. General Secretary Xi Jinping pointed out:

> China's ancient legal institution implied extremely rich wisdom and resources and the Chinese legal genealogy is unique among the major legal genealogies of the world. It is necessary to study the tradition of China's ancient legal institution and its success and failure, discover and carry on the essence of Chinese legal culture, absorb nutrition and choose and use what is good.[16]

As a dispute resolution institution with Chinese characteristics, mediation is also inevitably influenced by the traditional Chinese culture.

Starting with the world outlook of "nature-man unification," traditional Chinese mainstream culture pursued the harmony of the whole natural order. Therefore, the fundamental keynote of Confucian culture was to adhere to the "harmonious" thought of "holding the two and using the middle," "holding the middle for harmony" and the "Golden Mean." When reflected in the treatment of social interpersonal relation, such a comprehension is just "non-litigation" and harmony as precious. In the Chinese context, "mediation" itself has the meaning of harmony. According to the interpretation of *Annotations on the Chinese Characters: Yan Bu-Tiao (Mediate)*, "*Tiao* means *He* (harmonize)." In accordance with the common views of legal historiography circles, the embryo of China's mediation institution can be traced back to the period of Yao and Shun.[17] *Han Feizi-Difficulty I* and *Historical Records: Five Imperial Biographies* both recorded the deeds of Shun ruling the world with mediation. In the period of the West Zhou Dynasty, according to the record of *The Chou Rituals:·Local Official·Mediator*, the West Zhou set up "*Tiaoren* (mediator)" with the duty of "taking charge of mediating in the hatred of people." During the Spring and Autumn Period, facing the society of collapsed rites and music, the sage Confucius still held in esteem the governance of rites. *The Analects: Yan Yuan* said: "When hearing a lawsuit case, I am like others (without any brilliance). It is important to prevent any lawsuit case from happening." Hence, the pursuit of "harmony" is the target of traditional Chinese mediation.

The ethical standard provided the environmental soil suitable for the survival of traditional Chinese mediation. Under the social structure of "family-state cohesion," interpersonal relations are like family relations and all the social contradictions can be deemed as the internal contradictions of a family to be resolved through consultation. Such a society especially attaches importance to sensibilities and ethics. Mr. Liang Shuming pointed out: "In China's ethical society, what is precious can be briefly said as: respect the opposite,"[18] and in interpersonal communication, give priority to each other. Under the social concept of the ethical standard, China's traditional law was established on the basis of obligation rather than on the basis of rights. "The role of law is not to provide the legal channel for people to meet their selfish desire," but is to "try as much as possible to control the selfish desire of people and eventually achieve the purpose of making people not argue."[19] The prime task of everyone is to achieve harmonious coexistence with other people and nature. When a dispute takes place and cannot be settled at the discretion of the parties, the most important task of the third party is not to judge which party is legally correct or wrong, but to restore the harmonious status between the two parties. "The best dispute resolution method is not to correctly evaluate on who is right or who is wrong, but to make the two parties be satisfied and be happy in restoring their previous social relationship."[20]

The mediation tradition of Chinese legal culture formed a clear-cut contrast with the Western legal tradition that began in Ancient Rome. The Chinese tradition emphasized "keeping a good neighborhood to settle disputes" and the Western tradition emphasized "a struggle for one's rights." Western society has always lacked the legal tradition of mediation. According to research, the word mediation was sourced from Middle Old French *mediation/mediacion*.

The synonyms include *mediari* ("intervene") and *medius* ("intermediary"). The word in English appeared in about the fourteenth century, meaning the act or process of mediation, especially referring to intervening in the disputes of the parties for the sake of achieving conciliation, resolution, or compromise, but was not the cultural origin of Western ADR.[21] From the times of Ancient Greece, the Western thinkers started to think about such concepts as "law," "right," and "justice," and "*jus*" and "*Recht*" became the basis of the most important etymology in the Western legal culture. If the core thought in the tradition of China's Confucian legal culture is harmony, the core thought in the Western legal culture is right. Just as Mr. Zhang Zhongqiu said, "The legal culture of traditional China focused on order and thus led to non-litigation; traditionally, the Western legal culture took rights as the axis and pursued justice."[22] The Western type of "litigious system" formed the custom of litigation centralism, resolving disputes through competition and confrontation of right or wrong and success or failure. The treatment of disputes between Antonio and Sherlock in *The Merchant of Venice*, the famous play by Shakespeare, is just the vivid reflection of such a culture.

In 2012, at the "ADR Development Conference," Honorary President of the World Mediation Association, Michael Ris demonstrated the core thought of the Western ADR by citing the Chinese Confucian "Golden Rule" of "that is, forgive! Don't impose on others what you don't desire."[23] From this, it can be seen that the Confucian moral "Golden Rule" has a different approach but equally satisfactory results with Kant's absolute moral precept of "making your standard of conduct a universal natural rule," and this "Golden Rule" shared by the human society can be completely taken as the universal moral criterion widely applied in mediation practice.[24]

8.2.2 Contemporary Environment of Mediation: The Core Socialist Values of Standards for Society

After the New China was founded, the Communist Party of China established the new tradition of socialist law, but Chinese Confucian traditional culture still continued and, as injected with new elements and the technical combination of mediation and political mobilization of mass route, became the remarkable feature of the people's judicature, which is still full of vigor at the present time. The 18th National Congress of the CPC proposed the 24-word core socialist values, defining the target, value orientation and value criterion at three levels of state, society, and individuals. The core socialist values extended the traditional Confucian legal culture as well as integrated the new cultures of moral governance and legal governance corresponding to the spirit of modern legal governance.

Different from Chinese society, the mainstream value of Western society is liberalism, and such a liberalism is different from the value orientation of liberty in the core socialist values. What the Western liberalism pursues is a kind of liberty completely with personal freedom as the fundamental destination and a kind of liberty upholding the rights of personal liberty.[25] Based on pursuing personal liberty as the maximum value, the Western mainstream liberty theory emphasized the diversity and the relativity of morality and denied the existence of objective and absolute common social ethics and morals. From such a dividing line between the Chinese and Western cultures, it can be observed that Chinese society is based on the standards for society, while the Western society is based on the individual standards. Western society derived from the individual standard the tradition of a legal culture with a clear definition and standard of rights, while the Chinese standard for society emphasized the association of sensibilities and ethics:

> Everyone is relevantly obligated to ethical relations with everyone around him; in the meantime, those people around him are also respectively obligated to him in their ethical relations with him. All social members are, by chance, changeably and mutually associated, to form intangibly a kind of organization.[26]

Based on such an association, the society treasured the family, community, collective, public order. and communal cultural values more and preferred to do its best to avoid conflict and confrontation and actively consult in dispute resolution. This was the most favorable cultural factor in the effectiveness of the Chinese mediation institution.

The core of cultural self-confidence is the self-confidence of values. As a cultural ideology, the core socialist values are deemed to be the soul of the construction of socialist legal governance. In December, 2016, the General Office of the CPC Central Committee and the General Office of the State Council printed and distributed *The Guidelines for Integrating Further the Core Socialist Values into the Construction of Legal Governance*, defining the guiding significance of the core socialist values in the construction of legal governance. It advocated that mediation is an important measure in integrating the core socialist values into the construction of legal governance and the value idea of mediation completely complies with such core socialist values as “civilization, harmony, equality, justice, good faith, friendship, democracy, and legal governance.” Mediation pursued the interpersonal civilization and harmony in terms of a case closing for settlement; displayed the subject status of the parties, encouraged the autonomy and consultation of the parties, and reflected the freedom and democracy in social communication in terms of the dispute resolution process; emphasized that the parties should be honest and friendly and abide by the law and contracts, and reflected equality, justice, and legal governance in terms of the dispute resolution results. Among the numerous dispute resolution mechanisms, without doubt, mediation is the one that can best manifest the core socialist values as well as the institution that can best reflect the cultural self-confidence of socialist legal governance. Looking at the big picture, folk dispute resolution as well as political consultation on democracy and even international dialogue and communication have all implied the mediation idea. In terms of this significance, the Chinese contemporary mediation was based on the succession of Chinese Confucian cultural tradition as well as originated more from the scientific understanding of the human social governance law.[27]

8.3 Institutional Self-confidence of Mediation in China: The "Horizontal-to-Edge" and "Vertical-to-Bottom" Diverse Mediation System

During the period of the Republic of China, China transplanted Western civil procedure institutions with the judgment and mandatory enforcement as their axis, but such an aggressive reform was eventually replaced by the mediation institution created by the Communist Party of China, during the period of the new democratic revolution, due to the failure to meet the national conditions in those days. Faced with such objective environments in those days as the need for political struggle, shortage of judicial resources, and the demands of the people, the Communist Party of China, starting from the actual conditions, actively explored the new public judicial institution and thus the national people's mediation institution was generated[28] and became the main tradition of socialist people's justice. During the process of molding the new tradition of socialist law, the Communist Party of China skillfully combined the top-down policy with the bottom-up pilot experiment, compiling two popular "Chinese Stories" of mediation: the "Ma Xiwu Trial Mode" and the "Fengqiao Experience" and realized the creative transformation of the traditional mediation institution.

The "Ma Xiwu Trial Mode" was formed in the Revolutionary Base of the Shaanxi-Gansu-Ningxia border region in the 1940s, and was given instruction from Ma Zedong in 1943. Its main characteristics included: do not undertake passive court hearing, keep in close touch with the masses, carry out in-depth surveys and studies, combine judgment with mediation, and lay stress on resolution through mediation.[29] The "Fengqiao Experience" was formed in Fengqiao, Zhuji Community, Zhejiang, in the 1960s and was granted written instruction from Chairman Mao Zedong in 1963. In 2013, General Secretary Xi Jinping also gave an important instruction, emphasizing to insist on and develop properly the "Fengqiao Experience." The main characteristics of the "Fengqiao Experience" are: insist on the leadership of the Party committee and lay stress on resolution in collaboration, and rely on the masses and keep close to the conditions of the people; attach importance to the combination of prevention and resolution; emphasize systematic governance, legal governance, comprehensive governance, and source governance, prevent and resolve from the source of the contradictions and disputes by pushing forward the alternative dispute resolution with mediation as the main element, and realize the unification of autonomy and heteronomy, rigidity and flexibility, and management of the body and management of the heart.[30]

In a genetic sense, the "Ma Xiwu Trial Mode" in the period of Yan'an was different from the "Fengqiao Experience" in the socialist educational reform movement: the former was meant for the realistic need to effectively resolve the people's internal contradictions and disputes and the latter was the experience explored in the process of resolving the contradictions between ourselves and the enemy, but the two were both the vivid experiences of mediation in China, were both given the successive instructions and approval from the top leaders of the Party and state, both attached importance to such a "magic weapon" of winning the revolution as the popular line, and jointly constituted an important part of the socialist legal tradition, so that China's dispute resolution mode had the flexible structural feature of "convincing—genuinely convinced."[31]

Fifty years ago, the "Ma Xiwu Trial Mode" and the "Fengqiao Experiences faced the commune members and unit members in the period of collectivization and the simple disputes in the society of acquaintance. Fifty years later, facing the "atomic" individuals in the tide of the market economy and facing the complex interest disputes in the society of strangers, the rural "Charisma" authority was already disempowered along with the modernization of the state, the authority of the village and commune officials was greatly weakened with the state power withdrawn, and the traditional dispute resolution mode gradually declined. In the new era, to adapt to the changes in the major contradictions in society, the "Ma Xiwu Trial Mode" and the "Fengqiao Experience" advanced with the times, developed through innovation and were reformed by being upgraded, forming the "Grand Mediation" system, based on people's mediation and the advantageous complementary, organic combination and coordination of people's mediation, administrative mediation, arbitration mediation, and judicial mediation. Besides, different types of industrial and special mediation, commercial mediation, lawyer mediation, and other new types of mediation were also, in a broad sense, included in the category of people's mediation.[32] Such a diversified mediation system is observed as significantly different from the Western socialized and market-oriented autonomous mediation system. The Chinese mediation institution is advantageous and developed by relying on the strong organization and mobilization capacity of the Communist Party of China to grow deeper in the grass-roots society, forming the so-called "horizontal-to-edge" and "vertical-to-bottom" mediation organization system. With the economic and social conditions changing, the mediation organization and the mediation system in China are still in the process of continual self-adjustment, reform, and perfection.

First, the Chinese people's mediation institution is different from the Western community mediation institution. One important feature of Chinese grass-roots society different from the Western society is that, due to the long-term influence of the ethical tradition and "rural native character" in the society of acquaintance, Chinese grass-roots communities formed a community, as they were closely connected, the people in one community had the independence and mutual assistance for conscious participation in public life, and this made people prefer to seek self-resolution within the community if any contradictions and disputes arose. It is also the social foundation for China people's mediation to develop. China people's mediation played a fundamental role in the diversified resolution mechanism of contradictions and disputes, and the legal status of people's mediation committees was defined by the Constitution and *The People's Mediation Law*. As the grass-roots mass organizations, the people's mediation committees worked under the dual leadership of the judicial organs of the people's government above the county level and the grass-roots people's courts. Thus, the people's mediation institution has a strong feature of promoting the government and plays the role of "first defensive line" in the resolution of social contradictions. By 2018, China had in total nearly 766,000 people's mediation organizations, including 657,000 village (community) mediation committees, 42,000 township (sub-district) mediation committees, 43,000 industrial and special people's mediation organizations, and 16,000 people's mediation work offices found in the relevant departments. China had in total 3,660,000 people's mediators, including 3,172,000 part-time people's mediators, and 497,000 full-time people's mediators. Different disputes mediated annually by the mediators of these people's mediation organizations numbered more than 9 million cases, with a mediation success rate of more than 96 percent.[33] Now, under the strong promotion of the Party and the government, China has formed the people's mediation organization network at multiple levels and with wide coverage. This is a "horizontal-to-edge" and "vertical-to-bottom" organizational network system with the community mediation committees under "villager and resident committees" as the mainstay, with enterprise and institution mediation committees, industrial mediation committees and regional mediation committees as the supplements, and with the different villager (resident) mediation groups and people's mediation work offices (stations) as the nerve endings. Such a mediation network deepens the governance chain into the nerve endings of the grass-roots society and becomes the distinct characteristic of China's grass-roots social governance. However, as it is different from the people's mediation, the Western community mediation is not an institution based on the idea of social harmony, but a kind of forced adjustment under the condition of expensive litigation, which can only be an extremely limited role. With the American community (neighborhood) mediation mechanism as an example, it is mainly the folk, non-judicial dispute resolution mechanism with the community as the support and with community volunteers acting as the mediators, mediating free of charge in the interpersonal disputes that occur mainly in the community and neighborhood. The community mediation institutions have an independent status, are not under any administrative or judicial institution and are completely autonomous social organizations.[34] Since it is not actively used by people, community mediation is already observed with a trend of separating from its location and being brought into the court dispute treatment system.[35] In the state of

Virginia, in the USA, with a relatively developed community mediation institution, of 1.28 million civil cases in 2002, only 0.7 percent were mediation cases.[36] In terms of the orientation, nature, and actual efficiency of the mediation institution, the Western community mediation cannot compare with the Chinese people's mediation.

Second, China's court mediation differed from the Western court mediation institution. If the "Fengqiao Experience" is the typical sample of people's mediation, the "Ma Xiwu Trial Mode" is the successful sample of court mediation. The biggest feature of Chinese court mediation is "the combination of mediation and trial" and "the combination of mediation and judgment." In the process of a case trial, the judge in charge can help the two parties peacefully resolve disputes according to the will of the parties and based on proven case details and an adequate understanding of the appeals of the two parties. "Mediate as possible, judge as possible, combine mediation and judgment, and close cases for settlement" became the long-term basic policy insisted on in China's court civil judgments. The institutional structure of such a combination of mediation and trial violates the principle of procedural justice in the view of Western legal governance theory. Different from China taking mediation as the mode of exercising the adjudication power, the Western civil procedures almost all keep mediation outside the litigation procedure and work mainly in the mode of court-attached mediation, and mediation is deemed as a kind of managerial or looking-after judicial activity.[37] Due to the institutional structure of China's combination of mediation and trial, it is significantly advantageous in helping the parties reach conciliation. During the early period of the trial mode reform in the 1990s, of the civil cases handled by courts nationwide, more than 80 percent were closed through mediation, and only 20 percent through judgment. Afterwards, since the Western adversarial system was transplanted and the court trial reform started to intensify the responsibility of the parties to produce evidence, mediation was no longer placed in the prior position in the litigation procedure, but according to the statistical bulletin of the Supreme People's Court for the period from 2013–2018, the case closing rate of people's courts nationwide through mediation had always kept at about 30 percent. As the work report of the Supreme People's Court in 2017 displayed, local courts at all levels nationwide closed 5,321,000 cases using mediation, which is unique in the dispute resolution of courts worldwide. The academic circles called loudly for the reform of "the separation of mediation and trial," but in view of the latest development of reform, the Supreme People's Court has only taken a prudent stand of appropriate separation. Factually, the practical advantage of China's combination of mediation and trial is also unconsciously influencing the role of the Western judges in facilitating conciliation in litigation. When conciliating, some judges have also gradually changed their passive attitude and undertaken more actively the interposition or intervention in the conciliation negotiation of the parties.[38] In the opinion of German courts, in the circumstance where the conciliation judge is also the trial judge, there is no conflict of interest or tension in ethical roles.[39] Intriguingly, as the golden rule for Chinese scholars to criticize Chinese court mediation, "the principle of procedural justice that mediators cannot act as the trial judges" showed signs of being gradually loosened and softened in the Western court litigation institution.[40]

Third, China's arbitration mediation is different from the Western arbitration mediation institution. Similar to court mediation, over the last decades, arbitration mediation has also been widely applied in China's civil and commercial arbitration cases. China's arbitration procedure takes "the integration of arbitration and mediation." Article 47 of *The Arbitration Rules of China International Economic and Trade Arbitration Commission* provided the institution for the "combination of arbitration and mediation." With the consent of both parties, the arbitration tribunal can mediate the cases in the arbitration procedure. As one of the traditional dispute resolution modes in the West, like the litigation procedure, arbitration originally had no function of mediation. It was not until the 1980s that mediation rapidly developed in international commercial arbitration, but *The Model Law on International Commercial Conciliation*, adopted by the United Nations International Trade Commission, still strictly followed the procedural discipline of separation of arbitration and mediation. It was the unique creation of the mediation institution with Chinese characteristics to integrate mediation into the arbitration procedure and in the opinion of some scholars, China is the true place where arbitration mediation originated.[41] According to the statistical data of the Office of Legal Affairs under the State Council, from 2014 to 2016, the arbitration cases closed by the arbitration institutions nationwide through mediation and conciliation reached 41–65 percent. According to the statistics from *The Annual Report of the China International Commercial Arbitration*, in 2016 and 2017, the cases closed in the mode mediation and conciliation were 121,527 and 69,450 respectively, and this is the eye-catching achievement that the Western arbitration institution is unable to keep pace with. Factually, with foreign commercial arbitration growing in China, the Western arbitrators also started to gradually recognize the "Oriental experience" of the combination of arbitration and mediation. The voices opposing the combination of arbitration and mediation have already been gradually weakened and the opposition also started to be aware of the benefits of such a combination.[42]

Fourth, China's administrative mediation institution is also significantly different from the Western administrative mediation institution. Due to the influence of such administrative ideas as "minimum government" and "night-watcher," the Western state administrative institutions had always kept a passive and restrained attitude toward intervention in the resolution of folk disputes before the twentieth century. With the administrative power continually expanding, the administrative state and service idea drew attention and it was in the mid-twentieth century that the Western countries started to gradually break down the boundary between the state and society and the idea of "the separation of powers," and in terms of civil dispute resolution, to turn gradually from "administrative non-intervention" to "claim for administrative intervention" and ensure individuals were entitled to request the administrative organs to intervene in civil disputes.[43] However, completely differently, China's administrative mediation was mainly sourced from the combination of modern China' revolutionary political and judicial system and the community mediation tradition.[44] During the period of the planned economy, the government "intervened comprehensively" in the field of national social life with an omnipotent attitude. With the development of the market economy and the reform "streamlining government and delegating authorities, strengthening supervision and optimizing service," the administrative organs started to change their idea from "comprehensive intervention" to "limited intervention." Currently, most of the government organs in China have the function of mediating in civil disputes, and due to the influence of "big government and small society," China's administrative organs have relatively high credibility and authority. Due to such public power, the administrative organs have the natural advantage of authority in the mediation of civil disputes. In November, 2010, the State Council published *The Suggestions for Intensifying the Construction of Law-Based Government*, and more prominently proposed:

> [To] take administrative mediation as an important duty of the people's governments at all levels and relevant departments, and establish the administrative mediation work system with the people's governments at all levels taking the general responsibility, with governmental institutions of law leading and all functional department being the subjects.

This intensified the function of the administrative organs to resolve the civil disputes closely related to the activities of administration.

8.4 Theoretical Self-confidence of Mediation in China: Different from the Logic of Legal Formalism

When comparing the Chinese and Western mediation cultures and mediation institutions, it is not hard to discover the ideological difference between the two. Behind such a difference, it is actually the in-depth ideological difference of the Chinese and Western dispute resolution in society. We in China should have sufficient theoretical consciousness to discover our own unique experiences and theoretical discourse system from such a differentiation, and undertake dialogue with the Western mainstream theories.

8.4.1 Limitations of Western Legal Formalist Theory

In the context of Western modernity theory, the most influential theoretical school is the formalist theory, while the German scholar Max Weber is without doubt its most important spokesperson. Weber classified the development of legal institution into four different historical development stages and ideal types and viewed the legal rationalization developed from the formal irrational–substantial irrational–substantial rational–formal rational path and stated:

> only the formal reason (especially with the aid of logic abstract formalism) can realize the unique special and legal promotion and purification so that the legal rules are integrated into a complex of abstract method proposition in a modern sense without inherent contradictions.[45]

In the mind of Weber, the end stage of legal rationalization is the formal rationalization shown in Western capitalist society, which can meet, to the maximum, the predictability and stability required by the capitalist economy. Yet, China's traditional law is in the category of substantial irrationality and China's traditional justice is in the category of "Khadi justice" ("education-oriented mediation"). It does not treat the cases as per formalized provisions, but deploys the sensibilities, ethics, and morals outside law to mediate according to the actual conditions of particular cases and is full of free discretion and unpredictability.

For a long time, understanding in Chinese and Western circles of law about traditional Chinese society has always been dominated by Weber's theory. Under the premise of such a presupposition, mediation in China is deemed as the actual traditional approach used in the Middle Ages in the West and is the product of a backward culture that cannot fit into the modern legal governance. Only by replacing such a substantial irrationality with the law of formal reason can the modernization of legal governance be realized. This is a typical Western centralist stand. It regards the type of the Western modern law as an ideal type of non-Western social development. Weber's theory is actually supported by Western social culture with the ideology of subject-object dichotomy, this or that, and binary opposition. Being different from such Western thinking, what is seen in Chinese culture is "one-into-three" and the approach of the Golden Mean, is "holding the two ends but using the middle," and is the dynamic balance of thesis-antithesis-synthesis and left-middle-right.[46] Therefore, complete imitation of legal formalist theory to interpret the Chinese society's cultural thinking tradition of both this and that and binary co-existence obviously fails to hit the mark, leading to the lack of understanding the actual complexity of Chinese society. It fails to interpret why in China's contemporary legal practice, judgment and mediation can be in an easy-going co-existence and benign interaction and can still provide a market economy with predictable legal order and effectively resolve social contradictions and disputes. Obviously, high reliance on mediation will not necessarily result in the substantial irrationality of the "Khadi trial." In a word, the Chinese and Western different types of law should be deemed as different approaches of legal development rather than successive and straight-line evolutionary different stages.

8.4.2 The Logic of Chinese Law Is Led by "Pragmatic Reason"

When Chinese legal circles seek a theoretical basis for the legitimacy of Chinese mediation practice, currently, the most popular practice is to connect with the Western alternative dispute resolution (ADR) movement and take this universal discourse as the shortcut for a demonstration of China's contemporary mediation. However, mediation had originally no place in the Western justice system and with the legal formalist logic leading, Western society aimed to resolve social problems comprehensively through litigation, thus leading to "legal excess," "legal pollution" and "colonization of the life-world by the legal system" and resulting in the "legality crisis" of the Western social order.[47] Therefore, the Western trend of ADR arising in the 1970s was meant to cope only with the "litigation explosion," high litigation costs, and rigid judicial institution and thus failed to meet the increasingly flourishing demand for dispute resolution and was forced to take the judicial simplification measure of "access to justice." Yet even now, Western legal circles still fail to adapt to the disputes about this.[48] ADR is essentially still the product of the theoretical logic of legal formalism, with the rich legal centralist characteristic, and is still the ideological product of this or that, deeming mediation as the alternative mode of litigation. It emphasized "bargaining in the shadow of the law," orienting mediation as the class trial mode of "discovering legally correct resolution," rather than the target of pursuing the restoration of the harmony of the community social order. It only saw, in terms of "quantity," the alternative role of mediation as reducing litigation pressure and saving litigation costs,[49] but ignored its independent value of insisting on both this and that, balancing the diverse interests and pursuing the "comprehensive justice" in terms of quality.[50] Therefore, China's diversified dispute resolution mechanism has essentially an ideological difference from the Western alternative dispute resolution mechanism. China's diversified dispute resolution mechanism is essentially a kind of social adjustment system. It synthesizes different dispute resolution modes including mediation to facilitate different social relations achieve equilibrium. Mediation is the ideal mode of "source governance," while litigation is only the final dispute resolution.[51] Without doubt, according to Western ADR theory, it is to go south by driving north and climb trees to catch fish, in seeking the theoretical basis of mediation in China.

In recent years, some scholars have started to inspect the limitations of the formalist theory of Western law in view of the specialty of China's dispute resolution practice. By studying the law history of China since the Ming and Qing Dynasties, Chinese American historian Professor Philip C.C. Huang has extracted the concept of "a pragmatic moral" from the paradox of expression and practice and the interaction and integration of the formal justice system (trial) and the informal justice system (mediation).[52] In his opinion, the tradition of "a pragmatic moral" combined the moral expression and pragmatic practice, emphasized experiences more and actual effects, and was enough to compete with the modern Western formalist discourse hegemony. According to the harmonious idea of the Chinese mediation institution, it is possible to mediate in different circumstances in view of connecting closely with the facts according to one's pragmatic moralist thinking, so as to avoid pushing the law into the adversarial system of stacking up like the Western legal formalism that insists on identifying right and wrong.[53]

By studying the civil law sources in the Qing Dynasty, Japanese historian Shiga Shuzo discovered the importance of "sensibility" in China's law sources.

> The national law may be made into a metaphor of the floating iceberg sometimes visible in the sea of sensibilities. On the contrary, the Western European traditional legal order always attempted to cover the whole sea with ice, and when the spreading ice surface is observed with caves, try to expand the ice surface through proper arrangement so as to cover up these caves. This is the most fundamental difference of the two.[54]

The student of Shiga Shuzo, Hiroaki Terada used the metaphor of a moving "crowded train" to describe the traditional Chinese legal order. On the crowded public train, law cannot establish an equal statutory space for each person. The rights of different subjects are defined by fuzziness and symbiosis. It is also against common sense in society for individuals to claim, in this space, a vested right. In the crowded state of the train carriage, when being pushed or squeezed, every person can only first adjust himself and needs to squeeze back appropriately so that they continually give in and adjust. Through such convoluted mutual squeezing and giving-in, the order in the train can form an overall balance acceptable to all the parties.[55] The inference of Hiroaki Terada was meant for traditional Chinese society, but is still applicable to the present China and since the rapid urbanization and industrialization made the crowded feature of Chinese society more prominent, it is also more required to adjust through mediation.

On the basis of the work of Philip C.C. Huang, Shiga Shuzo, et al., Professor Lin Duan, the expert in Weber studies in the Taiwan Region of China, proposed the multi-value logic of traditional Chinese law and justice: the dispute resolution mechanism is diverse, such sources of law as emotion, reason, and law are diverse, and such legal procedures as official trial and folk mediation are diverse, as reflecting the diverse rational spirit of Chinese legal culture as

> unity of man and nature, morality given priority over penalty, Confucianism and law in parallel, opposite and complementary, harmony and easy-going, both this and that, integration of one and others, weighing the matter and deliberating on the reason, and law being nothing more than human relations.[56]

Professor Ji Weidong called such a thinking mode "situational thinking." He vividly described the fundamental features of Western modern legal thinking mode using metaphors of a "pyramid" and an "ATM" and described the features and principles of Chinese legal thinking mode with the metaphors "taichi diagram" and "random regulator." The latter does not take confrontation as the premise and dichotomy of this or that as the target. In the process of the trial, the judge runs through the gradual thinking and continual adjustment, on an attempt to restructure the adversarial factors so that "the opposing logic is transformed to continual logic, leading to the extensive middle entry and gray area" and the parties and judge both can, in such complex trends, expand the optional space and latitude and find the balance point acceptable by and satisfactory to all the parties in such a situation.[57]

In view of the universality of the foregoing theoretical logic, the theoretical vitality of Chinese mediation institution is based on the fact that it does not stubbornly generalize the abstract rights provided by the positive law, but emphasizes flexible contingency of "proceeding from reality all the work" and case by case, accepts the institutional arrangements for the coexistence of mediation and judgment in one litigation procedure and lays stress on the application of common and informal judicial techniques. It is a kind of theoretical logic different from the Western formal reason and a kind of "pragmatic reason" or "practical reason" starting from experiences, facts, and history.[58] Such a "pragmatic reason" is collectively reflected in the civil judgment policy of the Supreme People's Court:

> [The] "mediation-judgment combination" is the crux. It requires that when handling the particular cases, the people's courts should flexibly apply the modes and means of mediation and judgment according to the actual conditions of cases and should undertake mediation in a timely manner where it is possible for mediation, and should make timely judgment where it is impossible or unnecessary for mediation … Disregarding how to apply the modes and means of mediation and judgment while handling the civil cases, people's courts have only one target of "case closing for settlement." Case closing for settlement not only ends up as the end of litigation of the parties, but also ends up in being favorable to the social and economic development, favorable to the implementation of socialist morals, and favorable to maximizing the social harmonious factors.[59]

When "*Zuogongzuo* (persuading)," mediators will often place disputes in the multi-dimensional vision of economy, law, morality, habit, mentality and society for comprehensive investigation into such factors as the nature of disputes, the cause of disputes, and the extent of contradiction, emphasizing the multi-dimensionality of views, the variety of solution options, the flexibility of application of means and the comprehensiveness of interest adjustment for the sake of seeking the final resolution in compliance with emotion, reason, and law.

The unique value of such legal "pragmatic reason" logic is that it cares for the Chinese people's manners and hearts and justice concepts and even condenses the legal wisdom with the Chinese spirit. As discussed above, when the Chinese people "ask for an explanation" in the case of a dispute, the first impulse is often not to "struggle for rights," but to request the third party to "reason" or "reason out." This "reason" is not only limited to the legal principle of the positive law, but the unification of emotion (sensibilities), reason (heavenly principle), and law (state law).[60] General Secretary Xi Jinping emphasized: "Let the people experience the fair justice in each case." The content of such "fair justice" is different from the connotation of access to justice pursued by the Western legal formalist logic. The Chinese people lay more stress on the receptivity of justice. What is the appreciable justice? In the words of Shiga Shuzo, it should be a kind of "common justice balance feeling," i.e.,

> the Chinese people prefer not to view the dispute target in isolation, but apply the comprehensive and overall investigation into the social relationship of the two parties in opposition – sometimes involving thus the surrounding people. Furthermore, the Chinese people also are fond of the relative thinking mode and prefer to find out the equilibrium point from some losses or pains distributed and borne all by the two parties in opposition or sides.[61]

In such circumstance, the so-called "justice" in the mind of the Chinese people is actually an idealized compromise between the individual act and the act of others in the "crowded train." Therefore, being reasonable and fair, sensible and logical, and rational and acceptable forms the value rationality of the Chinese people to judge the right and wrong and the fair justice[62] as well as the value criterion of mediation in China.

In the meantime, China's legal practice with "pragmatic reason" as the leading force does not necessarily mean tenaciously defending the tradition or refusing the West, because "pragmatic reason" is not the theory resting complacently on its laurels or the model that never changes. With the complexity of modern industrial and commercial society, it is continually upgrading itself and developing and absorbing the advantages of the Western modern legal formal reason.[63] Particularly in the mediation practice, with the development in society from the traditional to modern, mediation in China no longer has a "suppression-oriented" and "education-oriented" face, but under the influence of formal reason, the extent of its legalization is continually promoted and the right consciousness and autonomous consciousness of the parties generally are intensified, thus forming a picture of mediation: the coexistence of "judgment-oriented mediation" (seeking the legally correct resolution), "education-oriented mediation" (seeking the restoration of the social community order), "negotiation-oriented mediation" (seeking bargaining at the minimum cost), and "treatment-oriented mediation" (seeking the mental emotional repair of interpersonal relationships) in China's contemporary dispute resolution practice.[64] Therefore, "pragmatic reason" will not constitute any barrier to the modernization of China's legal governance, but, on the contrary, provides the fully inclusive and equitable diverse logic for the modernization of China's legal governance.

8.5 Road to Self-Confidence of Mediation in China: Cooperative Interaction between State and Society

It is the treasured experience of China's social governance to push forward the alternative dispute resolution to realize the flexible governance, litigation source governance, and comprehensive governance through mediation. In recent years, it has been common for Chinese academic circles to interpret China's practice of social governance with such Western governance theories as "civic society" and "multi-center governance." The "civic society" theory originated in European society, claiming the independence of civic society and the political state.[65] The "multi-center governance" theory originated in the USA, with its institutional arrangement closely connected to American federalism, democratic politics, and public administration, also ignoring the subjective function of state power.[66] These social governance discourse systems all placed the "state-society" paradigm in a relationship of binary opposition and emphasized shaping civic society without the interference from the state power and with high autonomy.[67] These governance theories were actually still the product of the ideological trend of the Western liberalism theory, advocating the idea of "governance without government." Obviously, such a theoretical paradigm can hardly direct the path of China's social governance and cannot understand the inherent mechanism of "Grand Mediation."

Being different from the Western paradigm of keeping the state and society in binary opposition, China's social governance emphasizes the benign interaction of the state and society. In the practice of contradiction and dispute prevention and resolution, China recognized the benign interaction observed between the state and society and between the government and the people, combining the top-down policy and the bottom-up pilot experience. Professor Philip C.C. Huang was aware of the uniqueness of China's social governance practice and proposed the "Third Realm" theory, i.e., between the formal judicial judgment and folk social mediation, the state always first of all encouraged the parties to choose, as the first priority, the mediation mode for dispute resolution and only when the people's dispute resolution mechanism failed to cope would the state start to intervene. Even if the parties directly approach the state for public relief, the state will also hand over, in a certain way, the dispute to the spokesperson or the intermediary of the local grass-roots society for treatment, thus forming the semi-state and semi-social middle realm between the state and society.[68] China's "official approval and civil mediation" of mediating through village heads during the period of indigenous law, and the present mediation in China: entrusted to the courts, assigned mediation, special mediation and other socialized mediation practices and their judicial confirmation institution, can all be classified as the "Third Realm" of benign interaction between the state and society. Such a theory provided a new vision for interpreting the reason for the developed Chinese mediation institution, i.e., the wide application of mediation in China is not an issue of emphasizing judgment and ignoring mediation. The insistence and preference of the state for mediation come from the desire to "prudently save and allocate available rare judicial resources" and the popularity of mediation is not only because of traditional Confucian culture, but also because the minimalist governance model attempted to transfer part of the governance costs undertaken by the state to society.[69] To a great extent, the "Fengqiao Experience" reflected the simple governance of benign interaction between the state and society. Through the bottom-up mass participation and the top-down state mobilization, it effectively mobilized the resources on all sides and relied on the "Grand Mediation" system to realize "minor matters not beyond villages, major events not beyond township and non-submission of contradictions" and smooth the last kilometer of "access to justice." The theoretical contribution of the "Third Realm" is to consciously surpass the binary opposition between the state and society, but the "Third Realm" is actually still limited to the "public realm" theory of Habermas and has not yet completely displayed the particular ecology of the benign interaction between the state and society in China's social governance practice. Yet, the mechanism of the "Grand Mediation" has vividly manifested such a particular ecology and developed the social governance approach with Chinese characteristics, which has been called the model of cooperation of benign interaction between the state and society. The core elements of such a model are the state-leading, social diversity, and cooperation of the state and society, thus forming the governance community of diverse subjects. Some scholars called such a specific model of the relations between the state and society the "state-leading social pluralism."[70]

8.5.1 The State (Party and Government) Leading the Social Governance Community

To understand the particular style of China's mediation institution, mediation cannot be regarded only as an isolated dispute resolution mode, but it is necessary to place, in view of promoting the modernization of the state governance system and governance capacity, the mediation institution in the grand social outlook and grand governance outlook of "co-construction, co-governance and sharing." The report to the 19th CPC National Congress proposed: "build up the social governance pattern of co-construction, co-governance and sharing." "Co-construction, co-governance and sharing" emphasized national participation and encouraged the diversified and open governance idea of folk autonomy. The "Grand Mediation" is just the particular reflection of such an idea of governance. According to the official expression, the so-called "Grand Mediation" is

> the local Party committees and governments at all levels give adequate play to their political advantages to structure the mediation work system in which such departments as judicial and enforcement, comprehensive governance, stability, and complaint treatment coordinate comprehensively, the relevant departments and units act according to the duties and social sectors widely participate and people's mediation, administrative mediation, judicial mediation play their respective roles adequately as well as coordinate and cooperate mutually.[71]

From this, it can be seen that the Grand Mediation is substantially a kind of social governance institution "with the Party committee leading, governance taking charge, social cooperation, public participation, democratic consultation and legal assurance," and is a kind of alternative dispute resolution with the coordination, linkage, and cooperation of diverse subjects under the leadership of the state. In such an institutional framework, such diverse subjects as the Party committee, government, grass-roots autonomous organizations, social organizations, enterprises, and individual citizens participate jointly and seek the particular methods for resolving problems by continual communication and coordination. In view of such local samples promoted energetically by the state as Zhejiang's "Fengqiao Experience," Sichuan's "Meishan Experience," Shandong's "Weifang Experience," and Anhui's "Maanshan Experience," the prime common experience is "the Party and government leading first" and "total cooperation as one game." The Party and government leadership is the unique political advantage of the Grand Mediation mechanism as well as the endogenous institutional advantage. Under the people-centered ruling idea, public acceptance of the legality of the collective and uniform leadership of the Communist Party of China and the energetic support of the Party and government power can give proper play to the advantage of power resources not available to only folk powers, thus facilitating the mediation.

The Grand Mediation mechanism reflected the implementation without conflict of collaboration of the state as leader with social diverse forces: on the one hand, the state grants total support to the development of the Grand Mediation mechanism in terms of organizational building, institutional regulation, and allocation of resources. It is just because the state is leading (Party and government) that we can generalize and integrate the scattered social mediation resources, facilitate all the social sectors to cooperate and participate and promote the governance efficiency, avoiding the situation of letting the social forces "act completely on their own." On the other hand, as the buffer zone of the state power, social organizations also have the space to play an independent role. Through linking and the complementary aid, and the mediation-litigation matchmaking of such diverse mediation mechanisms as people's mediation, industrial mediation, administrative mediation, and judicial mediation, the flexibility of dispute resolution has been maintained as well as the maximum resultant force of dispute resolution has been condensed and the efficiency of dispute resolution has been promoted. The cooperative governance led by the state with social autonomy, forming the open and diverse social governance community, is a Chinese solution explored by China in the political and social environment of the transformation of society. It maintained the order and stability as well as kept the social vitality. Such a mediation institution surpassing the binary opposition of the state and society formed a totally different contrast to the social-autonomy mediation beyond the state, as advocated in Western society as well as the fundamental reason for the Chinese mediation institution to be more effective than the Western mediation institution which is promoted by completely relying on market-based forces.

8.5.2 Social Governance Complex of Integrating Three Types of Governance

The relationship of interaction and cooperation between the state and society is reflected not only in openness and diversity of mediation subjects, but also in the abundance and comprehensiveness of mediation. Different from the Western social governance highlighting separately the priority of legal logic, Chinese society especially emphasized "comprehensive governance." In the "administrative subcontract," the local officials, including the judicial organs, comprehensively undertook the governance tasks and the stability risk, and "legal logic" must take into consideration "comprehensive governance logic."[72] China's diversified dispute resolution mechanism is just the particular reflection of such an idea of the "comprehensive governance." It is not limited to the unitary legal logic, but encourages disputes to be resolved first through mediation and forms the governance complex of three governance models: (1) integrated, based on autonomy; (2) assured by legal governance; and (3) led by moral governance, thus realizing the target of "source governance."

First, for autonomy, China's Grand Mediation institution is the democratic and autonomous activity of people's self-management, self-service, self-education, self-supervision, and self-regulation. The state dominates the development of the Grand Mediation mechanism, but also respects the people's subjective status, respects the rule of mediation, intensifies the autonomy of the parties' wills, and encourages the parties to dissolve contradictions through independent consultation. The Grand Mediation mechanism based on autonomy filters disputes stage by stage, and makes disputes from more to less and from simple to complex, thus laying the solid foundation for the "three defensive lines" structure of social contradiction and dispute resolution with Chinese characteristics and making mediation (first defensive line) -- arbitration, notarization, administrative adjudication and administrative reconsideration (second defensive line), and litigation (final defensive line) show a funnel-shaped structure.

Second, for legal governance, China's Grand Mediation institution runs on the track of legal governance. It emphasizes legal mediation, opposes "mixing water into mud" that sacrifices the legal principles, guides the people to deploy the thought and mode of legal governance to protect their rights according to law and rationally express their appeals, and intensifies the leading, promoting, regulating, and safeguarding of the role of the people's court in the Grand Mediation system so as to correctly treat the relationship between right-safeguarding (vitality) and stability (order).

Third, for moral governance, China's Grand Mediation institution attaches extreme importance to deploying such informal norms as morals and customs to bind social conduct, regulate social relations, and maintain social orders and is adept at deploying the moral governance resources, moral governance forces, good faith system, and giving play to the educational role of the gentry culture, the clan culture, and lifestyle and customs. For example, such work models as Anhui Tongcheng Court's "Six Feet Lane Mediation Method" and Chengdu Pujiang Court's "Five-Elderly Mediation Law" have reflected the tradition of the legal culture with a combination of morals and law and with legalism in the name of Confucianism, and realized "keeping peace by law and nourishing people by virtue."

In a word, the difference in the development road of mediation in China from the Western approach is that the Chinese mediation institution not merely relies on "fighting alone" or the logic of unitary legal governance, but emphasizes the common action of autonomy, legal governance, and moral governance, especially attaches importance to the social conditions of facilitating informal cooperation, and is efficient at deploying multiple means, such as economic regulation, administrative management, legal regulations, moral binding, mental persuasion, and public opinion guidance, and nurtures people with culture to form the comprehensive mechanism of mediating and resolving social contradictions. On the one hand, folk mediation often cites national law to endow mediation with legality. On the other hand, official mediation also obtains social acceptance with the aid of such folk norms as articles of autonomy, local rules and regulations, resident convention, local customs and habits.[73] In the process of official-civil interaction and multiple-mediation links, the formal legal institution (national law) and informal institution (folk norms) exchange, impact and integrate mutually, getting rid of the unitary governance structure of the state and society and realizing the pluralistic governance of benign cooperation of the state and society.

8.6 Conclusion: Extend the Tradition, Keep a Foothold in the Native Land, and Turn Your Back on the West

The famous French thinker, Montesquieu once said:

> Since laws formulated for the people of a country should be very suitable for the people of the country, and if the laws of one country can be even applicable for another country, it will be only a matter of much coincidence.[74]

The legal governance approach of a country can only be rooted in the social soil of this country, the law discourse system of one country can also only be rooted in the legal governance practice of this country, and the simple doctrine of borrowing is not the reflection of cultural self-confidence. China has a vast territory that is unique in the world and the national conditions of China are complex and even surprising, thus the problems faced by vast China have vast complexity.[75] Therefore, China's legal governance construction must take a socialist legal governance approach with Chinese characteristics in terms of its own national conditions.

In the Axial Age, when human civilization achieved breakthrough and transcendence, the Confucian civilization held a place among the five major civilizations of the world and the Chinese law system was unique among the five major law systems of the world and has lasted till now in the long history of five thousand years of civilization. In the zig-zag historical evolution, by having a tolerant attitude and integrating Chinese and foreign different resources of the past and present, China explored its own approach of legal governance and thus formed the diverse and dynamic legal governance tradition, which has actually integrated the ancient Confucian tradition, the new tradition of socialist tradition and the tradition of Western rational law.[76] Mediation is the uppermost heritage of Confucian legal tradition as well as the most significant characteristic of the Chinese law system. This tradition has always run China's legal modernization and interacted mutually with the other two major legal traditions, thus forming the state-oriented, socially diverse, cooperative dispute resolution model, forming the Grand Mediation system of the benign interaction between the state and society and forming the new Chinese justice system, composed of informal (folk), semi-formal (semi-official and semi-civil), and formal (national) justice systems.[77] Therefore, the "Oriental experiences" of mediation are the crystallization of Chinese national rationality and wisdom, and the precious treasures that China's legal governance contributed to the legal governance of world civilization. As a legal institution of "harmony in diversity" and "seeking common ground while reserving differences," mediation reflected the variety of the human legal governance civilization. In the new era, we are in need of two different discourse systems, such as litigation and mediation, and make the two resonate simultaneously, mutually make up for their deficiencies, and adequately use their respective advantages in the state governance system.

The famous Chinese sociologist, Mr. Zheng Hangsheng, once said, those who create and update the academic discourse right need to have a wide vision of "keep a foothold in the native land and surpass the native land; value the tradition and surpass the tradition; draw from the West and surpass the West," and have the theoretical consciousness of "strive to become the theoretical innovator rather than merely a broker of the Western theory."[78] To structure the mediation discourse system with Chinese characteristics, it should: (1) develop the tradition, surpass the tradition, rebuild the Chinese law system from the profound mediation cultural tradition of the Chinese nation, and reflect its heritage and nationality; (2) extract and purify the reality and surpass the reality, extract and purify the new thought, new idea, and new method continually according to China's social development and reflect the originality and temporal spirit; (3) "draw from the West and turn your back on the West," when structuring the mediation discourse system with Chinese characteristics, walk out of the shadow of "Western centralism" as well as avoid declining to the extreme of "Chinese nativism," treat the relationship between mediation nativity and globalization properly and reflect the subjectivity and openness. Since mediation is a flexible dispute resolution mode with higher neutrality, as compared with litigation,[79] and the internationalization of legal affairs derived from economic globalization makes mediation become a cross-border dispute resolution mode that is more easily accepted by the parties,[80] the modernization of mediation in China is also the process of mediation globalization to some extent.[81] We should clearly understand that the Western mediation institution, especially commercial mediation, has already caught up from behind in terms of marketization, professionalization, and legalization and we can no longer be complacent over the "Oriental experiences" and immersed in the previous brilliance, but need to absorb the merits of the Western mediation institution development in comparison, reference, and criticism and realize the splendid transformation from traditional mediation to modern mediation through idea innovation, practical innovation, and institutional innovation. Only in this way can we make the nationality of mediation correspond more to the development requirements of contemporary China and the present world, tell a proper Chinese story of mediation and communicate properly the Chinese voice of mediation, and contribute China's legal wisdom in structuring the "community with the shared future for mankind."

Notes

1 Edward W. Said: *Orientalism*, trans. Wang Yugen (Beijing: SDX Joint Publishing Company, 1999), pp. 1–37.

2 "Legal Orientalism" was proposed by American scholar Teemu Ruskola. Legal Orientalism implies that a set of complete narrations on what is law, what is not

law, and who are its suitable subjects and who are not its suitable subjects are all dominated by the Western (American) discourses, and the legal practice of "others" is defined accordingly. See Teemu Ruskola: *Legal Orientalism: China, the United States, and Modern Law*, trans. Wei Leijie (Beijing: China University of Political Science and Law Press, 2016), pp. 4–31.

3 Zhang Guangxing: Studies on Law Science Should Intensify the Consciousness of Chinese Issues, *Chinese Social Sciences Today*, December 9, 2016, Edition 4.

4 In 2005, Professor Deng Zhenglai outlined the comprehensive introspection over the development of China's law since the reform and opening-up and proposed to structure "the ideal prospect of China's law science," arousing a strong echo in the circle of law science in China. Deng Zhenglai: *Where China's Law Science Goes to: Outline for the Era of Structuring "the Ideal Prospect of China's Law Science"* (Beijing: The Commercial Press, 2006), pp. 259–260.

5 Wang Xuedian: What Is "New Liberal Arts"?, *China Reading Weekly* June 30, 2020, Edition 5.

6 Wu Xinye: Contemporary Structuring of China's Social Governance Discourse System, *Social Sciences in Chinese Higher Education Institutions*, 2018 (3), p. 91.

7 Zhi Zhenfeng: Western Discourse and China's Legal Principle: Nonsense, Fairy Tales and Myth in the Research of Law Sciences, *Science of Law* 2013 (6), p.14.

8 Gu Peidong: Independent Approach of China's Legal Governance, *Chinese Journal of Law*, 2010 (1), pp. 3–18.

9 Wu Xiaoming: Contemporary Structuring of China's Academic Discourse System, *Social Sciences in China*, 2011 (2), p. 9.

10 Friedrich Karl von Savigny: *On the Contemporary Mission of Legislation and Law Science*, trans. Xu Zhangrun (Beijing: China Legal Publishing House 2001), p. 28.

11 In *From the Soil: The Foundations of Chinese Society*, Mr. Fei Xiaotong explained, with a vivid example, the meaning of "mediation": "in the countryside, the so-called mediation was actually a process of education … Mediation was a new word, while the old word was reasoning." Fei Xiaotong: *From the Soil: The Foundations of Chinese Society* (Beijing: People's Publishing House, 2015), p. 69.

12 Regarding the criticism on this concept misunderstanding, see Xiao Jianguo and Yang Bing: Conflict and Integration of the Adversary System and Mediation Institution: Enlightenment of American Mediation Institution for China, *Journal of Comparative Law*, 2006 (4), pp. 88–89.

13 The "three main systems" are the discipline system, the academic system, and the discourse system, and they complement each other. The discipline system is the foundation and source of the academic system and the discourse system, the academic system is the core and support of the discipline system and the discourse system. The discourse system is the expression and communication mode of the academic system and the link composing the network of the discipline system. Compared with the structuring of the discipline system and the academic system, it is more difficult to structure the discourse system because the key to structuring the discourse system is to generate the ideological system with charisma, influence, and persuasion. Xie Fuzhan: Accelerate to Structure the Discipline System, the Academic System, and the Discourse System of Philosophy and Social Sciences with Chinese Characteristics, *Social Sciences in China* 2019 (5), pp. 4–22; Zhang Wenxian: Where Will the Discipline System, Academic System, and Discourse System of China's Law Science Go?, *Guangming Daily*, May 20, 2020, Edition 16.

14 Liang Zhiping: *Cultural Interpretation of Law* (Beijing: Joint Publishing, 1998), p. 35.
15 Speech of Xi Jinping at the Seminar on Philosophy and Social Sciences (May 17, 2016).
16 The important speech of General Secretary Xi Jinping at the Second Meeting of the Fourth Plenary Session of the 18th CPC Central Committee (October 23, 2014)
17 Zeng Xianyi: Studies on Issues of Chinese Traditional Mediation Institution, *China Legal Science*, 2009 (4), p. 35.
18 Liang Shuming: *The Substance of Chinese Culture* (Shanghai: Shanghai People's Publishing House, 2011), p. 87.
19 Liang Zhiping: *Searching for Harmony in the Natural Order* (Shanghai: Shanghai People's Publishing House, 1991), p. 188.
20 Martin Shapiro: *Courts: A Comparative and Political Analysis*, trans. Zhang Sheng and Li Tong (Beijing: China University of Political Science and Law Press, 2005), p. 222.
21 Yu Xingzhong: Theorization of Medication Practice: From Concept to Philosophy, in Xu Xin (Chief Ed.), *Mediation: China and the World* (Beijing: China University of Political Science and Law Press, 2013), p. 21.
22 Zhang Zhongqiu: *Legal Culture in Comparative Vision* (Beijing: Law Press, 2003), pp. 225–271.
23 Michael Ris: ADR: Global Development Trend in 2020, trans. Long Fei, *People's Court Daily*, March 22, 2013, Edition 6.
24 Surely, Confucius' "don't impose on others what you don't desire" was only applicable to "gentlemen" (the ruling class) in the context then, but today, it can completely become a general moral rule under such premises as "man as the end." Deng Xiaomang: The Three Levels of Kant's Moral Philosophy, *Journal of Yunnan University (Social Sciences)*, 2014 (4), p. 24.
25 Xu Nengyi: How to Understand "Liberty" in Core Socialist Values, *Hongqi Wengao*, 2015 (2), p. 25.
26 Liang Shuming: *The Substance of Chinese Culture*, p. 79.
27 Li Yongjun: The Cultural Dimension of China's Legal Governance Subjectivity, *China Legal Science*, 2018 (5), p. 31.
28 Hou Xinyi: *From Justice for People to People's Justice: Studies on Public Judicial Institution of Shaanxi-Gansu-Ningxia Border Region* (Beijing: China University of Political Science and Law Press, 2007), pp. 259–312.
29 Zhang Xipo: *Ma Xiwu Trial Mode* (Beijing: Law Press, 1983), pp. 78–79.
30 For an outstanding practical summary and theoretical insight regarding the "Fengqiao Experience," see Shen Hongguo: "Fengqiao Experience" and Generative Model of Legal Governance with Chinese Characteristics, *Science of Law*, 2009 (1), pp. 17–28. In the new era, the "Fengqiao Experience" has been continually upgraded and it is described by Professor Zhang Wenxian as five elements: (1) party building and leadership; (2) people oriented; (3)"three governance" combination of autonomous governance, legal governance, and moral governance; (4) co-building, co-governance, and sharing; and (5) peace and harmony. Zhang Wenxian: Theoretical Propositions of the "Fengqiao Experience" in the New Era, *Law and Social Development*, 2018 (6), p. 2.
31 Takamieawa Osamu: *Disputes and Law in Modern China*, trans. He Qinghua, et al. (Beijing: Law Press, 2003), p. 1.

32 Liao Yong and Wang Chong: Self-examination on Generalization Phenomenon of People's Mediation and Remolding of Social Mediation System, *Law and Economy*, 2019 (5), pp. 67–80.

33 Fu Zhenghua: Insist on Development of "Fengqiao Experience" and Strive to Promote the Level of People's Mediation Work in the New Era: A Speech Made at the National People's Medication Conference (May 10, 2018), *Justice of China*, 2018 (6), pp. 7–13.

34 Wu Xiaoyan and Zhao Minxing: Features and Enlightenment of American Community Mediation Institution, *People's Tribune*, 2012 (11), p. 180.

35 Tanase Takao: *Dispute Resolution and Trial System*, trans. Wang Yaxin (Beijing: China University of Political Science and Law Press, 2004), p. 48.

36 Philip C.C. Huang: China's Ancient and Present Civil and Criminal Justice System: Chinese Law System under Global Visions, *The Jurist*, 2016 (1), p. 16.

37 Zhou Cui: Introspection and Restatement of the Relation of Mediation and Trial, *Journal of Comparative Law*, 2014 (1), pp. 46–63.

38 Fan Yu: Litigious Mediation: Trial Experiences and Legal Principle, *China Legal Science*, 2009 (6), pp. 134–135.

39 Nadjia Marie Alexander: *Global Trends in Mediation,* trans. Wang Fuhua, et al. (Beijing: China Legal Publishing House, 2011), p. 21.

40 Wang Chong: Mediation-Judgment Separation or Mediation-Judgment Combination: Re-exploration of China's Prospects of Court Mediation, *Hebei Law Science*, 2019 (9), pp. 193–195.

41 Zhao Xudong: *The Prototype Theory of Disputes and Dispute Resolution* (Beijing: Peking University Press, 2009), pp. 140–141.

42 Gabrielle Kaufmann-Kohler and Fan Kun: Combination of Arbitration and Mediation: Why It Is Successful in China, *Arbitration of Beijing*, 2008 (4), pp. 116–117.

43 Zhao Yincui: Studies of Civil Dispute Resolution Mechanism in the Process of Administration, *The Jurist*, 2009 (3), p. 149.

44 Philip C.C. Huang: Three Major Traditions of China's Justice System and Compilation of Present Civil Acts, *Open Times*, 2017 (6), p. 22.

45 Max Weber: *Legal Sociology*, trans. Kand Le and Jian Huimei (Guilin: Guangxi Normal University Press, 2011), pp. 27–31.

46 Pang Pu: *One-into-Three: Textual Research of Chinese Traditional Thoughts* (Shenzhen: Haitian Publishing House, 1995), pp. 3–6.

47 Ji Weidong: Diversified Dispute Resolution in the Society of Legal Governance, *People's Court Daily*, August 31, 2016, Edition 5.

48 Professor Owen Fiss of Yale University took a clear-cut stand against settlement in different forms, viewing it as having an impact on the judgment institution and being a kind of "second-class justice," and this mode should not be encouraged and praised. Owen Fiss: *The Law as It Could Be*, trans. Shi Shuai (Beijing: China University of Political Science and Law Press, 2008), pp. 117–138.

49 Fan Yu: *Diversified Dispute Resolution Mechanism and Structuring of Harmonious Society* (Beijing: Economic Science Press, 2011), p. 41.

50 Liao Yongan: Understand Scientifically the Value of Mediation and Promote the Innovation of Social Governance, *Chinese Social Sciences Today*, March 26, 2020, Edition 1.

51 Lu Yilong: *Disputes and Order in Transformational China: Studies of Legal Sociology* (Beijing: China Renmin University Press, 2015), p. 247.

52 Philip C.C. Huang: *China's New Justice System: Practice and Theory* (Guilin: Guangxi Normal University Press, 2020), pp. 1–10.

53 Philip C.C. Huang: *The Past and the Present: Chinese Civil Justice in Practice* (Beijing: Law Press, 2009), pp. 262–263.

54 Shiga Shuzo, et al.: *Civil Trial and Civil Contract of the Ming and Qing Dynasties*, trans. Wang Yaxin, et al. (Beijing: Law Press, 1998), p. 36.

55 Hiroaki Terada: The Crowded Train Model: The Concept of Society and the Maintenance of Order in Ming and Qing Dynasty China, trans. Ruan Yunxing, *Tsinghua University Law Journal*, 2010 (6), p. 170–171.

56 Lin Duan: *Weber on Traditional Chinese Law: A Critique of Weber's Comparative Sociology* (Beijing: China University of Political Science and Law Press, 2014), pp. 155–157.

57 Ji Weidong: China's Judicial Thinking Mode and its Cultural Characteristics, *Legal Method and Legal Thinking*, 2005 (3), pp. 74–81.

58 "Pragmatic reason" is a concept proposed by Mr. Li Zehou with reference to Kant's "Practical Reason" and Dewey's "Pragmatism." In the opinion of Mr. Li Zehou, traditional Chinese society had workmanship, but not science because China's traditional pragmatic reason ignored logic but emphasized experiences for the sake of serving the resolution of realistic problems. With Confucian ideology as the basis, "pragmatic reason" shaped China's unique thinking model of the Golden Mean. It emphasized the dynamic balance and harmony in diversity between different factors and attached importance to viewing things in the long term, a systematic and historic view with the purpose of keeping the harmony and stability of the existing system. It did not keep emotion and reason in opposition, but continually adjusted the relation of the two by linking theory with practice and emphasized the integration of emotion and reason. In the view of the author, China's mediation institution is just the reflection of such empirical reason. It differs from the Western law of formal rationality as well as is significantly different from law types of "substantial rationality" proposed by Weber. The latter characterized the status of no distinction between law and moral norms, dispute resolution is essentially the "paternalistic judicature" of resolving in accordance with the moral code, political criterion, and other special norms. Li Zehou: *Pragmatic Reason and a Culture of Optimism* (Beijing: Joint Publishing, 2005), pp. 3–54, 325–332; Li Zehou: *Chinese Ancient Ideological History* (Beijing: People's Publishing House, 1985), pp. 303–306.

59 For the official interpretation of the Supreme People's Court of "mediation-judgment combination," see Anon, Appendix to the Work Report of the Supreme People's Court, *Bulletin of the Supreme People's Court of the People's Republic of China*, 2008 (4).

60 He Yongjun: *The Spirit of Ancient Chinese Judicature* (Beijing: China University of Political Science and Law Press, 2016), p. 181.

61 Shiga Shuzo, et al.: *Civil Trial and Civil Contract of the Ming and Qing Dynasties*, trans. Wang Yaxin (Beijing: Law Press, 1998), p. 13.

62 Xu Zhangrun: *Outline of Chinese Law Science* (Guilin: Guangxi Normal University Press, 2014), pp. 43–55.

63 Li Zehou: *Pragmatic Reason and a Culture of Optimism* (Beijing: Joint Publishing, 2005), pp. 339–331.

64 As for the above four mediation classifications based on functions, see Tanase Takao: *Dispute Resolution and Trial System*, trans. Wang Yaxin (Beijing: China University of Political Science and Law Press, 2004), pp. 52–73.

65 Zhang Naihe: Notes on the Origin of Modern Civic Society and Contemporary China's Civic Society Structuring, *Journal of Jilin University (Social Sciences)*, 2016 (6), pp. 148–150.

66 Wang Chonghu and Wang Xipeng: "Social Comprehensive Governance": Discourse System and Empirical Theory of China's Governance: Comparison with "Multi-center Governance" Theory, *Social Sciences in Nanjing*, 2018 (6), p. 64.

67 Li Mei: Empirical Logic of Contemporary China's Social Governance Transformation, *Social Sciences in China*, 2018 (11), p. 69.

68 Philip C.C. Huang: *Law, Society and Culture of the Qing Dynasty: Expression and Practice of Civil Law* (Beijing: Law Press, 2014, pp. 91–111.

69 Martin Shapiro: *Courts: A Comparative and Political Analysis* (Beijing: China University of Political Science and Law Press, 2005), pp. 268–271.

70 Hu Jieren: *Perfect Social Contradiction and Dispute Resolution Mechanism: A Study on Contemporary China's "Grand Mediation"* (Shanghai: Shanghai Jiaotong University Press, 2017), p. 23.

71 Official website of the Political and Judiciary Commission under the CPC Central Committee interpreted the meaning of the "Grand Mediation" work system. See www.chinapeace.gov.cn/chinapeace/c28637/2012-07/24/content_12052535.shtml. "Grand Mediation" was first promoted by Nantong City of Jiangsu Province in 2003 and affirmed and propagated by the social sectors. At the National Mediation Work Meeting held in 2019, the Ministry of Justice expressly proposed: "By 2022, basically form the Grand Mediation work system based on people's mediation with the advantageous complementarity, organic connection, coordination and linkage of people's mediation, administrative mediation, industrial special mediation and judicial mediation."

72 Zhou Li'an: How to Understand China? Conversation with Mr. Philip C.C. Huang, *Open Times*, 2019 (3), pp. 37–63.

73 Yi Jun: A Study on the Hui-nationality Community Mediation Mechanism: Based on the Vision of Legal Pluralism, *Journal of North Minzu University (Philosophy and Social Sciences)*, 2016 (2), pp. 126–130.

74 Montesquieu: *The Spirit of the Laws*, trans. Zhang Yanshen (Beijing: The Commercial Press, 1961), p. 4.

75 Pan Weijiang: How to Understand China's Super-Large Scale? *Reading*, 2019 (5), pp. 3–11.

76 Philip C.C. Huang: *The Past and the Present: Chinese Civil Justice in Practice*, p. 5; Qiang Shigong: China's Legal Governance Approach and Legal Governance Model: Global Vision and Chinese Experiences, *Administration Reform*, 2019 (8), p. 26. Differently, in the opinion of Gan Yang, a famous scholar, contemporary China is composed of Confucian tradition, the tradition of equality emphasized in the times of Mao Zedong, and the market-based tradition since the reform and opening-up. This inference highlighted the difference of the two periods before and after the reform and opening-up, but ignored the historical process of "the spread of the Western influence to the East" in the late Qing Dynasty and early Republic of China, and the two historical periods before and after the reform and opening-up are a mutually connected entirety, composing jointly the socialist tradition. Gan Yang: *Through the Three Traditions* (Beijing: Joint Publishing, 2007), p. 3.

77 Philip C.C. Huang: The Past, Present and Future of China's Justice System, *Open Times*, 2018 (2), p. 144.

78 Zheng Hangsheng: The Key to Academic Discourse System Construction Is to Master the Academic Discourse Right, *Chinese Social Sciences Today*, January 1, 2014, Edition B02.

79 Takeshi Kojima and Makoto Itoh (Eds.): *Alternative Dispute Resolution*, trans. Ding Jie (Beijing: China University of Political Science and Law Press, 2005), p. 2.

80 On August 7, 2019, 46 countries, inclusive of China and the United States, signed in Singapore *The United Nations Convention on International Settlement Agreements Resulting from Mediation* (abbreviated as the *Singapore Convention*), indicating that the globalization of mediation had entered the new era.

81 Wang Fuhua: Dimensions for Transformation of Chinese Mediation System, *Legal Forum*, 2010 (6), p. 32.

References

Alexander, Nadjia Marie: *Global Trends in Mediation*, trans. Wang Fuhua, et al., Beijing: China Legal Publishing House, 2011.

Anon: The Appendix to the Work Report of the Supreme People's Court, *Bulletin of the Supreme People's Court of the People's Republic of China*, 2008 (4).

Deng Xiaomang: The Three Levels of Kant's Moral Philosophy, *Journal of Yunnan University (Social Sciences)*, 2014 (4): 24.

Deng Zhenglai: *Where China's Law Science Goes to: Outline for the Era of Structuring "the Ideal Prospect of China's Law Science,"* Beijing: The Commercial Press, 2006.

Fan Yu: *Diversified Dispute Resolution Mechanism and Structuring of Harmonious Society*, Beijing: Economic Science Press, 2011.

Fan Yu: Litigious Mediation: Trial Experiences and Legal Principle, *China Legal Science*, 2009 (6): 134–135.

Fei Xiaotong: *From the Soil: The Foundations of Chinese Society*, Beijing: People's Publishing House, 2015.

Fiss, Owen: *The Law as It Could Be*, trans. Shi Shuai, Beijing: China University of Political Science and Law Press, 2008.

Fu Zhenghua: Insist on Development of "Fengqiao Experience" and Strive to Promote the Level of People's Mediation Work in the New Era: A Speech made at the National People's Medication Conference (May 10, 2018), *Justice of China,*2018 (6): 7–13.

Gan Yang: *Through the Three Traditions*, Beijing: Joint Publishing, 2007.

Gu Peidong: Independent Approach of China's Legal Governance, *Chinese Journal of Law*, 2010 (1): 3–18.

He Yongjun: *The Spirit of Ancient Chinese Judicature*, Beijing: China University of Political Science and Law Press, 2016.

Hou Xinyi: *From Justice for People to People's Justice – Studies on Public Judicial Institution of Shaanxi-Gansu-Ningxia Border Region*, Beijing: China University of Political Science and Law Press, 2007.

Hu Jieren: *Perfect Social Contradiction and Dispute Resolution Mechanism: A Study on Contemporary China's "Grand Mediation,"* Shanghai: Shanghai Jiaotong University Press, 2017.

Huang Philip C.C.: China's Ancient and Present Civil and Criminal Justice System – Chinese Law System under Global Visions, *The Jurist*, 2016 (1): 16.

Huang, Philip C.C.: *China's New Justice System: Practice and Theory*, Guilin: Guangxi Normal University Press, 2020.

Huang, Philip C.C.: *Law, Society and Culture of the Qing Dynasty: Expression and Practice of Civil Law*, Beijing: Law Press, 2014, pp. 91–111.

Huang, Philip C.C.: *The Past and the Present: Chinese Civil Justice in Practice*, Beijing: Law Press, 2009.

Huang, Philip C.C.: The Past, Present and Future of China's Justice System, *Open Times*, 2018 (2): 144.

Huang, Philip C.C.: Three Major Traditions of China's Justice System and Compilation of Present Civil Acts, *Open Times*, 2017 (6): 22.

Ji Weidong: China's Judicial Thinking Mode and its Cultural Characteristics, *Legal Method and Legal Thinking*, 2005 (3): 74–81.

Ji Weidong: Diversified Dispute Resolution in the Society of Legal Governance, *People's Court Daily*, August 31, 2016, Edition 5.

Kaufmann-Kohler, Gabrielle and Fan Kun: Combination of Arbitration and Mediation: Why Successful in China, *Arbitration of Beijing*, 2008 (4): 116–117.

Kojima, Takeshi and Makoto Itoh (Eds.), *Alternative Dispute Resolution*, trans. Ding Jie, Beijing: China University of Political Science and Law Press, 2005.

Li Mei: Empirical Logic of Contemporary China's Social Governance Transformation, *Social Sciences in China*, 2018 (11): 69.

Li Yongjun: The Cultural Dimension of China's Legal Governance Subjectivity, *China Legal Science*, 2018 (5): 31.

Li Zehou: *Chinese Ancient Ideological History*, Beijing: People's Publishing House, 1985.

Li Zehou: *Pragmatic Reason and a Culture of Optimism*, Beijing, Joint Publishing 2005.

Liang Shuming: *The Substance of Chinese Culture*, Shanghai: Shanghai People's Publishing House, 2011

Liang Zhiping: *Cultural Interpretation of Law*, Beijing: Joint Publishing, 1998.

Liang Zhiping: *Searching for Harmony in the Natural Order*, Shanghai: Shanghai People's Publishing House, 1991.

Liao Yong'an and Wang Chong: Self-examination on Generalization Phenomenon of People's Mediation and Remolding of Social Mediation System, *Law and Economy*, 2019 (5): 67–80.

Liao Yongan: Understand Scientifically Mediation Value and Promote the Innovation of Social Governance, *Chinese Social Sciences Today*, March 26, 2020, Edition 1.

Lin Duan: *Weber on Traditional Chinese Law: A Critique of Weber's Comparative Sociology*, Beijing: China University of Political Science and Law Press, 2014.

Lu Yilong: *Disputes and Order in Transformational China: Studies of Legal Sociology*, Beijing: China Renmin University Press, 2015.

Montesquieu: *The Spirit of the Laws*, trans. Zhang Yanshen, Beijing: The Commercial Press, 1961.

Osamu, Takamieawa: *Disputes and Law in Modern China*, trans. He Qinghua, et al., Beijing: Law Press, 2003.

Pan Weijiang: How to Understand China's Super-Large Scale? *Reading*, 2019 (5): 3–11.

Pang Pu: *One-into-Three: Textual Research of Chinese Traditional Thoughts*, Shenzhen: Haitian Publishing House, 1995.

Qiang Shigong: China's Legal Governance Approach and Legal Governance Model – Global Vision and Chinese Experiences, *Administration Reform*, 2019 (8): 26.

Ris, Michael: ADR: Global Development Trend in 2020, trans. Long Fei, *People's Court Daily*, March 22, 2013, Edition 6.

Said, Edward W.: *Orientalism*, trans. Wang Yugen, Beijing: SDX Joint Publishing Company, 1999.

Savigny, Friedrich Karl von: *On the Contemporary Mission of Legislation and Law Science*, trans. Xu Zhangrun, Beijing: China Legal Publishing House, 2001.

Shapiro, Martin: *Courts: A Comparative and Political Analysis*, trans. Zhang Sheng, Li Tong, Beijing: China University of Political Science and Law Press, 2005.

Shuzo, Shiga, et al.: *Civil Trial and Civil Contract of the Ming and Qing Dynasties*, trans. Wang Yaxin, et al., Beijing: Law Press, 1998.

Takao, Tanase: *Dispute Resolution and Trial System*, trans. Wang Yaxin, Beijing: China University of Political Science and Law Press, 2004.

Teemu Ruskola: *Legal Orientalism: China, the United States, and Modern Law*, trans. Wei Leijie, Beijing: China University of Political Science and Law Press, 2016.

Terada, Hiroaki: The Crowded Train Model: The Concept of Society and the Maintenance of Order in Ming and Qing Dynasty China, trans. Ruan Yunxing, *Tsinghua University Law Journal*, 2010 (6): 170–171.

Wang Chong: Mediation-Judgment Separation or Mediation-Judgment Combination: Re-exploration on China's Prospects of Court Mediation, *Hebei Law Science*, 2019 (9): 193–195.

Wang Chonghu and Wang Xipeng: "Social Comprehensive Governance": Discourse System and Empirical Theory of China's Governance – Comparison with "Multi-center Governance" Theory, *Social Sciences in Nanjing*, 2018 (6): 64.

Wang Fuhua: Dimensions for Transformation of Chinese Mediation System, *Legal Forum*, 2010 (6): 32.

Wang Xuedian: What is "New Liberal Arts"?, *China Reading Weekly*, June 30, 2020, Edition 5.

Weber, Max: *Legal Sociology*, trans. Kand Le and Jian Huimei, Guilin: Guangxi Normal University Press, 2011.

Wu Xiaoming: Contemporary Structuring of China's Academic Discourse System, *Social Sciences in China*, 2011 (2): 9.

Wu Xiaoyan and Zhao Minxing: Features and Enlightenment of American Community Mediation Institution, *People's Tribune*, 2012 (11): 180.

Wu Xinye: Contemporary Structuring of China's Social Governance Discourse System, *Social Sciences in Chinese Higher Education Institutions*, 2018 (3): 91.

Xiao Jianguo and Yang Bing: Conflict and Integration of Adversary System and Mediation Institution –Enlightenment of American Mediation Institution for China, *Journal of Comparative Law*, 2006 (4): 88–89.

Xie Fuzhan: Accelerate to Structure the Discipline System, the Academic System, and the Discourse System of Philosophy and Social Sciences with Chinese Characteristics, *Social Sciences in China* 2019 (5): 4–22.

Xu Nengyi: How to Understand "Liberty" in Core Socialist Values, *Hongqi Wengao*, 2015 (2): 25.

Xu Zhangrun: *Outline of Chinese Law Science*, Guilin: Guangxi Normal University Press, 2014, pp. 43–55.

Yi Jun: A Study on the Hui-nationality Community Mediation Mechanism: Based on the Vision of Legal Pluralism, *Journal of North Minzu University (Philosophy and Social Sciences)*, 2016 (2): 126–130.

Yu Xingzhong: Theorization of Medication Practice: From Concept to Philosophy, in Xu Xin (Chief Ed.), *Mediation: China and the World*, Beijing: China University of Political Science and Law Press, 2013, p. 21.

Zeng Xianyi: Studies on Issues of Chinese Traditional Mediation Institution, *China Legal Science*, 2009 (4): 35.

Zhang Guangxing: Studies on Law Science Should Intensify the Consciousness of Chinese Issues, *Chinese Social Sciences Today*, December 9, 2016, Edition 4.

Zhang Naihe: Notes on Origin of Modern Civic Society and Contemporary China's Civic Society Structuring, *Journal of Jilin University (Social Sciences)*, 2016 (6): 148–150.

Zhang Wenxian: Theoretical Propositions of the "Fengqiao Experience" in the New Era, *Law and Social Development*, 2018 (6): 2.

Zhang Wenxian: Where Will the Discipline System, Academic System and Discourse System of China's Law Science Go?, *Guangming Daily,* May 20, 2020 Edition 16.

Zhang Xipo: *Ma Xiwu Trial Mode*, Beijing: Law Press, 1983.

Zhang Zhongqiu: *Legal Culture in Comparative Vision*, Beijing: Law Press, 2003.

Zhao Xudong: *The Prototype Theory of Disputes and Dispute Resolution*, Beijing: Peking University Press, 2009.

Zhao Yincui: Studies on Civil Dispute Resolution Mechanism in the Process of Administration, *The Jurist*, 2009 (3): 149.

Zheng Hangsheng: The Key to Academic Discourse System Construction Is to Master the Academic Discourse Right, *Chinese Social Sciences Today*, January 1, 2014, Edition B02.

Zhi Zhenfeng: Western Discourse and China's Legal Principle: Nonsense, Fairy Tales and Myth in Research of Law Sciences, *Science of Law* 2013 (6): 13–26.

Zhou Cui: Introspection and Restatement of the Relation of Mediation and Trial, *Journal of Comparative Law*, 2014 (1): 46–63.

Zhou Li'an: How to Understand China? Conversation with Mr. Philip C.C. Huang, *Open Times*, 2019 (3): 37–63.

Index

access to justice 74, 126, 138, 146, 156, 164, 193, 217, 222
administrative mediation 20, 45, 72, 73, 83, 91, 130, 131, 132, 164–6, 178, 185–90, 192, 193, 205, 214, 215, 223, 224
ADR 57, 120, 128, 166, 169, 180, 204, 205, 208, 217
appeal 1–3, 12, 14, 15, 20, 23, 25, 26, 48, 52, 64, 76, 81, 92, 99, 101, 134, 174, 213, 225
arbitration 5, 37, 110, 131, 148, 155, 166, 169, 179, 185, 186, 190, 194, 211, 214, 225
ask for an explanation 1, 72, 166, 220
authority 20, 21, 39, 43–6, 54–8, 60, 65, 71, 73, 74, 78, 81, 84, 93–9, 104, 105, 111, 117, 134, 141, 149, 157, 168, 175, 186, 190, 202, 215
autonomous 113, 114, 120, 166, 167, 178, 181, 211, 220, 223, 224

Chinese characteristics 3, 7, 9, 31, 73, 83, 114, 118, 164, 193, 203–6, 214, 222, 225–7
Chinese discourse system 202, 205
Chinese story 3, 227
combination of mediation and judgment 213
commercial mediation 72, 78, 83, 84, 86, 100, 105, 110–13, 115, 116, 118, 128, 130, 166, 169, 170, 175, 180, 185–9, 192, 227
common interests 62, 75, 174, 176
community mediation 72, 98, 100, 120, 211–13
conciliation 5, 13, 25, 37, 49, 50, 64, 82, 101, 143, 167–9, 208, 213, 214
confidentiality 13, 82, 101, 167, 179, 180
Confucian 8, 9, 12, 37, 40–2, 44–6, 48, 49, 51, 56, 70, 71, 84, 93, 95, 171, 193, 204, 206, 208, 210, 218, 222, 225, 226
The consensus induction mechanism 127, 129, 137, 145, 153
contradiction 5, 6, 11, 13–15, 17–21, 25–8, 46, 52–4, 65, 73, 75, 77, 83, 91, 92, 98, 99, 104, 105, 114, 117, 118, 120, 121, 127, 137, 143, 146, 151, 159, 164–8, 170, 172–5, 180, 182, 188, 190, 191, 193, 205, 207, 210, 211, 212, 216, 219, 221, 222, 224, 225
collaborate 16, 26, 27, 141
core socialist values 10, 170–2, 176, 206, 208, 209
cultural self-confidence 204, 206, 209, 226
customs 7–9, 21, 50, 55, 64, 78, 94, 171, 181, 182, 208, 225

democracy 73, 74, 171, 209
dispute resolution 3–9, 12, 14, 15, 18–21, 27–9, 37–40, 43, 46–9, 51, 54, 55, 57, 60, 66, 70–4, 77, 78, 80–7, 92, 94, 97, 100, 104, 106, 108, 109, 112, 114–18, 120, 121, 125, 126, 128, 131–3, 135–9, 141, 143–5, 150, 155–8, 164, 166, 167, 169–79, 181–4, 186–4, 204–7, 209, 212–18, 221–6
diversity 29, 53, 63, 83, 99, 105, 121, 125, 174, 187, 209, 222, 224, 226

economy 7, 38, 39, 44, 47, 53–6, 65, 66, 70, 72, 73, 75, 77, 92–6, 99, 104, 109, 135, 141, 172, 174, 186, 211, 215, 216, 219
efficiency 13, 41, 52, 61, 75, 111, 133, 137, 145, 147, 153, 154, 156, 167, 174, 186, 188, 191, 213, 223, 224

emotion 2, 3, 12, 14, 18, 19, 21, 48, 49, 51, 54, 63, 64, 71, 78, 92, 94, 96, 145, 172, 174, 175, 182, 218–21
equality 53, 70, 74, 171, 209

false mediation 139, 140, 148, 155
Fengqiao experience 72, 205, 210, 211, 213, 222, 223
flexibility 13, 44, 77, 116, 120, 121, 167, 174, 179, 184, 210, 224
flexible 3, 11, 13, 17, 29, 60, 76, 98, 174, 211, 219, 221, 227
freedom 59, 63, 70, 74, 171, 178, 179, 182

The golden mean 27, 207, 216

harmony 3, 7, 8, 11, 13, 20, 26, 28, 29, 38, 41–3, 46, 48, 49, 51, 65, 70, 73, 78, 114, 141, 167, 171, 175, 193, 206–9, 212, 217, 226
history 4, 9, 38, 40, 52, 97, 126, 203, 217, 219
honesty and credit 6, 182, 183

imperial power not reaching below the level of the county 38, 45, 94
industrial mediation 83, 86, 105, 109, 110, 112, 113, 115–18, 128, 130, 132, 164, 166, 168, 175, 185, 186, 188, 190, 192, 193, 212, 224
interests 2, 3, 5, 12–17, 20–3, 25, 28, 48, 51, 53, 55, 56, 58, 60–5, 74–6, 78–82, 84, 86, 95, 100, 101, 111, 113, 117, 129, 139, 140, 150, 170, 173–6, 178, 179, 217

judicial confirmation 127, 135, 142, 151, 157, 167, 189, 190, 222
judicial mediation 45, 73, 91, 165, 166, 193, 211, 223
judicial reform 80, 126, 133, 147, 158, 169, 179, 189
justice 1–3, 6, 7, 11, 13, 15, 16, 20, 24, 51, 59, 60, 67, 70, 73, 74, 77, 80, 81, 83, 96, 97, 100, 101, 104, 106, 108–10, 114, 121, 122, 126, 128, 129, 134, 136, 138, 139, 141, 146, 147, 156, 157, 159, 164, 169, 171, 173, 174, 176, 180, 187, 193, 208–10, 213, 214, 216–18, 220, 222, 226

lawyer mediation 72, 74, 83, 86, 115, 116, 120, 122, 164, 166, 168, 187, 192
legal principle 1–3, 28, 45, 48, 76, 94, 130, 154, 175, 176, 178, 220, 225
litigation explosion 146, 217
litigation idea 13, 70, 173
low cost 13, 127, 136

mandatory mediation 7, 23, 127, 129–31, 138, 146, 177
market economy 38, 53–6, 70, 72, 73, 75, 96, 99, 104, 109, 172, 174, 186, 211, 215, 216
Ma Xiwu trial 5, 210, 211, 213
mediation culture 10, 29, 64, 90, 191, 205, 215
mediation first 23, 25–7, 64, 138, 178, 181
mediation law 28, 116, 117, 164–74, 176, 182–5, 187–90, 192–4
mediation model 46, 90, 97
The mediation procedural prerequisite 125–31, 133, 134, 135, 138–58, 167, 178
mediator 4–6, 15, 18, 19, 21, 23, 27, 43, 46, 48, 51, 54, 56, 58, 59, 61, 62, 64, 65, 71, 73–7, 79–82, 84–6, 90–101, 104, 106–22, 127–40, 144, 145, 147, 148, 150–57, 168, 170, 174, 177, 179–82, 184, 186, 187, 190, 192, 193, 212, 214, 219
mediator-oriented mediation 46, 47, 90, 92, 93, 95–8
modernity 38, 40, 56, 74, 80, 98, 205, 215
moral 2, 3, 7–10, 14, 21, 24, 28, 41, 43, 45, 49, 51, 54–6, 58, 63–5, 84, 85, 94–6, 105–7, 113, 117, 171, 180–2, 185, 208, 209, 216, 217, 219, 224, 225
more cases but fewer personnel 27, 125, 128, 149, 156, 158

neutrality 4, 64, 75, 82, 86, 97, 100, 145, 227
new development idea 172, 176
nitiative intervention 96, 157
non-disclosure 81, 82, 101, 106, 176, 179, 180
notary 74, 83, 139, 141, 166, 185

one belt and one road 169, 170, 186
openness 13, 74, 83, 167, 174, 180, 186, 224, 227
oriental 38, 158, 202, 204, 205, 214, 226, 227

passive examination 151, 157
pauperization of consensus 5, 61, 82
people's mediation 4, 18, 45, 47, 72, 73, 78, 83, 86, 91, 95, 104, 105, 107–10, 112, 114–17, 120, 121, 127, 130–2, 159, 164–8, 175, 177, 178, 181, 184, 185, 187–90, 192, 193, 205, 210, 211, 213, 223, 224
The people's mediation law 4, 108, 110, 112, 114, 116, 117, 165–8, 184, 185, 189, 212
politics 7, 39, 54, 56, 57, 66, 93, 221
procedural justice 6, 59, 70, 80, 81, 96, 97, 100, 214
professionalization of mediation 1, 5, 84, 105–7, 111, 112, 114, 116, 118, 120, 168
professional morality 106, 111, 115
public credibility 111

rational mediation 38, 56, 57
reform and opening-up 48, 52, 54–6, 65, 72, 73, 92, 93, 95, 125, 158, 164, 166
relief 3, 23, 37, 98, 146, 168, 184, 221
reshape 56, 70, 83, 86, 164, 202
rights 2, 8, 16, 17, 19–23, 25, 28, 38, 48, 50, 51, 55, 59, 70, 74, 77, 78, 81, 96, 100, 101, 113, 119, 129, 141, 142, 146, 150, 152, 154, 156, 158, 166, 170, 175, 178–80, 182, 183, 188, 207, 208, 209, 218, 219, 220, 225
rigid 19–21, 26, 63, 174, 202, 210, 217
rite 2, 7, 8, 42–6, 51, 55, 92, 93, 95, 98, 207

social contradictions 14, 17, 21, 27, 65, 73, 98, 104, 105, 114, 118, 137, 143, 159, 164–8, 172, 173, 190, 207, 216
social control resources 52, 60, 83, 97, 98, 125, 131
socialist 3, 9, 10, 47, 92, 164, 165, 170–2, 176, 185, 186, 204, 206, 208–11, 219, 226
society of acquaintance 3, 9, 38, 47, 54, 55, 70, 72, 73, 78, 84, 94, 96, 98, 158, 171
society of acquaintance 3, 9, 38, 47, 54, 55, 70, 72, 73, 78, 84, 94, 96, 98, 158, 171, 211
stability 13, 17–21, 23, 26, 73, 85, 86, 90, 92, 97–9, 114, 119, 141, 167, 180, 188, 191, 216, 223–5
supervision 26, 55, 107, 134, 140, 154, 157, 180, 191, 215, 224

traditional mediation 10, 37, 38, 40, 41, 49, 51–4, 57, 65, 70, 71, 74, 80, 81, 83, 85, 90, 96, 104, 105, 113, 158, 168, 210
transformation 14, 15, 17, 28, 37, 38, 40, 54, 65, 66, 70–3, 84, 86, 90, 96–9, 105, 117, 125, 164, 167, 174, 186, 203, 224, 227

unification of mediation and trial 6, 7

variety13, 38, 46, 52, 77, 168, 219, 226
voluntary 4, 6, 13, 23, 47, 57–9, 72, 81, 91, 96, 101, 128, 129, 131, 133, 134, 137, 145, 146, 153, 167, 176–8, 186, 188–91

Western centralism 227
Western discourse system 158
Western mediation institution 13, 38, 224, 227

For Product Safety Concerns and Information please contact our EU representative GPSR@taylorandfrancis.com Taylor & Francis Verlag GmbH, Kaufingerstraße 24, 80331 München, Germany